WILD RIDES AND WILDFLOWERS

*Philosophy and Botany
with Bikes*

by
Scott Abbott and Sam Rushforth

TORREY HOUSE PRESS, LLC

SALT LAKE CITY • TORREY

First Torrey House Press Edition, March 2014
Copyright © 2014 by Scott Abbott and Sam Rushforth

Published by Torrey House Press, LLC
Salt Lake City, Utah
www.torreyhouse.com

International Standard Book Number: 978-1-937226-23-7
Library of Congress Control Number: 2013952250

Cover design by Jeffrey Fuller, Shelfish • shelfish.weebly.com
Interior design by Rick Whipple, Sky Island Studio
Cover image "Evening Landscape with Two Men"
        by Caspar David Friedrich
Author photo by Nancy Rushforth
Diatom photographs by Sam Rushforth

FSC
www.fsc.org
MIX
Paper from
responsible sources
FSC® C011935

For Lyn and Nancy

(if they'll have it)

—CREDOS—

Your ass back and your head down.
(mountain biking)

Both skis on the same side of the tree.
(backcountry skiing)

WILD RIDES AND WILDFLOWERS

*Philosophy and Botany
with Bikes*

TABLE OF CONTENTS

PREFACE

"Wildflowers" is self-evident. But so you don't waste your time reading this book if you're expecting a mountain-bike version of *Downhill Racer*, we'll explain at the outset that our goal is to "live to ride again." If you want to read about *really* wild rides, ask somebody who still feels immortal, one of the young guys at Mad Dog Cycles, for instance. We, after all, are academics with a hundred-odd years between us. We are saggy assed, long of tooth, and short of breath. "Wild," in our context, means—well, you'll see what it means.

In early 1999, Sam and I began writing a column called "Wild Rides, Wildflowers" for the *Salt Lake Observer*. I told the paper's editor, Brooke Adams, that she had been ignoring gardening and sports: "Sam and I can fill that niche with a single column." Brooke was skeptical, but finally agreed. Sam was harder to convince. "I'm no writer. There are too many words already in print. Count me out." He relented only when he read my first piece. "That's mostly horseshit you've written. If you're going to write about me with your misbegotten talent, I'll have to step in to protect myself."

Five months later, when the bi-monthly paper went under (not our fault), we were picked up by Salt Lake's monthly *Catalyst Magazine*, where Greta deJong published the column for more than three years.

Our intent was to ride a single portion of the Great Western Trail on the foothills of Mount Timpanogos again and again and again until we had seen its flora and fauna in every variation over the course of several years. We were looking for patterns, for meaning found only in repetition. We set out to catalogue our experiences with flora, fauna, weather, and geology, to see and hear and smell and taste everything along this trail so minutely, so sensitively, that our readers would be astonished.

Unfortunately, we are aging men with tics and foibles that preclude much sensitivity. So we wrote about what we knew: fear of aging, male behavior patterns left over from junior high, anguish at the relentless "development" of wild lands in the West, and about what Thoreau described as "wild and noble sights…such as they who sit in parlors never dream of."

Whether our story is read as a cautionary tale or an account of liberation will depend on whether the reader sees the authors as tenuous fathers, as inadequate husbands, as old and crotchety friends, as cantankerous Jack Mormons, as dedicated environmental activists, as heroic mountain bikers, or simply as that odd species called *Masculinus americanus*.

Scott Abbott

NOTE ON THE DIATOM IMAGES

While Scott and I were riding below magnificently bowed blue limestone cliffs and over quartzite outcroppings and through tenacious groves of scrub oak and past wildflowers beyond imagination, the beautiful Provo River was often in sight in the canyon below. In that swift water, a rarely witnessed botanical and geological drama was unfolding. I have spent my life studying that complex and shifting story, many of whose main characters are diatoms.

With a top-of-the-line Olympus microscope and a fine Nikon image capturing system, I took several hundred photographs of the organisms that exist and flourish in the river and nearby ecosystems. Each of the chapters of this book features a photograph of one such diatom (1/10 the diameter of a human hair).

Sam Rushforth

Year I

Here the land always makes promises of aching beauty and the people always fail the land.

Charles Bowden, *Blue Desert*

Art, science: to invent connections, matrices, balances, measurements, instruments of repetition, to give meaning. To fill the horrible void.

Jean Frémon, *The Botanical Garden* (translation by Brian Evenson)

ONE

Lumpers and Splitters

26 February, Great Western Trail, Mt. Timpanogos

On the foothills of Mount Timpanogos, in late February, it's rare to find a dry and rideable trail. This winter, however, has been sudden, short, and moody. The jeep road at the mouth of Provo Canyon, climbing through dormant cliff rose and sage, skirting cliffs of muscular blue limestone, is passable today. Unfortunately, after three months of freezing and thawing the switchbacking trail is as soft as our bellies. Tough going for the first ride of the year.

Where the trail levels off, Sam drops his black carbon-fiber Trek to the ground and leans over to hide the fact that he's sucking air. Even *in extremis*, he can't take his eyes off the view. Utah Lake's slate-grey waters slice the valley from north to south. The Oquirrh and Lake Mountains form the western horizon. Santaquin Peak and Mount Nebo dominate the southern end of the valley. Cascade Mountain is a massive snowy presence to the southeast. Provo Canyon cuts through the folded limestone to the east. The snow-covered escarpments of Mount Timpanogos, 11,749-feet high at the peak, rise abruptly above us.

I lay down my red Specialized Stumpjumper M2, a bike much heavier than Sam's (as I often point out), and take in the view myself.

"Damn!" Sam exclaims.

"Damn!" I wheeze.

A flock of mountain bluebirds (*Sialia currucoides*), their color an exact match of the sky, bursts out of the sage. The birds call to one another as they sweep across the gibbous moon hanging heavy over the canyon.

"Gibbous," Sam says. "I love that word. It means swollen or humped."

"Etymology from a botanist!" I exclaim.

Sam replies with wounded dignity: "You have forgotten, Scott, that I am a professional botanist. I studied Latin for a full year. 'Gibbous' is from the late Latin through Middle English and is often used in plant and animal formal species definitions."

Overlooking the final hills above the city of Orem's last orchard, we hear and then see a motorcycle and a four-wheeler screaming across the rocky terrain. Dozens of mule deer (*Odocoileus hemionus*) break in waves before the maniacs, retreating, splitting into smaller groups, rejoining, bouncing up hills, breaking through oak brush.

"You bastards!" Sam yells, and speeds down the hill. I join the breakneck descent, ready to protect Sam or the maniacs, whoever needs it most. The infernal combustionists see us coming and disappear around a switchback. On the flat, the two man-boys (*Homo erectus*, obviously not yet *Homo sapiens*) are waiting for us.

"What the hell are you doing?" I shout.

"It's a misdemeanor to harass wildlife," Sam bellows. "We'll have you sons of bitches hauled into court."

"We weren't hurting them," the four-wheeled maniac says flatly.

"The hell you weren't," Sam blusters. "It's the end of the winter and they're in compromised condition. The stress you're causing will kill them. You understand the word *compromised*, dipshit?"

The steely eyes of the motorcycle rider reveal only disdain. His bike spits dirt as he leaves us standing. His buddy follows, blatting a foul exhaust.

We head home through an apple orchard, then cross 8th North into the Orem neighborhood where we both live.

"Those boys will find it hard to discount our well-reasoned arguments," Sam deadpans.

"As do our children," I add.

2 March, Great Western Trail, Mt. Timpanogos

Sam has a rough ride up the steep track near the mouth of the canyon. In the early going, he falls twice, both times into oak brush (*Quercus gambelii*) that embraces him with a brittle crackling. At the top, mounting his bike after standing for a while on winter-matted grass to admire the view, he falls again. "That ties our record," I tell him. "Three falls in a single ride. But neither of us has done it in a hundred yards before."

"You know," Sam says from the ground, "I think I fell that last time out of pure wonder. Who gets to witness this glorious landscape again and again and again?"

I point to green tips of new grass, drawn out of the earth by lengthening days, warming temperatures, and new angles of sunlight. "Harbingers of spring," I observe.

"Harbingers my ass," Sam replies. "You've spent too much of your life in eighteenth-century Germany. This new-looking cheatgrass has been here since mid-fall, waiting under the snow for an early start, aiming to bear seed before the heat and dryness of summer and before its later-emerging competitors."

"I study the German Enlightenment," I respond proudly. "You've lived your life hunched over a microscope counting diatoms, whatever the hell those are!"

"Add this to your so-called enlightenment," Sam says. "A diatom is a single-celled alga, common in any wet or moist habitat in the world. Nearly all are photosynthetic, and it is estimated that diatoms produce up to half of all the oxygen on Earth. Diatoms are beautiful, ranging from round to elongate in face view, with thousands of shapes and sizes. They produce glass cell walls and can last in sediments for millennia. Furthermore, diatoms grow preferentially in habitats with different chemical or physical extremes. You can identify changes through time—climate change, for example—by studying density of diatoms in sediments and cores."

Dumbfounded, I respond with a non sequitur: "Where did the word 'dumbfounded' come from?"

"Same family as 'thunderstruck,'" Sam answers, climbing back onto his bike.

6 March, Great Western Trail, Mt. Timpanogos

We ride along the Provo River into the canyon, turn up a dirt road that leads to a snaky green aqueduct, and then follow the pipe to where a single-track trail bisects the road. Erosion this winter has left the trail narrower than ever, but this section of the Great Western, an ambitious trail projected to reach from Canada to Mexico, widens some as it makes a double dogleg up over a bed of what we call shale but that is really quartzite. If you're still on your bike when you reach these loose rocks on the steep part of the trail you have lost much of your momentum and your legs and lungs are burning but since you have made it this far you try to power your way up onto the rocks, feeling in your legs for that tricky point beyond which your efforts will make your back wheel spin out and finally, the bike gods willing, you make the sudden climb up from the quartzite onto the gentler trail that skirts the hill until it swings away from the precipitous edge (fortunately, there are tall herbs and a fringe of oak brush to shield your vision of the drop-off to the river five hundred yards below) into a beautiful forty-acre bowl of native grasses bordered by scrub oak.

"Johnson's Hole," Sam says at the top of the treacherous trail. "Empty now, but homesteaded more than a century ago by early pioneers."

It's easier for me to nod than to use my lungs for speech. Notch one up for Sam.

"I've always been interested in places folks homesteaded and then abandoned," Sam says as we ride on up the ridge. "Did they survive? Did they leave for a better place? Years ago,

I was collecting algae from ultra-saline habitats at the north end of the Great Salt Lake. Along a lonesome dirt road was a brown-grey, disintegrating wooden slab home leaning east into four huge, half-dead cottonwood trees. An old-fashioned rose bush, still producing a few blossoms, slumped to each side of the front doorway. And in the middle of what used to be the front yard was a three-wheeled wagon, rusted, battered, apparently not worth taking with the family when they pulled stakes. Why? Did they lack room? Was the wagon too 'used up'? I sat by the wagon to eat my lunch, a buzzard overhead. I found myself spinning the one wheel that was still mobile. Ever since, I have wondered about who and where the little girl is who had to leave her wagon, and, by god, I have longed to take her a new Radio Flyer 'fat-tire' and ask about her life."

On our way down, I remind Sam that after his discourse on diatoms I was dumbfounded. "So I looked up the word 'dumbfounded,' I say.

"Where does the word come from?" Sam asks.

"It's a marriage of the adjective 'dumb'—unable to speak—and the verb 'confound,' which originally meant to throw into disorder. Learning new things makes me rethink old ideas and, for a blessed moment, I'm silent. Dumbfounded."

8 March, Great Western Trail, Mt. Timpanogos

Yesterday's rain and snow are long gone by the time we reach the trail on this Monday afternoon. A new storm is blowing in from the south. Streaks of rain shroud Mt. Nebo. Utah Lake is troubled, a rumpled grey slate to the west. Far to the south, the sun breaks through and spotlights the valley floor. Sam gestures at the gully-slotted hillside: "Greys, browns, and yellows. Colors that match my mood over the last month—maybe my whole life. Did you see the *Zigadenus paniculatus*?"

"Huh?"

"Death camus, the spiky-leafed plant emerging in the middle of the trail."

I had missed it—but, alerted to the possibility, I spy a second one thrusting its sharp leaves through the loose dirt of the trail.

"*Zigadenus,*" Sam says, "is in the family *Liliaceae,* the lilies. Most of the members of this family are non toxic and several are edible—onions and garlic, for example."

"Why *'death* camus'?" I ask.

"The generic name," Sam explains, "refers to the active agent, an alkaloid called zygadenine that makes this perhaps the second most poisonous plant in the west, after hemlock. It causes a quickening and irregularity of the heartbeat, slows respiration, and brings on convulsions, just like riding this damned trail does. Because it is one of the first plants to appear in the spring, livestock sometimes eat it. Lois Arnow, author of *Flora of the Central Wasatch Front,* says sheep are the only animals she knows of that are routinely poisoned by Zigadenus. That makes death camus a fine selective sheepicide. Every year I gather seeds and scatter them across our territory. What a lovely task."

"On another note," I say, "thank you again for helping me with my appeal of the decision not to promote me to the rank of professor. I'll send you a summary when I get home. If some patriarch complains about your lack of citizenship, you can show him what you did for me and for the university. Our reasonable arguments, our silver-tongued eloquence, and our 'civility that becomes believers'—to quote the university's citizenship policy— ought to get me promoted, don't you think?"

"All things being equal," Sam answers, "the BYU administration should promote you and give you a big raise. But when they accused you of 'kicking against the pricks' I figured it was over. Anyone who could categorize your arguments against them as 'kicking against the pricks' has no sense for language, no sense for irony, and no sense of humor. I'm afraid you may have kicked against your last BYU prick."

8 March, Orem *(by email)*

Sam—Here is my summary of the appeal. There are probably psychological reasons why I put it in third person. Whatever the case, thanks again. It was nice not to have to stand alone. And best of all, we had a hell of a good time saying what we think in a place where that is anathema.

To ground their allegations of "contentious criticism," university officials cited the following statements from Scott's publications:

"There is a virulent strain of anti-intellectualism in the Mormon Church...and its purveyors are, among others, members of BYU's Board of Trustees...The Department of Religious Education has hired teachers who fit the unctuous seminary teacher mold rather than teacher-scholars...BYU is a sanctimonious edifice, a formalistic, hyper-pious community."

The Dean of Humanities wrote that through "Scott's actions as co-president of the BYU Chapter of the American Association of University Professors [which had investigated allegations of infringements on academic freedom at BYU], the university and the Church have been held up to national ridicule."

"A more circumspect Scott," he asserted, "would think twice, then thrice about taking his grievances to a national organization that regards academic freedom as the only true God."

Holy shit! Scott thought. There was not—and he knew this for a fact—a "more circumspect Scott." The "University Representative" for the subsequent appeal wrote that Scott's work had been "disruptive, manipulative, and contentious," whereas BYU faculty "*assume an obligation of dealing with sensitive issues sensitively and with a civility that becomes believers.*"

HOLY SHIT! *Scott thought.* I need help. *And who better to help him than his partner in godless academic-freedom crime: Sam Rushforth. Sam was, after all, co-president of the BYU Chapter of the AAUP. And he was not unctuous.*

Sam was not sympathetic, either (he alleged that sympathy *could be found between* shit *and* syphilis *in the dictionary). He agreed, however, to be Scott's "faculty advocate." As the two men prepared the appeal, they found it difficult to summon the "civility that becomes believers." Some things are simply beyond belief.*

Scott and Sam collaborated on the arguments they presented to the members of the appeal committee. Sam told the committee that, when he and Nancy were advocating stricter clean-air standards for Utah, "someone thought we were being contentious and threw a brick through our window. The people who have denied Scott's application for promotion have, in effect, thrown a brick through his academic career."

Scott concluded the appeal: "You have argued that I am a bad citizen because I used the word 'unctuous' in reference to hires of non-scholars and because I called BYU 'sanctimonious.' The Dean has argued that I am a bad citizen because I held the university up to ridicule. You haven't, however, addressed the question of whether an 'unctuous' and 'sanctimonious' university is ridiculous."

12 March, Great Western Trail, Mt. Timpanogos

Bright sun this afternoon, glorious but still chilly for the light cotton shorts we both wear. A shiny black deposit on a rock proves to be relatively fresh fox (*Vulpes fulva*) scat. "A touch of diarrhea," I observe.

"Here's a set of paw prints." On his knees, Sam points to small, rounded depressions in yesterday's mud. Around the corner, we pass the scat of a more regular fox, a tight twist of black "tobacco," also deposited conspicuously on a rock. Two years ago, we surprised a pair of red foxes dancing circles here, rising on two legs to paw at and dance with one another. A few weeks later, we looked down on a golden-brown fox backlit by a brilliant sunset, lighter hair marking a cross down the length of its back and across its shoulders. And that fall, we stood and watched the same cross-phase fox trot slowly away, watching us warily as it traversed a draw and bounded up a hill. At the top, it sat back on its haunches and watched us pass.

Since then, over the course of several hundred rides, we have seen many signs of foxes—but no actual foxes. Scat and tracks have served as the presence of an absence. We have come to relish this indirect, mediated relationship, to respect the intimate distance. Whenever we top a rise from which we have seen foxes in the past, our eyes scan the landscape. When no fox appears, we breathe a sigh of relief.

Relief?

It's complicated, but maybe we're relieved because we recognize ourselves as forerunners (foreriders) of the human wave encroaching on Utah's wild places. If the foxes can slip our sight, they will be better off.

Grass is beginning to fill openings between the oak brush. Spears of death camus dot the meadow, a few of them cropped by browsing deer, we surmise, although that perplexes us. I try to dig up a bulb.

"Careful," Sam warns.

It's a double warning. There is the poison, of course. But Sam is sensitive to intrusion, to human hubris in the face of nature. I've heard him argue that we would have a better world if we accorded legal standing to trees. Last summer, when I plucked a blooming stalk of hound's tongue to take home to draw, Sam couldn't suppress an "awwww!"

The pointed leaves of the death camus rise a couple of inches from the ground. I dig for more than four inches and still don't reach the bulb. When I pull on the plant, it breaks off.

"The bulbs will be deep," Sam explains. "Maybe a foot down."

I wipe my fingers carefully on my sweatshirt.

Sam points to another plant. "Look at this little umbel. The yellow buds in the center are already open."

The inconspicuous plant hugs the ground, the yellow mass of tiny flowers surrounded by almost fern-like green leaves, streaks of purple along the triply forked stems. "Maybe a carrot," Sam surmises. "Or a parsnip. At least some sort of umbel. The first spring flowers on the foothills of Mt. Timpanogos this year!"

"By the way," I tell Sam on the ride down, "there was a quick response to our appeal. The letter from the Chair of the panel came yesterday. 'We regret the disappointment,' he wrote, 'and we hope for a day in which you will be able to understand and appreciate the perspectives of all your colleagues here.'"

"He's got a point, Abbott," Sam says. "What we have here is a failure to communicate how much you understand and appreciate the self-righteousness of the so-called leaders who are destroying what had the potential to be a decent university."

18 March, Great Western Trail, Mt. Timpanogos

A dark velvet, blue-spotted mourning cloak butterfly flits across our path. I chased these as a child at my grandparents' farm in Windsor, Colorado. Childhood memories are powerful. When I decided to move from Tennessee to Utah, the Dean of Vanderbilt's School of Arts and Sciences asked if Brigham Young University was offering me more money. "No," I said. "I miss the scent of sage." Visceral childhood memory trumped academic prestige. And, of course, there's the matter of public lands. Tennessee, though exquisitely beautiful, is almost entirely privately owned. The federal government controls sixty-four percent of Utah, and ten-percent of the landscape is state controlled. That means it belongs to us and not to someone with money to build a big fence.

Another insect flashes past, a brilliant scarlet-orange patch under its wings. "Boxelder bug," Sam says. "'*Boisea trivittata*.' Named by Thomas Say, an American entomologist who was part of an expedition to the Rocky Mountains in 1819 and 1820. He was the first to classify and name the coyote and the lazuli bunting as well. The bright red of this bug, like the red of many species, warns predators that there's a foul smell and/or taste waiting for them if they attack."

Up the trail, a tank-like ladybug (*Hippodamia convergens*) splits its red-orange shell (more foul odor!) to reveal black wings. Small spiders dodge our tires. When I think I have found the first tender green leaf on the still barren oak brush, it turns out to be a lime-green stinkbug (*Acrosternum hilare*). Another stinker.

At the top of the hill, Sam points to a tiny plant with red leaves. "Some plants use this red coloring to protect themselves from the bright sunlight that bleaches their chlorophyll. The pigment is in a class known as anthocyanins, the same pigments that, along with tannin, may make red wine good for the heart and cause the red coloring in fall leaves."

"Thanks for the lecture," I tell Sam. "But help me with something else. Last night I looked up death camus in both of my field guides to wildflowers. The one lists only meadow death camus, *Zigadenus venenosus*, and doesn't mention any other variants. The other book describes mountain death camus, *Zigadenus elegans*, and notes the existence and characteristics of *Zigadenus gramineus*, *Zigadenus venenosus*, and *Zigadenus paniculatus*. What's the deal?"

"You've stumbled onto something controversial and interesting here," Sam says. "It's a classic disagreement between the lumpers (me included) and the splitters. Your second guide was written by splitters and your first by lumpers. Lumpers see splitters as scientists who proliferate species endlessly on the basis of insubstantial differences. Splitters see lumpers as scientists who are too lazy or conservative to pay attention to the importance of detail. Actually, the trick is in understanding what details matter in separating taxa. Dandelions, for example, are a great source of tension between splitters and lumpers. They grow from Alaska to Patagonia and most lumpers call all or most of them *Taraxacum officinale*. Because dandelions are self-fertilizing, mutations tend to "stick," and splitters distinguish hundreds of species. Check your guides and see what you find."

At home, I open Carl Schreier's *A Field Guide to Wildflowers of the Rocky Mountains*. The common dandelion, *Taraxacum officinale*, is listed as a single species. Craighead, Craighead, and Davis's *Rocky Mountain Wildflowers*, however, lists three dandelions that occur in the Rockies, and states that "close to 1000 species of *Taraxacum* have been described, but conservative botanists now recognize around 50." Schreier is a lumper, Craighead and friends splitters. It's that simple—once Sam points it out. I bought these guides expecting scientific facts. Instead, I get judgments, assessments, interpretations built on biases. "Truth," Nietzsche wrote, "is a mobile army of metaphors." I'm fifty years old and have known this for decades. Now I know it again.

I try to explain this epistemological rediscovery to Sam and he has a sage reply: "Truth is relative for folks comfortable with dissent and argument, but solid as concrete among ideologues."

Two

Biker lycra siticus

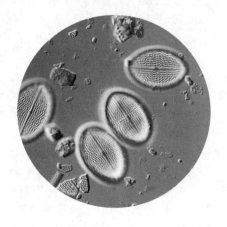

21 March, Great Western Trail, Mt. Timpanogos

A storm during the night has scoured the air! The sun burns with a rare clarity, north of the equator for the first time since the fall equinox. We leave civilization and climb the mountainside. Restraints slough from minds and bodies. We ride over the quartzite, past Johnson's Hole, along the limestone ridge, not stopping to catch our breath till the trail meets the fire road. We look again at the umbel.

"I did some reading," Sam says. "I think this is *Cymopterus longipes* (spring parsley)—because of the bluish green coloration of the leaves. If I'm right, in the next couple of weeks the floral stalk will raise off the soil several centimeters on a stemlike structure known as a pseudoscape.

Near the spring parsley stands another tiny white flower. "They're fourmerous," Sam indicates. "And see how each of the four petals is split in two? I'd guess them to be mustards, the Brassicaceae family, genus *Draba*."

We are down on our knees, our faces inches from the ground, our asses pointed skyward. I take my reading glasses, sans earpieces, from my shorts pocket and hold them to my nose. The tiny flowers are delicate and beautiful. Like us.

"By the way," Sam says, "I checked on the death camus we thought had been cropped. Came up with a couple of different stories. First, some people believe deer will not browse death camus. Second, some suggest deer browse on *Zigadenus* when it is young and tender and there isn't much else to eat. They may be able to get by with this as long as they eat other forage as well. Valerius Geist—who studied with Nobel Prize winner Konrad Lorenz and has become a wonderful biologist with a focus on large North American mammals—argues that the mule deer's rumen and bacterial flora can detoxify plant poisons, helped by its large liver and kidneys. He also points out that overgrazing has reduced the abundance of many good forage plants, making way for death camus and other toxic species."

We've ridden the lower section of the Great Western Trail a dozen times since it dried. Today we'll try a higher stretch, a challenging single-track trail winding up the flank of Mt. Timpanogos toward two pyramidal humps that protrude from the mountain's southwest slope: Little and Big Baldy. Bikers at Mad Dog Cycles call this semi-hidden trail "Frank"—a nonsense code name—hoping to keep down the number of riders.

Frank begins with an abrupt approach through overhanging oak brush, jerks up a steep, tight C-turn, thrusts up two linked chutes so rocky we call them creek beds (with shifting adjectives to suit how badly they're beating us up), and follows a relentlessly climbing ridge for miles. It doesn't really need a code name to keep riders away.

I can't find a line through the loose rocks just above the C-turn, and in the second creek bed Sam loses his balance as well. We remount and pedal up the ridge as slowly as the requirements of balance allow. In a meadow where the trail flattens just a bit, we stop for a moment (this has nothing to do with how my lungs are burning) to watch six heavy-bodied, spindly-legged elk (*Cervus canadensis*) slip out of the meadow and over a ridge. Creatures rightly wary of our presence. Specters of beauty and grace. Can they admire our forms? Find humor in our two-wheeled contraptions?

Not far below where we ran into the toe of a late avalanche last spring, wet snow halts our progress. Clusters of pink and white flowers bobble on their stems at the snow's edge. The blossoms are fivemerous and have five pink-tipped stamens. "Spring beauties," Sam exclaims. "*Claytonia lanceolata*. What a nice find!" On that same snowy ecotone, we discover flat little organisms that remind me of Lilliputian lily pads made of salamander skin. "An ascomycete," Sam observes. "It's a beautiful little fungus related to the morels we could find here later. The fungal flora of Utah is not well known, and I don't even know the genus of this beauty." I'll ask Larry St. Clair at BYU, one of my colleagues who has become an expert on fungi and lichens in the West.

Heading back down the trail, working our brakes now instead of our pedals, we hear unexpected voices. Two young bikers appear on the trail below us. We pull our bikes off the trail, respectful of the wheezing, perspiring, climbing riders. The scent of onion engulfs us. We're standing in a patch of wild onions (*Allium cepa*)!

Having descended to the top of the final hill, an orchard stretching in orderly rows beneath us, deeply satisfied by this equinoctial adventure, we stand down and let the sun touch us. Sam's body turns suddenly and I watch him listen intently. It comes again, the complex, liquid warble of a meadowlark (*Sturnella neglecta*). The lark, its fat yellow belly brilliant in the sun, perches on a tip of silver-green sage. It calls again and again, swelling and contracting with the effort. From an adjoining hill, another meadowlark answers, filling the draw with echoes as warm as the sunlight.

Sam's standing form, silhouetted against the valley below, reminds me of early nineteenth-century paintings by Caspar David Friedrich. Responding to the new sense among German Romantics for the importance of the subject as it relates to objects of perception, Friedrich painted human figures from behind, their gazes turned to nature. "Nature," Friedrich's contemporary Schelling wrote, "is visible spirit, spirit is invisible nature."

27 March, Orem, Utah

"Sam," I say when he answers the phone, "the *Salt Lake Observer*'s out, and our first column shares the paper with Terry Tempest Williams' 'A Letter to Edward Abbey on the

10th Anniversary of His Death.'"

"You mean *your* first column," Sam answers. "I'm glad none of my prose is up against Terry's. There's no way she'll think I wrote any of that, is there?"

"Not a chance," I reply. "She's known you a long time. She knows you can't put two sentences together. But get this, she tells Abbey things have changed since he died: "There is a new species that has inhabited Slickrock Country: *Biker lycra siticus*. It is everywhere on Porcupine Rim, White Rim, Slickrock, Sandpoint, the River Road, Behind the Rocks, wherever there is flat red rock or an incline or decline wide enough for a mountain bike's tire, *Biker lycra siticus* is there."

"Ah, shit," Sam opines. "That's a harsh judgment from a woman we've always been half in love with. Guess we'll have to sell the bikes."

"Maybe we're different from the bikers she's writing about," I venture. "Maybe we ride more responsibly, more respectfully."

"All I know," Sam says before hanging up, "is that you'll never see me in Lycra again. And I'm taking over half the column. This is too important to leave to your misperceptions and sorry lack of talent."

28 March, Great Western Trail, Mt. Timpanogos

The male boxelder trees (*Acer negundo*) are boldly in flower now, extruded stamens drooping conspicuously from long reddish pedicels. While we sit in the grass at the top of our lower loop, we notice several early grasshoppers. Last summer, following an extraordinary growth of yellow sweet clover, the grasshopper population exploded. The winter has been unusually mild. Grasshopper apocalypse approaching?

"Let's do Frank," Scott suggests, and we start up the unrelenting trail. We both make the early hills and are feeling good— small pleasures for half-grown children. As I approach the top of the second chute, an oak brush hand reaches out and grabs my bar-end and over I go. "Nice ride," I tell Scott as he powers by. Farther up the trail, much farther than we expected to get today—a lot of snow has melted since last Sunday—we get off the bikes and walk among the naked scrub oak. "Oregon grape," Scott shouts. "Isn't March early for this?" He has discovered an entire hillside of *Mahonia repens*, thousands of yellow buds ready to burst into blossom and later make fruits that have long been important as native dyes.

I range across the hill, looking for the glacier lilies we ought to see here. Nothing. On the way back to the trail, however, I stumble across a single, elegant *Dicentra uniflora*—steershead. This unusual flower is pinkish white and really does look like the head of a lollygagging Jersey cow. It's an unexpected and startling find, this single flower nestled among the resurrection green of a burgeoning hillside meadow. Scott has never seen a steershead, and bends over it enthusiastically, peering through his funny reading glasses.

I tell Scott I've been thinking about our earlier conversation about lumpers and splitters—and about ideologues. "I just re-read your 1996 essay about BYU—"Clipped and Controlled." You pointed out that, in his inaugural address, BYU president Merrill Bateman plagiarized his whole diatribe against moral relativism. You quoted him as saying that 'If university scholars reject the notion of truth, there is no basis for intellectual and moral integrity…The university becomes a politicized institution that is at the mercy and whims of various interest groups.'"

"He's right," Scott says. "If we have our way, the university will be at the mercy of immoral advocates of academic freedom. But enough of that. Let's ride on up the hill."

Spring beauties spread across whole meadows still matted from the snow. We ride higher and higher, wind through a still leafless maple grove, and halt where the trail cuts across the mountainside just before turning back into a series of final snow-packed switchbacks below the saddle between Little Baldy and Mount Timpanogos. Scott finds a bright yellow violet blooming on the trail, Nuttall's violet, *Viola nuttallii*. After basking shirtless in the sun for a while, we swoop down the Great Western Trail, reveling in the precision of our fine machines and bursting with the magnificence of this mountain landscape.

THREE

Ed Abbey Had a Mountain Bike

30 March, Great Western Trail, Mt. Timpanogos

All morning the sky has thickened and thinned with chasing clouds, an unsettled and unsettling day with moderate wind out of the north. "Must say this matches my mood," Sam says. Timpanogos is veiled behind a thin white scrim of clouds. Colors today are heightened by patches of sunlight that race across meadows and up the slope of the mountain. Silhouetted against the slate-colored western sky, a dozen mule deer stand on the spine of the ridge, their enormous ears working the landscape of sound—elegant, rotating antennae scanning for danger. Standing for a moment to let our hearts slow down after what turned into a competitive sprint (Sam won, as he usually does), I spot blue flowers growing on the hillside. "Bluebells," Sam reports. "*Mertensia oblongifolia*, perhaps. They're in the borage family, related to forget me nots and hound's tongue."

Why do these deep blue flecks against a dark hillside have our hearts pounding again? Beauty may be the simplest answer. But why do we then stop and look into the blossom and count the stamens? Why do we speak to one another about this blossom? It's because we want to know, I surmise. For a moment, this perfect natural thing overcomes our anger at the ongoing human destruction of the Earth. Good lord, these flowers are beautiful. And infinitely complex.

Our children will worry us again when we return home. What future will they have in an overpopulated world where greed is the rule? Frustrations spawned by our own inadequacies will quickly engulf us. Unfulfilled desires will return before the evening is through. Newspaper headlines will provoke anger or despair. But for this moment, in this moment, we stand fulfilled by perfection of nature.

On the way down from the top of Frank, we ease past a small herd of elk drifting down through the oak brush—dark shadows against the white, barkless hearts of oaks stripped by the fire that swept these hillsides two years ago. In today's patchy light, the mountainside alternates between muted greens and greys. When we reach the overlook at the canyon's mouth, Utah Lake is again a disturbed dark slate to the west, silvered in places where the sun slants through a heavy western sky.

"The color of steel," Sam muses.

"Bad metaphor," I say. "The Geneva Steel Plant is a polluting cancer on the lakeshore."

"Pewter," Sam says. "A pewter lake."

5 April, Great Western Trail, Mt. Timpanogos

It's Monday afternoon and we haven't ridden since last Tuesday. Timpanogos is pristine under the brilliant white blanket of snow that was our April-fools' surprise. Banks of grey and black clouds scallop the sky. A cold wind blows from the south. We head toward the canyon wearing the tights and wicking underwear and vests and gloves we thought we had put away for the season.

At the canyon's mouth, a harsh, descending *kreeeeeeer* draws our eyes skyward. Two red-tailed hawks (*Buteo jamaicensis*) circle just above us, calling, diving, swinging up, diving, hanging motionless against the canyon wind, playing the mating game so precious and familiar to living beings. While neither of us can dance in the sky, we understand the mating dance and have done our best, each in his own way, to perfect it.

As we pedal along, I tell Sam that BYU decided yesterday not to retain a Jewish colleague because members of the Board of Trustees were afraid that, with only 98% of the faculty as practicing Mormons, we were in grave danger of becoming a secular university. "Arkady told me it was no big deal. He was used to being kicked out of Russian universities for being a Jew."

"Arkady Weintraub," Sam says. "One of the best math pedagogues in the world. Why do we keep working for these guys?

You remember the Christmas fiasco when Ernest Wilkinson, the President of BYU at the time, wrote his own self-congratulatory history of the university and gave it out instead of the customary turkey? Someone renamed the book *Mein Kampus* and figured that the sequel ought to be called *Free Agency: And How to Enforce It.*"

I remind Sam that the title of my essay, "Clipped and Controlled," was a quotation from the grounds-crew mission statement. "It felt like sphincters were tightening all around. Why do we work for these guys? Remember the dean who said you had been seen in the bookstore wearing shoes without socks, a clear violation of the BYU dress code?"

"Sure do," Sam smiles. "I told him I had been wearing pantyhose. And when the same poor guy called me in to say students complained when I swore in class, I answered repentantly: 'Sorry, Dean. I'm so sorry. I really fucked up. And, by god, it won't happen again.' Many deans, it turns out, don't realize that swearing is a disciplinary requirement meant to supplement the precise descriptions and Latin names we use professionally. When I was still a graduate student, my thesis advisor, recently returned from military service, told me about a lunch with a visiting expert who had come to help determine the location of some very important fossil plants and who was looking to donate some money to BYU. My advisor absent-mindedly said, 'please pass the horsecock…Oh my goodness, I sure fucked up there.' Didn't faze the donor a bit."

A blue bird brings our attention back to the here and now. Seeing only the first flash of blue, we anticipate a mountain bluebird. When the bird alights atop the scrub oak just below us, we note its elongated head, long round beak, long tail, and large size. A scrub jay, *Aphelocoma californica*. The bird's eyes flash as it looks us over—two scrub bikers.

7 April, Great Western Trail, Mt. Timpanogos

We set off under a darkening sky. Halfway up Frank, Sam bends over the bluebells, none the worse for their blanket of snow. "There are maybe five species of these along the Wasatch Front," he tells me, examining the center of the flower, "with an additional species occurring south of here. Two of these, *Mertensia brevistyla* and *Mertensia oblongifolia* are perhaps most common. They are quite similar, differing mostly by fine characteristics of the flower, including the length of the style, the elongated structure between the stigma and ovary. This one is short-styled, it's *Mertensia brevistyla*, the Wasatch bluebell."

At the mouth of the canyon, the storm whipping in from the southwest strikes us head on. With sleet dripping from my exultant face and a wide stripe of sop up my back, bucking, slipping, and sliding down the final knife edge ridge, I hear snatches of song behind me: "Amazing grace…sweet…wretch like me…" It's Sam, celebrating the wonderfully depraved human condition and the splendor of our wild ride.

10 April, Great Western Trail, Mt. Timpanogos

It doesn't take long to reach snow, so we ride toward the mouth of the canyon along the dirt road built to service the big green aqueduct that has radically changed the region's ecosystems by shifting the flow of water. We get off our bikes to sit on a sunny rock and watch a flock of robins.

"*Turdus migratorius,*" Sam notes. "The common robin. It's odd that we learn to consider these wonderfully sonorous, brilliantly colored birds common. Perhaps it's the old story of familiarity and contempt. Were we careful and attentive enough, familiarity would deepen our awe. That, of course, is the guiding principle of our daily rides up and down the same trail: meaning arises out of thoughtful repetition."

My attempt to see the large orange breasted birds with new

eyes is cut short by a fleck of purple on the hillside next to my rock. It's a tiny, five-petaled flower rising on a long stem out of a cluster of even tinier leaves. Alongside the flower, a single distinctive fruit gives the plant its common name: storksbill. Sam confirms my assessment: "Yes, it's storksbill. I've been expecting it all spring, a geranium, *Erodium cicutarium*. It is thought to have been introduced from Europe, though that's something of a mystery since it was noted in the west by Fremont as early as 1844."

12 April, Great Western Trail, Mt. Timpanogos

We turn up Frank with some trepidation. It has been two weeks since we tried this upper section of the Great Western Trail, and at our age, muscles seem to atrophy overnight. Mine, in fact, are not quite up to the first steep corner. From where my head has struck the ground, I'm face to face with unfamiliar brilliant yellow flowers at the end of horizontal stems that snake through last year's dry grass. A pair of cupped bracts frames each blossom like the frills on an exotic lizard. "I'm stumped," Sam admits while I dust myself off. "Let me do a little research." He tucks a piece of the plant into his shorts pocket.

Near the top of Frank, we spot a white patch across a gully on a south-facing slope and step off our bikes. When the patch turns slightly and catches the late-afternoon sun broadside, we recognize it as a venerable elk, white-sided and black-caped. It steps back into the oak brush, joining two smaller darker elk, and together they high-step to the top the hill and disappear.

On the way down, we stop to watch an orange-breasted bird with a black head and white slashes on its wings and tail: a Bullock's oriole, *Icturus bullockii*.

13 April, Orem, Utah

The phone rings. It's Sam, who has a copy of the new *Ob-*

server. "Scott, we're vindicated! Ken Sanders, the rare book Ken Sanders, wrote a letter to the editor defending us. Get this:

> I would like to remind Terry Tempest Williams and Scott Abbott, both of whom I consider friends, and the mountain-biking, botanizing Sam Rushforth, that Ed Abbey had a mountain bike. He rode a red one in the '80's, while he was holed up at Pack Creek Ranch writing his fat masterpiece, *The Fool's Progress.* I even remember a photo of him astride it, replete with his shit-eating grin. After observing mountain bikes and their damage, near Arches, Wendell Berry remarked that riding mountain bikes is 'a hell of a lot of work to go to, just to give your ass a ride.'"

"So Wendell Berry doesn't like us either. This is no vindication."
"Sure it is," Sam explains. "We're okay as long as we ride with shit-eating grins, which come natural to us. But get a load of this second letter:

> Dear Editor, I can't believe you let Sam and Scott misspell camas ('death camus') numerous times. It wrecks their credibility and yours. The column they write is interesting to me. People are trying to extend the Great Western Trail in Cache County, and I worry about Terry Tempest Williams' *"bikers lycra siticus"*—people who zip by the botanical beauty without seeing it. Now I know some see it, but I hope they do their homework next time before they write it in the paper. Star Coulbrooke of Smithfield, Utah

"Abbott, what happened? You misspelled the word in the first draft, and I corrected it. How the hell did it get back to the French existentialist?"
"Sam, I saw your correction when I was going through the

final draft, but I changed it back. Must have been a subconscious indication of how I view your intelligence, or maybe the "death" part of the name triggered the existential part of my brain."

"Brain?" Sam replies. "Camus' fiction is much scarier to me than death camas. Remember that last sentence from *The Plague*: '…the plague bacillus never dies or disappears for good'? In any case, we'll have to thank Star for pointing out our mistake and you'll have to promise not to amend botany with philosophy in the future."

14 April, Great Western Trail, Mt. Timpanogos

For the first time in too many days, we're able to climb back up to where we saw the steershead. Although there is still a lot of snow, that particular south-facing slope is dry. The yellow flowers of Oregon grape are everywhere. Nuttall's yellow violets are plentiful. Spring beauties are recovering from two weeks under the snow. But we can't find the little steershead. Its elusiveness today reminds us that we were lucky.

"Scott," I say as we sit on a sunny hillside, "the other day I was talking about wilderness with Jim Harris, Dean of Science at Utah Valley State College. 'More and more,' he said, 'wilderness for me is about small wild places, even wild moments, rather than wilderness designated on maps.' Jim is one of Utah's strongest wilderness advocates. But he also understands that along with designated wilderness we must have wild hearts if wilderness is to survive. I think that there are places along our stretch of the Great Western Trail that are wild in every way imaginable."

We ride on up the trail and stand finally in a two-acre swale that burned hard two years ago. Skeletons of Gambel oak skirt the trail, ten feet tall, crooked-branched, silhouetted against the eastern sky. At the feet of fire-blackened trunks, hundreds of root sprouts have erupted, some of them already several feet tall, their leaf-buds swelling. In the crook of a dark oak branch, last year's hummingbird nest is perfection in miniature, a soft bed of woven yellow grasses for tiny hummers.

On the way down, we are forced to slow at a dangerous curve made even more difficult by horse traffic in mud. Scott notices a flash of blue and we skid to a stop. An early larkspur, *Delphinium* species, unexpected at this time of year. "Another plant dangerous for livestock," I tell Scott. "Early settlers used a tincture of delphinine to eliminate lice. The name *Delphinium* comes from a Greek story about a dead fisherman carried to shore by a dolphin and then restored to life as a flower the color of the sea with a bud shaped like a dolphin carrying a load on its back. Some Greek looked closely and named the flower after the shape of the bud—as did some English speaker who was more partial to larks than to dolphins. And now you and I are telling our own stories about flowers, by damn."

"Stories deeply colored by the Greeks and Romans," Scott replies. "Stories guided by Thoreau and Goethe, by your botany textbooks, and by the fact of growing up white and male and Mormon in the mountain west. Are we telling stories or are the stories telling us?"

"You're talkin' like a book, Abbott," I say. "Let's drop the bullshit and see if we can get off the mountain alive."

FOUR

Testiculatus

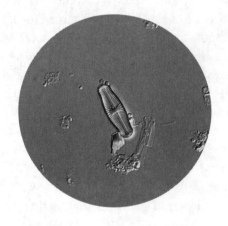

15 April, Great Western Trail, Mt. Timpanogos

Taxes due tonight. I tell Sam I generally like the feeling of being a productive citizen of this country, but the idea of writing a check today to a government that will use it, however indirectly, to drop bombs on people I care for in Belgrade pisses me off.

We ride slowly in the canyon, limestone cliffs protecting us a bit from the cold wind blowing from the northwest. The sun warms our backs. A red-tailed hawk hovers above us, a lethal living presence that disappears as suddenly as it appeared. We get off the bikes to watch a swarm of black butterflies swirling around a maple tree just starting to bud. A hillside blooms with hundreds of bluebells: blue bluebells, lavender bluebells, pink bluebells. Walking among them, we raise the scent of wild onions. Mule deer watch us from above and below, their scruffy grey-brown winter coats sloughing off to reveal slick brown undercoats. We engage in a pleasant and desultory conversation. A fat ground squirrel scuttles down from a high perch in a dead tree. We lie on a grassy hillside and soak up the sun.

War rages in what was once Yugoslavia.

16 April, Great Western Trail, Mt. Timpanogos

Scott and I are both on edge today, worries about children the immediate cause. He's got seven, I've got four. How the hell did that happen? Slipping gears on my bike feel like a metaphor. While I have tried to be a fine father, it is perhaps difficult beyond my abilities. We exchange stories, express concern, venture the only advice we can muster: they have to live their own lives. Small comfort.

A purple flower rising above wrinkled silver-green leaves changes our focus. Locoweed, the year's first *Astragalus*. "This is a difficult genus," I tell Scott. "Stan Welsh, the world's expert on these plants, recognizes over 110 species and many varieties of *Astragalus* in Utah. We are going to tear our hair over these before the year is over. Today's plant is most likely *Astragalus utahensis*, variously known as Utah milkvetch, early locoweed, or lady's slipper."

"I never had a botany class," Scott breaks in. "How the hell do botanists deal with so many names for the same plant?"

"Naming," I reply, "is a tricky business. Each member of the Earth's biota is formally named using a Latinized binomial— the genus and species names. It's a system devised by Carl von Linné, or Linnaeus. Any plant (or animal) may have a whole slew of common names and these often vary locally. But the Latin name is constant and must be used in scientific studies. Formal rules exist to name a species, and they are rigorously followed. Still, there is plenty of room for error. For example, some years ago I named a new fossil holly I had collected from the Cretaceous of southeastern Utah. I published a short article naming this plant *Ilex serrata* for the saw toothed leaf margins. Trouble was, I had not checked previous literature closely enough, and this name was already occupied by a living species of holly. So, a friend of mine published another article in which he changed my fossil's name to *Ilex rushforthii*. This happens all the time, but it tends to embarrass biologists."

"That story," Scott smiles, "confirms the vague sense I've always had of you as related to a saw-toothed fossil."

17 April, Great Western Trail, Mt. Timpanogos

Another peaceful ride today—warm, sunny, lazy. Three teen-aged boys race past on their bikes. Normally we would respond by picking up our pedaling cadence and pass them when they start to feel the climb. In our mellow mood, however, we maintain our speed. "We're figuring this out," Sam says as he pedals a little faster. "We're learning to control our competitiveness."

"I was thinking the same thing," I reply, shifting up a gear.

"We're pretty smart to make that decision while it's still a matter of will." Just before the top of the relentless hill, we pass the panting youngsters.

Hundreds of white-spotted black butterflies flutter around a budding maple tree. I am tempted to grab one to examine it more closely. I remember a painting I saw in the National Gallery: John James Audubon's "Golden Eagle." Audubon bought the live eagle in Boston, agonized over whether to kill it or set it free, made several attempts to kill it without harming its appearance, then worked so feverishly on the painting that he suffered some kind of seizure. In the bottom left-hand corner of the painting, Audubon depicted himself high in snowy mountains, crawling across a chasm on a tree trunk with a rifle and a golden eagle strapped to his back. I leave the insects alone.

A pair of yellow and black Bullock's orioles. A meadowlark. And on a high electrical wire near town, tail bobbing, the first kestrel we've seen this year—*Falco sparverius*, American kestrel. We sit our own tails on a warm slab of blue limestone.

"What the hell are we going to do?" I ask Sam.

"Do about what?" he responds. "About our kids? About the planet?"

"I mean about BYU," I say. "We've got colleagues who are just keeping their heads down till they can retire. We, in contrast, have raised our heads so high that everyone would notice if they fired us. And it hasn't been exactly easy. Remember when we were preparing for the arrival of the AAUP investigators? I dreamed I was holding a lit stick of dynamite. While the fuse burned, and it was burning way too fast, I made excruciatingly slow calculations to figure out how long I could hold on before throwing it into the administration building."

"Yeah," Sam adds, "and I dreamt that Nanc and I were tending to a sick horse. I had a monster syringe full of medicine that was sure to cure the horse. Before I stuck in the needle, Nanc warned me to move away from the horse's ass. 'When the cure comes,' she said, 'the horse is going to blast shit everywhere.'"

"We've had some fun," I say, "and we've done what we thought was right, but I'm not looking forward to spending the next decade working for someone who doesn't want me around. You should know that I've applied for a couple of jobs, even had a campus interview. Hope something pans out."

Sam is quiet for a minute. "Shall we soak up a little more heat from this wonderful limestone?" he finally asks. "And then let's get our asses off this mountain."

18 April, Great Western Trail, Mt. Timpanogos

The inconspicuous yellow flower we've seen several times during the past couple of weeks is common today—bur buttercup, *Ranunculus testiculatus*. If we weren't such delicate fellas concerned about the sensibilities of our readers, I would mention the shape of the fruit for which this plant is named. Have a look next time you are on the hillside. It's a common early flower, often emerging with storksbill. Bur buttercup is another introduced species, entering the U.S. in the last century from southeastern Europe. Like several others we have seen this spring, this species is toxic to sheep.

We've been looking for glacier lilies along this upper trail for three weeks now. Scott and I split up to scour areas near several small patches of remaining snow. Scott shouts—he's found something. It's not a glacier lily, but equally wonderful: a yellow bell, *Fritillaria pudica*. It's a fine discovery for me, a plant I have seen only a few times across the years. Surrounded by spring beauties, the striking flower with its three solid yellow petals and three identical sepals nods on a single stem. I tell Scott the spring beauty bulbs are edible and he soon grubs a thumbnail-sized bulb out of the black earth. "Are you sure about this?" he asks. I tell him grizzly bears love them. I clean it and we each eat half. Scott thinks it tastes like a hazelnut. When I remind him I am primarily a stream ecologist and that I'm dredging notions of all these plants out of deep memory, he blanches.

19 April, Great Western Trail, Mt. Timpanogos

Riding this afternoon, having learned the name "bur buttercup," I have a new eye for these rather inconspicuous plants with their testicular fruits. Names can abstract from the thing and thus deflect careful observation, but in this case the name helps me see more exactly.

I find a five-petaled pink flower.

"The first phlox of the year," Sam says. "We'll see a bunch more of these in the next few weeks. *Phlox longifolia*, I think. Sweet William."

"Phlox! Phlox! Phlox!" I explore the feel of the word in my mouth. I see the odd-looking word in my mind. "Where does the name come from?"

"It's the Greek word for flame," Sam answers.

We stop at the maple tree that attracted so many butterflies the other day, hoping to get a better look at the insects. A few of them are still around, but in two days the scene has changed drastically. Prominent buds have opened fully and bundles of flowers hang down from long stems. Today the tree swarms with shiny orange ladybugs, most of them copulating. One male wiggles his hips energetically and we laugh aloud. "We are not even in their conscious world," Sam says. "We are nothing to them. We don't exist for them. I like that feeling."

FIVE

Weeds of the West

29 April, Great Western Trail, Mt. Timpanogos

Sam's in New York City for a conference on biodiversity, so I'm riding by myself today. My mood is tending to a not unpleasant melancholy when a skunk (*Mephitis mephitis*) ambles out from behind some rabbit brush next to the trail. Its small head swings around, its tail swings around, I swing around. The skunk makes its way back into the brush with an undulating gait that makes the white stripes on either side of its fat back ripple like waves.

I ride out of the canyon ahead of a rain squall. The air above the river is alive with swallows. I stand and watch the long forked tails open and shut like scissors as the agile birds fly jagged lines from insect to insect. They are barn swallows (*Hirundo rustica*) with red-orange chests and dark heads and backs, recently back from Argentina. How is that possible?

I've been jealous of Sam's reference library, so today I bought *Weeds of the West*, now in its 5th edition. What is a weed? the authors ask. "A plant that interferes with management objectives for a given area of land at a given point in time." The Mormons who settled the Great Basin believed God wanted them to make "the desert blossom like a rose." This meant that many native desert plants became weeds. Similarly, Sam and I have become weeds at BYU. My plan to help educate my fellow Mormons hasn't worked out, I think. Somehow, the expansive theology behind the church university ("the glory of God is intelligence") has given way to doubts about free inquiry and demands for absolute obedience.

My thought turns to my brother John. He grew up Mormon, went to BYU, served a mission in Italy, trained as a chef, and then came out as gay. Talk about interference with LDS management objectives! He lived in near exile from the family until he died of complications related to AIDS. In 1995, four years after John's death, the Church released a statement on the family. "Gender," they proclaimed, "is an essential characteristic of individual premortal, mortal, and eternal identity and purpose." From this premise, and from the commandment to "multiply and replenish the earth," they argued that marriage should be heterosexual and that John was thwarting God's plan. As a professor at BYU, I have been lending my name to a religion that denigrates my brother and others like him. That can't continue.

1 May, New York City *(by email)*

Scott—the New York biodiversity conference is good. Plenty of folks who know what they are talking about are discussing worldwide biodiversity loss. On a global basis, habitat loss or damage is the most important factor causing the loss of native species. Second is the invasion of exotic species. These two are related, since exotic species often invade areas with degraded habitat. Global or local, the perturbations are the same.

In Utah, we have had a century and a half of habitat destruction. Livestock overgrazing and mismanagement are among the top causes. Even many years after livestock are removed, their impact remains, including soil erosion by wind and water, stream gullying, degraded water quality in our streams and lakes, the loss of wildlife, and the loss of native plant species. Many of the invasive exotics are well suited for life in disturbed habitats. For example, they often tolerate reduced or periodic moisture, infertile and compacted soils, high soil temperatures, and so forth. Many reproduce rapidly and produce copious seeds. Furthermore, such plants are often more resistant to the various local pathogens and pests that have evolved with native species. All in all, invasive species are scrappy and tolerant of a wide variety of ecological conditions. In undisturbed habitats, exotic species have a harder time. There simply is less room for them, fewer open niches. So, the trick to saving native species is to protect native habitats. And in order to protect habitat, we need to have a close look at grazing management in the West. There are some places, including much of the Colorado Plateau, where livestock should not graze.

2 May, Great Western Trail, Mt. Timpanogos

Hoping the trail will have dried off after three days of rain, I head off for a Sunday ride, alone again. Sam's not back from New York. Low on the mountain, I spot the first paintbrush on the slope this spring—*Castilleja miniata*. Its muted red-orange bracts *cum* flowers are the perfect complement to the silver-green, three-toothed leaves of *Artemisia tridentata*, the sage growing next to it. The paintbrush is semi-parasitic, living in part from water and nutrients it draws from sage roots. Near the paintbrush, the small yellow flowers of another three-toothed plant: bitterbrush, *Purshia tridentata*.

I think about my family as I ride. They are in church this morning. For more than four decades, I have attended church every Sunday, happy to be there, grateful for the company of people trying to improve themselves and determined to serve one another. I paid a generous tithing. I observed the "Word of Wisdom": no smoking, no tea or coffee, and no alcoholic drinks. But last year, when the BYU Board of Trustees announced a new policy that required a bishop's certification that faculty were obeying those commandments, I balked at the requirement. Unless my bishop certifies my worthiness, I'll lose my job. I know myself well enough to predict I won't succumb to coercion. What I don't know is where this will lead. Today it has led me to the mountain.

I climb past bur buttercup, spring parsley, Wasatch bluebells, Oregon grape, storksbill, loco weed, sweet vetch, phlox, leafy spurge, larkspur, Nuttall's violet, and spring beauty before I see the next new flower: ballhead waterleaf, *Hydrophyllum capitatum*. The golf-ball-sized sphere of tiny lavender flowers bristles with stamens and stigmas. High on the mountain, my legs showing signs of palsy, I come across some kind of composite, a sunflower-like flower. Its silver-green, arrow-shaped leaves help me identify it as arrowleaf balsamroot, *Balsamorhiza sagittata*.

Hell, maybe I can do without an accompanying botanist.

5 May, Great Western Trail, Mt. Timpanogos

I've been off my bike for a week in Mexico and a week in New York. I was nervous about riding with Scott, figuring he'd be poised to demoralize me on the trail. Fortunately for me, Scott is feeling dreamy today. He has just been offered a job at Utah Valley State College and is full of the possibilities.

Sitting in the meadow, Scott wonders aloud what it would be like to teach at a place where you were rewarded, rather than punished, for pushing the limits of the known and accepted, for arguing against the status quo, for questioning political and religious certainties. "What will it be like," he asks, "to teach at a school that would welcome my gay brother?"

6 May, Great Western Trail, Mt. Timpanogos

A plant I have been trying to ignore all spring is abundant along the trail today—cheatgrass, *Bromus tectorum*. First named by Linnaeus from European specimens and first collected in Utah in 1894, this grass is native to Eurasia but is now widely distributed throughout the Americas. In our foothills and mountains, cheatgrass grows and sets seed early and turns reddish brown as it matures in the late spring and summer. Most hillsides in the west are abundant with cheatgrass, often a result of disturbance from livestock, which prefer native species until they are decimated. Look east to the Wasatch Range this summer, and the reddish cast you'll notice on the hills is due to senescent cheatgrass. Some argue that it protects disturbed soils from erosion and has forage value for wildlife and livestock.

While this is marginally true, cheatgrass is a miserable introduction that represents all that is problematic about exotic invaders.

Scott hears quail (*Callipepla gambelii*) chattering. Below us, high-pitched motors scream. Motorcycles, we think, or four-wheelers. But it's worse than that. When we cross the last ditch, we see two men with chainsaws systematically felling the orchard we have ridden through for the past decade. Five rows of trees are already gone.

6 May, Great Western Trail, Mt. Timpanogos

Five inches of wet snow yesterday morning, and this afternoon we are riding the Great Western Trail! I spent the morning at Utah Valley State College negotiating the details of a job and am full of the energy that comes from being wooed. Sam is quiet today. As co-founders of the BYU Chapter of the American Association of University Professors and as co-instigators of an AAUP investigation which determined that "at Brigham Young University infringements on academic freedom are distressingly common and the climate for academic freedom is distressingly poor," we have worked together for over five years on academic freedom issues. It must seem to him like I'm a rat leaving a sinking ship.

"This almost didn't come off," I tell Sam. "You know the BYU retirement plan is a disaster unless you put in thirty years. With my eleven years, I'd walk away with nothing. I sat down with the academic vice president and laid out the problem: 'I have a job offer I'd like to take, but I can't leave BYU unless you give me a retirement package—a year's salary added to my TIAA-CREF retirement account.' He said they could come up with half of that, at most. 'In that case,' I said, 'I'll have to stay here.' After some overnight calculations, he offered me the whole amount. They're damned happy to get rid of me."

"I'm sure the feeling is mutual," Sam surmises.

Back from the ride, remembering that Carl von Linnaeus first named cheatgrass, I pick up a new book by Linnaeus, edited by Wolf Lepenies. Not only did Linnaeus classify plants, he thought he could discern divinely guided patterns in human tragedy as well. In the collected accounts of what he called *Nemesis Divina*, he recounts this story:

Jacob of Saanas (community Stenbrohult in Smaland) lived badly with his wife. One Christmas (in my youth) as she wanted to walk over the ice to church, she breaks through the ice, holds on, 1/4 hour, to the edge of the ice with her hands, calls for help. Her husband stands on the bank, for it happened close to the yard, and says he doesn't dare to venture out on the ice (because he would be happy to lose her). She drowns. Five years later Jacob's fingers begin to rot, the fingers with which he could have helped his wife; and they continue to rot on both hands. Finally he dies of the disease.

Linnaeus collected hundreds of these stories, proof that GOD is watching you and will avenge. Our human obsession with meaning and order has a productive scientific component, but Linnaeus's search for cosmic order also resulted in superstitious bullshit that is simply embarrassing. And psychologically unsettling. His *Nemesis* story feels like a metaphor, of sorts, for my own marriage. It has been a decade since our relationship settled into nothing but a shared concern for our children. We have been drowning one another in icy neglect and soul-rotting anger.

7 May, Great Western Trail, Mt. Timpanogos
Today, the first fully open white flowers of death camas. In one inflorescence, we find a large, solid-red ladybird beetle. A

scrub jay flashes blue as we ride past, scolding us harshly. These jays form long-term attachments between males and females and they have been observed to share lives with a third adult "helper" that aids in raising and protecting the young against predators. There's a wide range, we note, of possible "natural" families.

"Let's issue a 'Proclamation to the World,'" Scott suggests. "A manifesto to rebut the Mormon one with that title that says the only natural family involves marriage between one heterosexual man and one heterosexual woman. Ours will argue that natural families are evolutionary experiments of the widest imaginable variety. We'll make our case with science rather than theology."

Butterflies are abundant again. I mention to Scott that identifying all of them is going to be difficult. "Why do we have to know or identify everything?" he asks. "For everything we know, there are fifty things we don't." His suggestion that we don't have to identify them all is a momentary relief. But backing off that compulsion is not easy for a professor whose role in life is to have the answers.

9 May, Orem

"What a symphony of crickets," Sam exclaims.

"What crickets?" I ask.

Last summer, Sam stopped suddenly and backed his bike away from a chunk of blue limestone. "What's up?" I asked. "It's a rattlesnake!" he said. "It's buzzing like crazy. Back away." I stepped off the bike the wrong way—toward the snake—and Sam said nonchalantly, "I'll take good care of your bike after you die." I eventually saw the snake, but I never did hear the high-pitched rattling. And now I can't hear the crickets.

Faced with a steady decline of the various senses, it makes sense to start pairing up. Sam, for example, can protect me from rattlesnakes. And I see better than he does. It's like the eighty-year-old man who announces his engagement to his friends. "Is she beautiful?" they ask. "No," he answers. "Is she a good cook?" "Can't cook a lick," he says. "Is she nice to you?" "Not especially." "So why are you getting married?" "She can drive at night," he explains.

Six

Beauty is as Beauty C'n Do

11 May, Teasdale, Wayne County, Utah

Last night was cold and cloudy. Nanc and I wake to a dusting of snow across the sage and piñon landscape. On Thousand Lake Mountain to the north and the Boulder to the south, lava flows are accented by the new snow, and the reds and yellows of the Mesozoic rocks have been delicately frosted. As we stretch awake in the thin and melancholy blue and orange light, fourteen deer cross a hundred yards in front of us after a night of good food in the alfalfa fields east of Teasdale.

There are robins here, several sparrows, an American kestrel, a few mountain bluebirds, a red-winged blackbird, two starlings, and several common ravens. I don't agree there is much common about the raven. These birds (*Corvus corax*) are very smart—some say as smart as a good dog. They apply logic to problem solving and seem to be constantly running a con or just playing for the hell of it. A couple of years ago I stood at the South Rim of the Grand Canyon at sunset and watched a raven rise a thousand feet above the rim, fold its wings, fall like a bullet below the rim, catch itself, and start over again.

14 May, Great Western Trail, Mt. Timpanogos

The day began with neon and ended with iridescence.

My eighth-grade son, Ben, appeared this morning wearing a neon-green shirt and bright purple pants and left home fifteen minutes before the bus was due. "My friend and I have to coordinate outfits," he explained.

Late this afternoon I took my first bike ride in a week—alone, because Sam and Nancy are spending the week in Teasdale. After days of alternating rain and sun, the hills are furry with fresh grasses. New scrub oak leaves give whole hillsides an orange-brown hue. The first flax of the year, *Linum lewisii*, blue as a robin's egg. Riding toward the canyon's mouth, I wondered when the lazuli buntings would appear from their winter range in the mountains of Mexico. My notes from last year show our first sighting on May 17th. On cue, just before breaking out of the canyon, I heard a familiar call. Putting down my bike, I walked back toward the quick, high-pitched song repeated every fifteen seconds or so. An iridescent blue head shimmered at the top of a still leafless scrub oak. A male lazuli bunting, *Passerina amoena*. The familiar bright cinnamon breast above a white belly. Two white slashes across the dark wings. The bird sang again and again, and from the hill above, another voice answered with its own version of the song. I stood between the communicating birds, silent, thinking about my own pending migration.

Later I stopped at the ditch above the disappearing orchard (ten rows of trees now gone) and bent to look at the emerging dusky-purple clustered flowers and slender curved lingual leaves of the year's first hound's tongue, *Cynoglossum officinale*. Another European introduction. I straightened up to see a flash of yellow, then a second one. Two male western tanagers (*Piranga ludoviciana*) chasing a single female. The bright yellow breasts of the males contrast with their black wings and backs and are accented by their brilliant red heads. They, too, have returned from wintering in Mexico, albeit somewhat farther south than the buntings.

So much color! And to think that the evolutionary forces that developed the colorful buntings and tanagers are also at work in Ben's choice of his own eye-dazzling plumage, meant to impress the girls and boys of the eighth grade.

15 May, Wayne County

On the road near Grover today, we are stopped by a herd of maybe 150 cows taking their time up the middle of Highway 12 on their way to Miner's Mountain. I step out of the car. Two cowboys, one old, one young, ride at the back of the herd. The young cowboy sits a big buckskin. "Good-looking horse,"

I tell him. "Thanks," he nods and rides on. The other cowboy, who won't see seventy again, rides over and smiles. "Beauty is as beauty c'n do," he says. "I got horses back in my barn prettyr'n that horse and they don't look half as good." This while a cow pisses next to me, a great yellow gusher that splashes me up both legs.

Makes an old green activist wonder about the future of the cowboy, about the interactions between the old west and the new. Makes me wonder how we can learn to talk together long enough to solve our differences.

21 May, Great Western Trail, Mt. Timpanogos

An early morning canyon wind. This routine draining of cold air to our lower valley creates a small delta of unusually clean air at the canyon mouth where Sam and I both live. It's a steady wind this morning, a constant presence that flavors every aspect of our ride. Standing, for instance, just above the quartzite that has knocked us off our bikes again this morning, we watch eight gulls (*Larus californicus*) fly up canyon. Headway is possible for them only in furious spurts, followed, always, by a sudden veering away, a sliding downstream.

The wind is at our backs as we swoop up the knife-edged ridge. We talk about the return of the buntings from Mexico, look across the canyon at the greening scrub oak, feel the systematic breathing of the canyon. Above us, a dark-feathered hawk toils against the wind, lumbering upcanyon. It draws our attention into the sun hanging just above the canyon's highest eastern notch. The hawk disappears into the sun and Sam marvels at the sundogs crouching to either side. We remember the winter morning when we stood on our skis high in Hobble Creek Canyon and looked into the sun to the south to witness two full rings, the larger of which shimmered colorfully down into the gully at our feet. Sam swore it was a visitation of the Virgin Mary.

22 May, Great Western Trail, Mt. Timpanogos

From time to time, for the past several years, a bird has puzzled us here. It's a bit smaller than a robin, but with that same sort of substantial presence. We've never seen it close enough to identify it. Today, one perches in a trailside tree. "Turn around, you sonofabitch," Scott says. "Show off your plumage! Don't you know we're trying to commune with nature here?" It's in no hurry, but finally complies. It has a velvety black head, short conical beak, dark wings with white dashes, orange sides, a white breast, and a sharp reddish eye. A rufous-sided or spotted towhee (*Pipilo maculatus*). *Chirpchirpchirp—trillllllllll!*

24 May

New flowers everywhere: purple Wasatch penstemon (*Penstemon cyananthus*), yellow Dalmatian toadflax (*Linaria dalmatica*), delicate white woodland star (*Lithophragma parviflora*), spiky yellow goatsbeard (*Tragopogon dubius*), mellow orange globemallow (*Sphaeralcea coccinea*), and purple northern sweetvetch (*Hedysarum boreale*).

Enough said.

SEVEN

The Prostate Saver

25 May, Provo

Nancy, Scott, and I have lunch at a Provo café. I mention that I'm thinking of cutting off what remains of my hair and being done with it. "I don't want to be one of those guys who combs three strands of hair left to right and pretends he has hair." Scott says he has just seen a "Propecia" ad in the newspaper's sports section (where else!) that asks: "Tired of those bald jokes?" He wonders, however, about a treatment for baldness that has impotency as a possible side effect: "So who would risk potential impotence in order to look more potent?"

Nancy chimes up: "Speaking of impotence..."

Scott looks at me and cracks up. My reply is just a beat late: "Nancy, I saw you reading the Viagra ads yesterday. But I have to say I'm doing my best."

Nancy laughs out loud, "No, no, you've got me wrong. I just wanted to mention I think you should get one of those bike saddles that protects against squashing the pudendal artery. They're made to prevent impotence. Statistics show a four percent impotency rate among frequent bike riders."

What's a guy to do? I head to Mad Dog Cycles and buy a Specialized Body Geometry Comp Saddle. I suggest to Randy and Josh that Specialized ought to sponsor Scott and me, a couple of old guys using their prostate-protector saddles. We could wear jerseys that say "Fifty and Perineally Fit" or "The Prostate Saver, Don't Leave Home Without It," or even "Don't Kiss Your Ass Goodbye, Ride Specialized Body Geometry Comp." No luck interesting them in a sponsorship, so I shell out the money. These babies are not cheap, ninety dollars even with a discount. But if they work, I don't suppose there is a guy on the planet who would complain about the money. "Designed to reduce genital numbness that may be linked to male impotency," the label on the saddle says. "Designed by Dr. Minkow with firmer, more supportive foam and a flatter top, to help elevate the rider off the perineal area and onto the ischial tuberosities." God bless Dr. Minkow.

Later that afternoon I head to Scott's for a ride. "You show up without a helmet but with your new prostate saver. How bright is that?" he asks.

"Gotta have your priorities straight," I reply.

26 May, Great Western Trail, Mt. Timpanogos

Newspapers report this morning that cosmologists have a new fix on Hubble's constant and now estimate the age of the universe as twelve billion years. "That figure shocked me," I tell Sam as we ride into the canyon. "I had a sense of the universe as infinite, and suddenly it turns out to be only a few years old. That's unsettling."

"My colleagues are talking about this cycle of the universe," Sam replies. "The ongoing expansion since the Big Bang. But the twelve billion years may be just the beginning of the cycle. If there is enough matter in the universe, everything will contract and we will start over. You're still okay with your comforting sense of infinity. On another note, Dr. Minkow's prostate saver is killing me. I'm black and blue after yesterday's ride. If today's ride beats me up as bad, I'll have to move from body geometry to body calculus."

The first tiny blossoms of yellow sweet clover, *Melilotus officinalis*, are evident today. As the clover matures, so do the grasshoppers—each step into the grass disturbs a hundred of the fast-growing insects, maturing rapidly to take full advantage of the coming clover. And, as we noted from their scat last year, the foxes will take full advantage of this bumper crop of insects.

27 May, Great Western Trail, Mt. Timpanogos

I hate gravel pits. I hate rock crushers. I hate the fact that zoning laws in Utah County allow anyone with a few bucks to dig out entire mountainsides and leave the place scarred for centuries. But this morning I hate the gravel pit and rock crusher at the mouth of Provo Canyon for another reason. When Sam hears the machine across the canyon, he grits his teeth and doubles his speed. I'm feeling puny today and muster what may be my last breath to ask Sam why I have to pay for the sins of the gravel pit owner. He rides on at a furious pace. By the time I reach the meadow at the top of Frank, I have fallen three times and Sam, who has had a splendid ride, has been waiting so long that his sweat has dried.

On the way down, we stop in a protected grassy swale surrounded by oak brush, halted by a powerful birdcall. "A ring-necked pheasant," Sam says. "I hunted them with my dog when I was a kid."

"For a vegetarian, you've got a checkered past."

"I've got a checkered ass as well," Sam says. "This new saddle has seen its last ride on my bike. Do you want it? Maybe your body geometry is better suited to the good Doctor's calipers."

The year's first lupine (one of the varieties of *Lupinus argenteus*) is in purple bloom. Lupine is another fine plant," Sam says. "It causes birth defects and death in cows and sheep alike. Maybe we could make some lupine soup for the gravel pit owner."

29 May, Great Western Trail, Mt. Timpanogos

Cloudy this Saturday morning as we set out on an early ride to see and hear the birds at a different time of day. By the time we are halfway up the lower loop, it is raining just enough to make things slick. We make it up the quartzite and start up the next hills. Halfway up a steep reach, my back tire slips off a large rock and I fall hard into oak and rock. "Well," Scott says, "at least that wasn't half-hearted."

Evening primrose, *Oenothera caespitosa*, white succulent blossoms brilliant with raindrops, draw our attention. "Like something from the deep south," Scott says. From a thick stand of scrub oak and maples comes a raucous and varied set of calls: a chirr, whistles, a squawk, a couple of linked notes. In the rain, steaming from our climb, we stand on both sides of the grove and try to see the birds making the noise. Fifteen minutes later, chilled, we give up and head back to the mouth of the canyon.

30 May, Great Western Trail, Mt. Timpanogos

Another of those blessed Sunday morning rides. The rock crusher is silent. The traffic across the canyon road is still. After yesterday's rain, the birds are in joyous voice. A bushy-tailed, golden-shouldered fox slips up a slope and into some brush. My legs feel strong this morning and so do my lungs. Evening prim-rose, their large, heart-shaped flowers a milky, silky white, line the trail after their one-night stands. We stop to look at a single plant that produced five of the big flowers last night. Nineteen wilted pink flowers remain from previous nights' orgies. The profligacy is overwhelming.

"There are two major strategies for living organisms to sur-vive," Sam points out. "Some plants and animals put their entire reproductive investment into a single flower or offspring which they care for intensely. Others simply produce flowers and seeds and offspring profligately and depend upon one or two of them catching hold. Some biologists have suggested humans are the epitome of care of few offspring, although your seven kids and my four may undermine that theory."

"I've been wondering," I tell Sam, "whether I'm the epitome of anything in regard to my family. Susan and I can't get along and I spend more time on my bike than with my kids."

"You're good with your kids," Sam says. "Ease up on your-self. You know I've got similar worries about myself as a father. But when the two men from the church who have visited us for years stopped by for the last time and told us they felt bad our

kids had left the church, that they wished they had done a better job as 'home teachers,' I told 'em to fuck off. My kids are full
of life and moral commitment and I'm proud they have found
their way. Self-righteous sons of bitches! Leave us alone! We're
doing the best we can and it's better than most, no thanks to you
and your kind."

Back at the scrub oak and maple grove, we hear the same set
of varied calls we heard yesterday. A lazuli bunting sings from
a high branch, but he's not what we're hearing. Nor are the two
western tanagers we see and hear from the same grove. Finally,
Sam and I each catch a single glimpse of the noisy bird. It is large,
dark-backed and yellow-breasted, and seems to be making the
whole range of calls all by itself.

At home, we look through our field guides and come to the
same conclusion: a yellow-breasted chat, *Icteria virens*. The book
describes its "unmusical song" as "a jumble of harsh, chattering clucks, rattles, clear whistles, and squawks." It also mentions
"white spectacles," which neither of us saw. "Chat," the book
says, may be derived from "chatterer."

31 May, Great Western Trail, Mt. Timpanogos

A quick ride this morning before Sam and Nancy head
south to spend the week in Teasdale. We're rewarded with two
sightings of the yellow-breasted chat, and note the white markings on the head. It feels like we've found a new friend. Goat's
beard (*Tragopogon dubius*) is the flower of the hour. Wherever
you look, the yellow flowers dot the hillside. As the summer
continues, they will transform themselves into puffy white
balls of seeds. For the first time this year we also see the erect
yellow inflorescence that inspired someone to call the stately
mustard "prince's plume" (*Stanleya pinnata*). It is named after
Sam's dear friend, Stanley Welsh.

1 June, Teasdale

Near the trailhead in Teasdale, two or three northern harriers (*Circus cyaneus*) hunt low above the fields. These birds, often known as marsh hawks, fit Utah mores perfectly. Up to fifteen percent of the males and forty percent of the females are polygamous. According to one study a few years ago, males preside over "well-structured hierarchical harems of two to five females." The marsh hawks ought to be our state bird. Forget the California gull (which, by the way, has a relatively high incidence of homosexuality). Another couple of examples for our natural family manifesto.

EIGHT

The Bird that Eats Shit

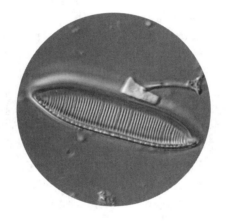

5 June, Vienna *(by email)*

Sam—I arrived okay, and have checked into the Pension Falstaff, just around the corner from Sigmund Freud's home in the Berggaße. On the plane, migrating from west to east across the Atlantic, I read the first half of Scott Weidensaul's *Living on the Wind*: "Marginal habitat is the wave of the future, as the last pristine forests disappear. The chainsaw and the machete are always busy, the smoke is hanging in the air, and *la selva Maya* is a little smaller now than it was when you started reading this chapter."

On the train from the airport into town, I watched a hawk hanging over a field of hops lined with brilliant red poppies and blue flax. It was a beautiful sight until my mind's eye saw the hawk as a NATO jet over a fruitful Yugoslav landscape.

7 June, Vienna *(by email)*

Sam—Elections this week for the European Parliament. Advertisements for the FPÖ (Freedom Party of Austria) feature its clean-cut, right-wing, xenophobic leader Jörg Haider and claim that EUROPE NEEDS CONTROL. It doesn't say over what, but the subtext is control over the foreigners who represent chaos, control over those who are different, control over the Weeds of the East.

How is it, Sam, that you and I—who would like to see those who exploit the planet and pollute the earth controlled, but who want more freedoms for difference, less control over individuals—how is it that we ended up teaching for an institution whose conservative leaders and guiding principles require more control over individuals and less over exploitative corporations, more control over those who are different and less over those who exploit the environment?

I wish you were here to see the current exhibition in the Belvedere: 19th-Century Paintings from America. It's instructive to see how European-American painters saw the new country. Asher Brown Durand's "First Harvest in the Wilderness" (1855), for example, depicts a wheat field in a clearing, tree stumps still sticking up through the wheat. The site is a minor ecological disaster, but a divine light shines through the clouds to make the clearing glow. An accompanying quotation from de Tocqueville justifies the European rape of the continent: "In the moment God refused to give the native inhabitants the ability for civilization, he predestined them to certain ruin. The true owners of this continent are those who know how to use its riches."

8 June, Great Western Trail, Mt. Timpanogos

Nancy and I walk the Great Western Trail starting at Canyon Glen. We saw sego lilies (*Calochortus nuttallii*) near here about a week ago. Today, these three-petaled, three-sepaled beauties are everywhere—abundant between sage, emerging from cheatgrass fields, accompanying declining evening primroses. A mile up the trail Nancy shouts, "Sam!" and throws her arm out to bar my path. As I regain my balance, I see she is pointing at a small, silvery snake, shaded greenish and yellowing toward the underside. A yellow-bellied racer (*Coluber constrictor mormon*), a snake I love. Our Utah subspecies was purportedly named by a biologist not particularly enamored of the local Mormon population.

Black-billed magpies (*Pica hudsonia*) are plentiful today. I once told a visiting Native American historian that indigenous people referred to these birds as black-and-white long tails. "That's true," he said. "The more common name, however, is the bird that eats shit." Magpies are gregarious birds that form long-term pairs, and males feed females throughout the laying and incubation periods. In the winter, magpies form groups of twenty-five pairs or so that travel and roost together. It is comforting to think of groups of magpies that know each other and prefer each other's company through the winter's dark.

9 June, Vienna *(by email)*

Sam—I ought to go to bed, but I'm still reeling from the events of the day. A couple of hours ago, NATO and the Yugoslav Parliament came to some kind of agreement that stops the bombing. And I'm just back from the world premiere of Peter Handke's play in Vienna's Burgtheater. It's called "The Play of the Film of the War," and has the filmmakers John Ford and Luis Buñuel in a Serbian town ten years after the war trying to decide how to make a film of the war. Interesting for you and me, Sam, was the scene when the really bad guys of the play, three "Internationals" who know all the answers, who dictate all the terms, and who can think only in absolutes, appear on the stage as follows: "Three mountain bike riders, preceded by the sound of squealing brakes, burst through the swinging door, covered with mud clear up to their helmets. They race through the hall, between tables and chairs, perilously close to the people sitting there. 'Where are we?' the first International asks. 'Don't know,' the second answers. 'Not a clue,' the third says." Sam, the American moralists—people without a hint of self-irony or humor, absolutists who run the world because of their economic power, clueless idiots—were depicted this evening as mountain bike riders. Same genus as us—but by god I hope they're another species.

19 June, Teasdale

Several sage thrashers (*Oreoscoptes montanus*) sing at dawn in the flat on the north side of Boulder Mountain. They alternate for an hour or more with a meadow lark and a couple of mourning doves from the nearby grain field. An hour of melody, filling the cove with melancholy. Sage thrashers are shy birds that hide their twig-and-grass nests beneath sagebrush. Last time Nanc and I were in Teasdale, a male thrasher sang through most of the night, even though the moon was dark. I joined him in the sage, naked, and listened with attention for most of the hour or two before dawn, wondering if he had received "The Message," "The Truth," a "Portent of the Apocalypse," and was singing it my way.

21 June, Great Western Trail, Mt. Timpanogos

This afternoon as I bike up Timpanogos on the Great Western, still without Scott, I run into mourning doves (*Zenaida macroura*). I have always been partial to these birds, whose haunting call is unmistakable. Three fly off the trail in front of me. Even though I have not lifted a shotgun for three decades and have no desire to hunt again, in my mind my .410 single shot snaps to my shoulder and I follow the last of the three, squeezing the trigger just after my barrel passes the bird. "Think of watering your bird with a hose," I hear my dad, nearly twenty-five years dead, tell me. Mourning doves are our most widely killed game birds. I find this a bit difficult to understand, though, after having shot a bunch as a kid and trying to make a meal of ten or fifteen. "Hell," my dad said, "just as well eat hummingbirds."

It's the last summer solstice of the millennium this afternoon. I'm on the trail the very moment the Earth begins to tilt back toward the north, shortening the days in the Northern Hemisphere. I ride into dark black thunderheads on Timpanogos. Light slants under the clouds. A bit of rain blows hard from the northwest, silvered by the low sun. Birds are everywhere. All of the spring's players sing for me, one by one, as I ride along. It is as though the spring birds take a curtain call and prepare for Act II, Summer.

NINE

Murderers, Fornicators, and Coffee Drinkers

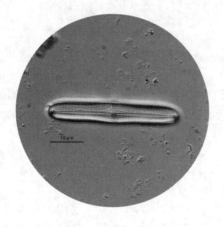

June 25, Great Western Trail, Mt. Timpanogos

Death close to hand on two fronts today. Someone has driven a blade along our low trail for no reason we can tell, snapping down several large box elders and oaks, leaving their shattered stumps and carcasses along the trail. And a lazuli bunting lies lifeless on the trail. No signs of struggle, no evident wounds. Its head and back still shimmer with turquoise color, and the orange patch burns bright on its throat. We lift the bird off the dusty trail and lay it into a patch of yellow sweet clover. It reminds me of another corpse I saw some years ago on this trail, and when I get home I look up the event in my notebook:

2 September 1993 – On a trail high in the canyon lies a mouse. Stretched taut with the gasses of putrescence, its skin shines with a healthy grey luster. The tail is a thin pole, and the two hind legs poke out stiffly to finish the tripod. There are no front legs. No head. The body has formed a new neck around the wound. Sucking on that tight pucker is a swarm of aggressive yellowjackets, bright yellow, dangerously quick, ominously thirsty.

At the time, BYU was losing its intellectual nerve, and Sam and I and several others were beginning to protest infringements on academic freedom. I saw the corpse as an omen.

26 June, Brighton

Sun setting at the end of a beautiful day. The nearly full moon rises while the sun sets. Standing on Nancy's and Sam's balcony, I'm east of the sun, west of the moon. For the first time in my forty-nine years, I understand that the phrase is a reference to evening. Before we go to bed, Nancy reads several of Shakespeare's sonnets. I'm struck by two lines that remind me of the headless mouse and aggressive, ecclesiastical hornets:

"And art made tongue-tied by authority, / And folly (doctor-like) controlling skill…"

It's an old problem.

27 June, Great Western Trail, Wasatch Crest—west of the sun, east of the moon

This will be our first high-altitude ride this year, much of it above ten thousand feet, a stretch of the Great Western Trail called the Wasatch Crest. We climb from Brighton to Scott's Pass, where we look down over Park City's highest slopes. For some reason (it may have something to do with the two athletic young women riding aggressively behind us), Sam doesn't stop at the pass, although we usually do, nor does he stop at the top after the old mine shaft, although we always have. To take my mind off the pain, I chant lines from a poem by our friend Alex Caldiero:

he wonders if it was worth while making a good impression
on the beautiful lifeguard who invited him out to where
the waves were tall and the undertow unforgiving.

The red rocks where we finally sit in the sun are accented blue, orange, and yellow by tiny penstemons, a paintbrush and a daisy. Higher on the Wasatch Crest, five or six deep snowbanks cross the trail. Slogging through the last one, knee deep in melting snow on the Park City side, we find glacier lilies (*Erythronium grandiflorum*) in a small fellfield. A couple of hundred plants, yellow petals turned back on themselves, rise from the wet soil at the edge of the snow.

A young golden eagle lifts off a cliff beneath us and rises to our height. He circles us and stands still in the air, occasionally adjusting a wing. With a quick turn of his body, the eagle becomes a diagonal line against the sky and is instantly a half-mile across the ridge.

Main Street in Park City is surreal after three hours of isolation on the trail. We feel like country boys misplaced to fashion city. We stop in Swede's Alley for a half-hour of shade and a half-gallon of rehydration. We can't help but notice the steady flow of folks walking past us into the local liquor store. Thinking about his childhood Sunday school lessons on the evils of alcohol, Sam opines that "they don't look like murderers, fornicators, and coffee drinkers to me."

Muddy, bloody, wet and tired, we climb past the silver mine, cross over Guardsman Pass, and drag back to Brighton. Twenty-eight miles round trip, several thousand feet total climb. Nancy has fixed us what Alex calls "food to fit the hunger."

1 July, Great Western Trail, Mt. Timpanogos

Ninety degrees Fahrenheit when we start riding in the late afternoon. This south-facing hillside has changed dramatically in just two weeks. The yellow sweet clover, for instance, bursting with new growth ten days ago, is spindly and shrunken—at least those stems that haven't been stripped by voracious grasshoppers. The yellow, spurred flowers of the Dalmatian toadflax hang limp and shriveled. The vigorous new penstemons look tired. The grasshoppers don't have it easy either. We see a big brown hopper, upright and seemingly intact, caught in a web. Beneath the insect, upside down, its bright red hourglass catching the sun, hangs a black widow spider (*Latrodectus mactans*). Its shiny black abdomen is taut with the grasshopper's life.

Higher on the hill, with the big green aqueduct acting as a fence on one side, we come face to face with a doe. She wheels around and jumps off the road, straight into a barbed-wire fence. She thrashes, falls onto her back, kicks and pulls, and breaks free. She jumps up and has another go at the fence. Her front legs clear it this time, and her body and hind legs crash over. She disappears into the thick oak brush.

"I was rooting for her," Sam says. "She would have kicked our heads off if we had had to help her."

Everything is new and fresh and hopeful and fecund in the spring. By this time of year, everything is simply eating everything else. As if to drive the point home, we find the last row of trees cut down in the orchard.

Ten

Hardtail or Doublesprung?

3 July, from the Great Western Trail to Mad Dog Cycles

This is going to be a hot one—that's evident the minute the morning sun breaks from behind Cascade Mountain at seven a.m. When we finally stand in the meadow at the top of Frank, trembling from heat-exacerbated exertion, I exclaim, "Well, that's the worst of it." Two hundred yards down, riding swiftly on a smooth trail, I find that that wasn't the worst of it at all. I catapult over the front wheel and skid on my back across ground that looks grassy but feels like a gravel pit. Sam rounds the corner to find me apparently taking a rest. I remount and bounce my way down a rocky trail. At some point, I realize that my front wheel has lost its true and is banging against the brakes with every turn. The wheel has split, thinned by hundreds of miles of brake pressure. I nurse my way down the remainder of the trail, getting off to walk down the last steep stretch. When Sam pulls up beside me, I step aside to let him pass. He is dusty and sports a deep red scratch from elbow to armpit and down the side of his chest to his waist. "Just a little trouble getting over those rocks at the top," he explains.

My next stop is Mad Dog Cycles. I have no hankering to die of equipment failure. Besides, a guy can go only so long without new gear. "Hardtail or double-sprung?" Randy asks.

From the bike shop, I limp over to Utah Valley State College where I sign a contract. I'll be an Associate Professor of Integrated Studies and Philosophy, which will expand my work from the more narrowly focused discipline of German language and literature that has been my academic home. And, at a state school protected by laws a private religious school can ignore, I'll enjoy the full fruits of academic freedom and a wider range of colleagues and students. That's the theory, at least.

5 July, Orem

How do you like that? Scott falls off his bike on Friday, tacos his front wheel a little bit, and goes right out and buys a new bike. Hell, if I bought a new bike for every little fall I took, I would have a house full of bikes. (Nancy says I already have a house full.)

"I could have structural stress throughout my bike," Scott says. "Can't take chances with old gear."

Such a deal, this new bike. A Specialized Stumpjumper FSR XC Comp with sapphire Superlight A1 welded frame, FSR XC suspension and sealed bearing main pivot, STOUT hubs, Mavic 222 rims, ForeArm Elite crankset, alloy HeadFirst headset, XT/XTR 0sp transmission, Avid 25 v-brakes, Kevlar-bead Dirt Control/Master Comp tires, not to mention the TPC-cartridge Manitou SX-R fore and Fox Air Vanilla FLOAT aft.

This is a shock. But if it is any consolation for me, Scott is now riding the best gear on the trail and he can't hide it. That means every bike jock we see expects him to be a hell-of-a-rider just to be the equal of his gear. That's no small burden for an old guy. I guess I'm looking for a new bike myself. With my proceeds from this column, I am onto one after 120 more months.

10 July, Great Western Trail, Mt. Timpanogos

Dry and hot. We ride listlessly, not paying much attention to anything but our overheated bodies. The trail is littered with smashed grasshoppers, corpses alive with hungry fellow grasshoppers sucking out the juices, recycling scarce moisture. "It's reasonable," Sam says, "but repugnant nonetheless. Why does it seem so macabre?"

"Because of how we feel about cannibalism?" I wonder.

"Or because we know it is our ultimate end as well?" Sam offers.

The grasshoppers that aren't dead or feeding on the dead hug bare stems of sweet clover in stacked pairs, hundreds of thousands of conjoined couples. Chewing, sucking, copulating insects. "I hope I don't fall," Sam says, "I wouldn't want to go down among those ravenous, fucking bastards."

We pick up our pace and for the first time since last year we both ride Frank from bottom to top without touching down. We stand in the high meadow sweating and puffing and try to analyze our unexpected success. The luck of the bounce, we decide, lacking any other possible explanation. Near the mouth of the canyon, large and brilliant yellow flowers stop us. Five pointed petals frame a riot of bristly yellow stamens. Blazing star (*Mentzelia laevicaulis*).

11 July, Great Western Trail, Mt. Timpanogos

Neither of us touches down—the second time in a week that we have both ridden Frank perfectly on the same day. We are jubilant. In case the bike-hubris gods are looking on, we try to look nonchalant. On the way down we stop to look at the trumpet-shaped blossoms of salmon gilia, and at the mullein stalks filling with yellow flowers (*Verbascum thapsus*). A light rain begins to fall. A marvelous scent rises from the dry, spent, yellow sweet clover, a pungent odor that like many other precious scents seems to rise out of childhood memory.

12 July, Great Western Trail, Mt. Timpanogos

Yesterday Scott and I came across our first salmon gilia of the year. This plant is a dead ringer for scarlet gilia except for its rich salmon-pink color. For several years I have thought of these two as separate gilias, plausible since Stan Welsh recognizes 25 species in Utah. But it turns out scarlet and salmon gilia are variations on a theme and both belong in *Gilia aggregata*. A couple of ecologists from Northern Arizona University recently discovered that the scarlet-colored phase is pollinated by hummingbirds and the salmon-colored phase is pollinated by hawk moths. The proportion of floral color depends on the proportion of pollinators. In the autumn, hummingbirds often migrate to lower altitudes or southward and the gilias may begin to produce more salmon-colored flowers to attract the remaining hawkmoths. Attracting two pollinators is not a bad strategy in a fickle world.

17 July, Great Western Trail, South Fork of the Provo River

Today we cross the Provo River to explore the section of the trail that winds up a canyon on the east side of Cascade Mountain. It's seven a.m. and overcast when we start up Provo Canyon, eight a.m. and drizzling when we reach the trailhead several miles up the South Fork of the Provo River. It's a cool and beautiful climb up to Big Springs. Along the spring banks stand masses of yellow monkey-flower (*Mimulus guttatus*), expanses of white geraniums (*Geranium richardsonii*), stretches of purple and aptly named monkshood (*Aconitum columbianum*), and rivers of yellow columbine (*Aquilegia flavescens*).

We look up at the snow-capped crest of Provo Peak. We breathe deeply, stand silent.

From the springs, the trail climbs more steeply. Sam points ahead. Five wild turkeys (*Meleagris gallopavo*) rise tentatively from their pineneedle beds, stretch legs and wings and long necks, and slip into the woods. We continue the climb, grateful for our extra-low "granny" gears. We suck the thin air deep into burning lungs, will trembling legs to push and pull us up one more climb, then another climb, and another. The trail wins, as it always does, and we stand down without having reached any specific destination. We are soaked, less from the intermittent light rain and more from the thick wet grasses that have crowded the trail. After an easy ride down the canyon, four-and-a-half hours after setting out, we are home again. Wet, tired, and jubilant.

ELEVEN

6,047,086,034
6,047,086,035

19 July, Great Western Trail, Mt. Timpanogos

Showy milkweed (*Asclepias speciosa*) all over the place. The flowers are thick with milkweed bugs (*Oncopeltus fasciatus*), bright red-orange copulation machines dedicated to turning the world's biomass into insects. These bugs have few predators, since their diet is comprised entirely of the poisonous milkweed plants. The same holds true for the monarch butterfly, whose larvae feed on milkweed. Oddly enough, this summer's grasshoppers are eating milkweeds. They seem to avoid the leaves and stems, focusing on the flowers. We suspect this is because the rather meager crop of yellow sweet clover has been eaten to the ground. Sheep, on the other hand, are not so smart and will eat the whole plant. A couple of pounds of showy milkweed will kill a full-sized ewe. Symptoms of milkweed poisoning include wheezing, labored breathing, and "recumbence"—similar to the symptoms induced by riding up Frank.

In Hindu mythology, Soma, one of the most important Vedic gods, is a personification of the soma milkweed. This plant contains a milky sap from which a world-class, euphoria-inducing intoxicant is derived. Indra created the universe under its influence and placed Earth and sky in their proper positions. I gotta say, milkweeds are among my favorite plants. What else do you know that has the potential both to kill sheep and set the world right?

21 July, Great Western Trail, Mt. Timpanogos

Sitting in my lab thinking about last night's ride. We snaked through a group of maybe forty riders of all ages waiting at a starting line to race up the lower part of our trail. No kidding—starter's pistol, entrant numbers, staggered starts, age classes—the whole deal. This spectacle poses at least two dilemmas for me. First, although this is not my trail, as I ride through the sea of expensive bikes and colorful Lycra butts I feel like saying,

"Hey, we've been riding this trail for many years in all seasons, even in snow over our shoes—long before any of you had the foggiest idea about mountain bikes, let alone about this place. Move the hell over and let two old men pass."

A second more urgent issue is brought home by the human population counter sitting behind my computer, ticking off the growth of the human race on Planet Earth. I had this two-foot-long electronic counter built a few years ago to remind me of what I think is the central issue of our time. As I sit here, the counter reads 6,047,086,034…6,047,086,035… 6,047,086,036— in just over one second. Correcting for death, we add about 2.6 new persons to the Earth each second—relentlessly. That's about 156 new people per minute, more than 9000 per hour, nearly a quarter of a million per day and more than 80 million per year. Trouble is, all of them want to eat well, enjoy adequate housing, and ride the Great Western Trail.

22 July, Great Western Trail, Timpooneke to Provo Canyon

Just after eight a.m., Nancy drops us off at the Timpooneke Trail high in American Fork Canyon. We'll ride the section of the Great Western Trail that circles Mount Timpanogos from north to west to south to east. It's a high alpine singletrack, soft in places with pine needles, rocky in others. The one constant on the ride is the show put on by wildflowers: white Colorado columbine (*Aquilegia coerulea*), scarlet gilia that gives way to salmon and white, red paintbrush extruding lascivious fruiting tongues, tall green gentian (*Frasera speciosa*) that's perennial for some years but dead after once flowering, showy larkspur, wild rose, sunflowers, yellow wallflowers, sego lily, mullein, white and pink geraniums, pale wild hollyhock, blue flax, fields of yellow daisies, masses of blue penstemon, and western coneflowers (*Ratibida columnifera*).

We have stopped to look more closely at some brilliant penstemons when Sam motions for me to look behind a rock. "Is it a blind snake?" I ask when I see the snake's smooth reddish skin. "No," Sam says, "it's Utah's only native boa constrictor, a rubber boa." The boa slowly insinuates itself back into its hole.

"Look at the stump of a tail," I say.

"They often present their tails as their heads in the face of danger," Sam says. "Unlike most Utah politicians, this snake knows the difference."

We're well aware of the difference in our legs by the time we finish the ride five hours after we began. And the difference in our minds, as well.

27 July, Great Western Trail, 7:00 a.m.

Heading up Provo Canyon, we talk about obsessive-compulsive behavior and anxiety. Sam wrote a book about the subject, which he knows from personal experience, and he once lectured up and down the Wasatch Front to rapt and anxious audiences. Our conversation turns to the embolism in Sam's rear tire that threatens to end our ride at any moment, to dear friends who are breaking up after long relationships, to the complexities of my own disintegrating marriage.

"After twenty-five years we share only a rancorous partnership that involves a house and children," I tell Sam. "It frightens the hell out of me to look into the future. I try to visualize twenty-five more years and I see only black. But when I try to visualize life after a divorce, I see black as well. I can't live without a companion. I won't live without physical and emotional intimacy. And yet I tend to silence, to solitude, to the self-enclosed world of a compulsive reader and writer, to solitary travel—all behaviors that preclude intimacy. Susan is as frustrated as I am. And we can't find a way past it."

"I feel for you both," Sam says. "You start out with high hopes for melding two lives into a joint life. If you're lucky, as circumstances change and as you both change, you make the same turns. If you're unlucky, you find yourselves heading in opposite directions. Your increasing unwillingness to go to church, for instance, has to be difficult for Susan. Both Nancy and I are finding church increasingly troublesome and are able to take this turn in our lives together. It's all going to blow up, however, when BYU figures out where I've got to and fires my ass. And while we're confessing our fears—you know I've always worried with Paul Simon I would end up being a cartoon in a cartoon graveyard. I've been thinking about my lack of ability and potential fraudulence more and more with the passing years. I'm not the botanist I could have been. Rather than give my life to the discipline, I have tried to live a life. But I end up second-guessing myself, wondering what if…"

"For all practical purposes, I've just abandoned my own discipline," I respond, "hoping to write more personally and more broadly. It's a risky move."

Our mood is grim until two young men on new bikes sprint past us on the trail. We up our speed a notch, confident that the long, steep climb will take its toll. We keep talking, not because we need to talk, but for the effect the talking will have on the riders in front of us as we catch up. It doesn't take long. Conversing, we sweep past them in grand style. Such pleasures for old men are short-lived, however, and we are quickly back to our gloomy conversation. We turn up over the quartzite at the end of the aqueduct, Sam riding first over the most difficult section of today's ride. Loose rocks knock him off his bike. He stands, and in one swift, violent motion swings his bike over his head and lets it fly into a stand of oak brush far down the hill. The bike settles gently into the deeply notched leaves. An hour later at the mouth of the canyon, sweaty and tired, Sam smiles and says, "Short of Soma, that morning's about as good as it gets."

TWELVE

This is True Worship

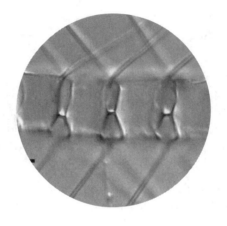

30 July, Teasdale and Orem

Ravens wake me this morning. After standing in sage, listening and watching for half an hour not long after sunrise, I notice they are fussing around two or three coyotes on the mountainside. It isn't clear what the commotion is about, but it's certain the ravens aren't happy. After an hour, the coyotes cross to the east, low and careful. These boys have seen airplanes with state and federal gunners shooting their compadres as they tried to escape.

I startle an old raven hopping across the road at the edge of the feedlot. This old boy has a bad wing, can't fly, and is perfectly aware of what that means. I meet his left eye as he looks back over his broad, black wing, assessing his chance for escape, sizing me up as a potentially lethal opponent. He's about to meet his end. I wish him a good death.

Back home, back on my bike, I tell Scott, "I couldn't help thinking about this brother's chances for the future—and you know, I got breathlessly, deeply melancholy. I thought of running him down and breaking his neck, but I'm not certain I could have done it."

"You're thinking about yourself in the raven's position," Scott replies. "You can't bear being helpless. Maybe this guy will find some way to survive for a while among the cows. Maybe he's not willing to be dead yet. And maybe it's not your place to decide for him."

"All right," I reply, irritated that Scott did not get my drift. "Remember, I didn't kill the sonofabitch. I only thought about it. I can't get over his eyes—apprehension maybe, and some sort of deep knowledge of our lives and common ends. This guy knew stuff and it was all I could do to walk away."

2 August, Great Western Trail, Mt. Timpanogos

The afternoon ride is a mistake. Most everything is blasted, hot, withered. The countryside is sighing, waiting for rain and the cooler air of autumn. "I read this morning that India is about to pass the one-billion human population mark," Scott says. "In a few years it will eclipse China as the world's most populous country. All of this in the face of vanishing water, diminishing fossil fuels and food, increasing pollution—the potential for all-out ecological collapse."

I add to his misery: "Utah County has a birth rate right between India and Pakistan. How can that happen? The keynote speaker at last week's International Botanical Congress stated we are racing toward worldwide poverty in a monstrous, poisonous garbage dump. The guy's right. Why in hell don't we see it as a people? How do our political and cultural leaders ignore this? How did we end up with eleven children between us? Jesus!"

"Yes," Scott agrees, "it was our version of what we believed Jesus wanted for us. That and simple, unadulterated desire. After the fact, however, I couldn't do without a single one of them. They worry me, of course—and they are a powerful, abiding source of meaning for me."

6 August, Great Western Trail, Mt. Timpanogos

Lisel Mueller's poem "Losing My Sight" begins with this observation: "I never knew that by August / the birds are practically silent, / only a twitter here and there. / Now I notice."

The birds are silent today. Along the trail are a couple of praying mantises (*Mantis religiosa*), one a bright green, the other a yellow-brown that blends with the mature August grasses. "Praying mantises have felt sinister to me," Sam says, "ever since I caught one in midair on Strawberry Reservoir and it took a chunk out of my palm."

"Remember the first lines of our friend Susan Howe's poem, 'Mantis'?" I ask Sam.

"Sure do," he says. 'The mantis affects an attitude of prayer. / 'Oh Lord,' it seems to say, 'I thank thee / I am praying and not prey.'"

"Since I was preyed on with prayer," I say, "I've never felt quite the same about prey or prayer."

"What happened?" Sam asks.

"You know my stake president, who is also a professor of religion. He was trying to force me to retract my claim in an essay I published in *Sunstone* that three Mormon apostles were pitting faith against reason. He required regular meetings to keep up the pressure. One night I entered his office in the Stake Center to find him waiting with both his counselors and my ward bishop. All four men looked like undertakers in their black suits, white shirts, and dark ties, and when I looked around there was in fact a mortuary calendar on the wall. The stake president asked one of his counselors to pray, an eighty-year-old orchard owner I had never met. We knelt on the office floor. The counselor prayed that God would 'soften Brother Abbott's heart so he would listen to council.' As you can imagine, a string of salacious curses ricocheted through my mind. Nothing but curses. You suppose that was the spirit of the Devil?"

"Knowing you, I don't suspect there was any devil necessary," Sam says.

"This is the stake president, by the way, who told the men of the stake gathered for a priesthood meeting that the trouble with the stake's women was that they were not priesthood broke."

"It's the luck of the draw," Sam says. "Another president might well have been a priesthood whisperer."

Sunflowers are losing their petals to grasshoppers. Not so the curlycup gumweed (*Grindelia squarrosa*) whose smaller yellow flowers are protected by a sticky extrusion that earns the hardy, drought-resistant plant its name. *Weeds of the West* points out that extracts of the plant are used in modern medicine to treat bronchial spasm, asthma, whooping cough, and poison-ivy rashes.

On the way down from the mountainside, we disturb a large flock of starlings, black birds that flash ominously against a hillside of bright yellow grass. Ominous, I tell Sam, "because that's how Vincent Van Gogh taught me to see black birds against yellow grass. Goethe was so worried about seeing through the eyes and descriptions and metaphors of predecessors—and even through mental structures like time and space—that he eschewed microscopes and telescopes, hoping to see things directly, immediately, unaltered—the things in and for themselves."

"Slow down," Sam says. "Mental structures like time and space?"

"Yeah," I answer. "We construe everything we know based on the mental tools we have to work with. That's one of Immanuel Kant's main ideas. Time and space don't exist anywhere as things. But we see and know through structures like time and space. They're like tinted glasses that color our observations even while they make them possible. Are things really that color, or do the glasses make them look that way? Thus, Goethe's interesting but doomed attempt to see things without mediation."

"Is that Kant's analogy?" Sam asks. "The tinted glasses?"

"No, that comes from a letter Kleist wrote to his fiancé trying to explain why the certainties of his moral universe had just exploded. All of his good work, you should know, was written after this crisis. I thought it might be as good an example for a botanist as it was for a fiancé."

21 August, Great Western Trail, Wayne County

Scott Carrier, a friend who writes for *Esquire and Harpers* and *Mother Jones* and does pieces for National Public Radio, rides with us up a track on the north slope of Boulder Mountain strewn with black volcanic rocks and rutted by heavy rain. Juniper and piñon trees replace sage as we climb, and by the time we reach the saddle between the Donkey Creek and Fish Creek drainages, aspen and ponderosa pine are part of the mix. I mention that "the Boulder"—Boulder Mountain—is unusually wet this year, and Scott (Carrier) tells about an interview he did with an anti-wilderness activist in the town of Boulder: "If the Boulder wasn't the Boulder this wouldn't be Boulder," the man said, as a final explanation of his position.

We push our bikes up Donkey Creek. If we had a bushel basket, we could fill it in minutes with mushrooms, with heavy and spongy brown-to-red boletes, with little brown mushrooms, with delicate grey mushrooms, with frilled white mushrooms, and with my favorites, parasites that are not mushrooms at all— the tall, reddish-white pinedrops with their hanging bell-like flowers.

On the other side of the saddle, we bushwhack our way down through pines till we reach a sagebrush flat on top of sandstone cliffs. Scott (Abbott) leads us down through a notch in one cliff, slipping and sliding on the loose wet stone with his bike slung over one shoulder. We ride down a sandy wash, densely packed from all the recent rain, winding through high sage while rain falls again and lightning and thunder burst from a dark cloud descending off the Boulder. By the time we reach the brilliant ochre-and-black pictographs of horned human figures near the base of a high cliff we are soaked and smiling.

THIRTEEN

A Carbolic-Acid Enema

27 August, Great Western Trail, Ridge Trail

Today Scott and I plan to ride along the ridge and over the mountain from Sundance to Brighton. We try to do this thirty-mile ride once a year at summer's end. Last summer, the day before our ride, we were in Mad Dog Cycles getting some extra tubes and patch kits and told Randy, with some pride, what our plans were. "I've got a guy working in the back, Jeff," Randy said, "who rides that nearly every weekend. That's his bike against the wall." He gestured toward a heavy downhill bike. "Can we talk with him?" Scott asked. Jeff came out and we compared notes. "It's a tough trail alright," he said. "How long does it take you from the top of the Alpine Loop to the pass overlooking Brighton?"

"About seven hours," we answered. "How long does it take you?"

"About the same," he said.

"Does someone pick you up at Brighton?"

"No, seven hours round trip."

Outside, Scott argued that it's not a fair comparison. "He's half our age."

"Yeah," I said, "but his bike is twice as heavy."

It is a multi-splendored ride today—sun, rain and hail, thunder and lightning—weather alternating precipitously between late summer and mid fall. We ease through inch-deep flour dust sporting recent cougar tracks, slide up and down muddy trails, bump over rock and swing through forest, sweating, swearing, puffing, panting. Exulting.

The high mountain landscapes along this ridge are unparalleled—fifty-mile vistas in all directions. The alpine flora is rich and fecund. Scott and I each carry two 100-ounce water bladders in our CamelBaks. We suck water continuously to maintain our strength for the final push up the cliffs to Catherine Ridge between Alta and Brighton. PowerBars go down in hourly doses.

On our last two rides, we took unexpected and costly detours over peaks called the Ant Knolls. This year we pay closer attention and find the trail skirting the knolls. We stop and celebrate by taking off our shoes and wringing out our sweaty socks. There's a stink in the air beyond our own considerable odor. A herd of sheep has denuded the hill across from us. Land maggots! Not a plant left standing—with the exception of ten or twelve short stalks of blue flowers. We look closer. Larkspur. Smart sheep.

Finally, the cliffs at the blind end of Mineral Basin tower over us. We climb toward the ridge, pushing our bikes up much of the ascent. At the top of the final ridge, we stand gasping, our hearts pounding, and I think of how Shackleton must have felt standing on top of the last mountain on his return to South Georgia. Then I remind myself that we have just traversed, in six hours, only the last quarter of the Wasatch 100, the ultra marathon that will be run on this trail Saturday and Sunday. Tarahumara Indians from the Sierra Madre Mountains near Copper Canyon, sponsored by a doctor we know from our visits there, have won this hundred-mile test of endurance wearing tire-tread sandals! We're no Shackletons, nor are we ultra-marathoners. But by god, here we are.

Because the trail into Brighton is marked for hiking only—NO BIKES!—we bump the bikes over granite outcroppings and roll them over pine needles past a moose and her gangly calf till we get to the little Brighton store. Scott has a fiver in his pocket, which buys us a large-can six-pack of hydration. On the cabin deck, our cramping legs stretched out, backs to the wall, late sun warming our faces, we gulp the weak but plentiful brew and have an increasingly profound conversation that would certainly solve most of the problems of the universe if we had thought to record it.

For dinner we sauté a softball-sized *Boletus edulis* we collected just past the Ant Knolls. The flesh of the heavy brown-topped mushroom also known as King Bolete, Cep, Steinpilz, or Porcini, is firm and white and smells faintly of trout in the frying pan.

30 August, Orem

Seven or eight friends sit around a table heavy with good food and drink. We talk about John Berger's new book *King*, a bleak look at the underbelly of human existence from the perspective of a canine narrator. Especially troubling is the futile battle at the end—homeless squatters against the bulldozers and riot-control vehicles of the powers that be. "It's an important book," I say. "Berger's focus on the disenfranchised and his narrative ability will make a difference in this world."

"Not a chance," Sam cuts in. "You're deluding yourself."

"The stories we tell do make a difference," I repeat.

"I've done green activism in Utah for decades," Sam argues, "and it hasn't made a damn bit of difference. We're in a worse place ecologically today than we were when I started."

Sam's declaration leaves me reeling. My arguments fall away. A chasm opens in my soul. I feel the emptiness and futility of my life in a dark, suffocating flash. I won't climb out of this hole for days.

5 September, Great Western Trail, Mt. Timpanogos

A Sunday ride, not the testosterone-laced race we often do to the top of Frank. Competition is low, conversation is paramount, and life seems to have eased up. We both are well beyond the life expectancy of our sort merely a century or two before. We realize just how quickly our final act will play.

"How old was your dad when he was killed in the car accident?" I ask.

"Younger than I am now," Scott replies. "How about your dad?"

"The old bastard was only sixty when he gave it up," I reply. "I would have given my right nut to have him around for a while. I've been aching to listen to his stories, to ask him questions, to find out what he thought about things. It seems so damn pertinent, now that I'm his age."

"Did you get along with your dad?" Scott asks.

"When he was alive and before I married Nancy, I didn't think much of him. He and Mom didn't do well together and things just went a lot better when he was off in Washington. It wasn't until I married Nancy that I found out he was a hell-of-a-lot better guy than I thought. By the time I figured that out, we only had a couple of years together before he went over.

"He was a funny sonofabitch. When he was in the hospital for the last time, he couldn't breathe and had an emergency tracheotomy. He was scared and sad and couldn't talk much, though he plugged his trach one evening and told me he was dying. While I knew this was true, I denied it. I told him we had too much to do yet. I could see in his eyes his love for me and his sadness for living a life he would've liked to have been different and for not telling me that he loved me—and for dying before he could change any of that.

"We started fishing Strawberry Reservoir a couple of years before he died, sometimes with my brothers, sometimes just the two of us. Damn guy would show up at my bedroom window at 4:00 in the morning and start banging. 'Gotta get breakfast at the Hub,' he would say. So it was eggs sunny side up, brown toast, a quart of coffee for Dad, and then half a pie each. 'That'll get us started,' he'd say.

"When Dad was dying, he took a substantial dislike to a night nurse on his case—on his case in both meanings of the word. One day, he asked her to close his trachea so he could speak. She did and he mumbled, 'I'd...I'd like to give you a carbolic acid enema.'"

"Plenty of people I'd like to give carbolic acid enemas," Scott replies, "and I'm not dying just yet."

"What about you and your dad?" I ask.

"We did okay," Scott replies. "He was a good father. I was caught up in the sorts of things a young guy thinks are important—girls, tennis, books. My dad was busy doing church work—he was the bishop some of those years—and trying to keep a family together on a teacher's salary. I admired his dedication to what he thought was important and I admired his work ethic. I like to think he knew I admired him…but we didn't talk much."

10 September, Great Western Trail, Mt. Timpanogos

Happy to be out this afternoon, we scoot up the trail, slide up through the debris below the quartzite, clamber up into Johnson's Hole. The old jeep road shows fresh scars. We climb the ridge to find a big rotary drilling rig flanked by a house-sized compressor. Next to it stand a bulldozer, three pickups, and a panel truck. The trail we have made our own over the course of a thousand rides has been obliterated. Savage bulldozer tracks straddle the trail, cross the trail, swing wide, and return to what was once the trail. Deep tracks from the truck-mounted drilling rig crisscross the dozer tracks. We ride past hundreds of yards of crushed oak, the earth scalped of grasses and flowers and brush, the outcropping blue limestone powdered.

Sam wheels his bike around. I follow him breakneck back down to the drilling rig, wondering what the hell he has in mind. Two muscle-bound men in hard hats and white shirts sitting on the tailgate of a pickup eye us as we ride up. Sam throws down his bike and asks who the hell drove the dozer down the trail.

"Not us," one of the men says. "We came down the road back there." He jumps down from the tailgate and walks us over to the driller, a powerful man of maybe thirty-five. I recognize his type. One summer I ran a Bucyrus-Eyre cable-tool rig outside of Park City drilling water wells, and I put myself through college as a roughneck on oil rigs in northwestern New Mexico. This guy's not going to be impressed by our bikes and shorts and half gloves. He's gonna think we are Tinker Bell and her friend. "Who drove the dozer down the Great Western Trail?" Sam asks him, fire in his eyes.

"I did," the driller says. He tells us his equipment was too heavy to go round the road and that someone working for the Central Utah Project gave him one-time permission to drive his rig down the trail. They are drilling through the overburden, he says, to see whether a tunnel for irrigation water will be feasible here.

Not willing to exchange blows after such a reasonable explanation by such a powerful man, we head back up what's left of the trail. We have knelt on this ground in reverence to tiny flowers. We know where the rattlesnakes sun themselves. "Why can't we figure out a better way to live?" Sam spits. "It's the end of the twentieth fucking century."

18 September, Great Western Trail, Wasatch Crest

I can hardly ride through the meadows of yellow-brown, shin-high grasses, between golden current and snowberry mingled with scattered sage. I feel heavy with a sense of finality and missed opportunity. These alpine fields disarm my verbal and logical self, exposing me to some part of myself I prefer to avoid. It is a visceral reaction that spider-webs through my brain and heart, causing me to lose all pretext of competence or connection. It makes me feel more akin to the creatures of the high forests facing the coming winter than to my relentlessly stupid own kind and my own stupid self.

Scott has been keeping track of the grass heads as we ride along. He reckons each small meadow contains two billion seeds and uses that fact to counter my debilitating pessimism. "The biota on the Provo Canyon stretch of the Great Western will be back," Scott says. "One damned bulldozer can't obliterate what has evolved there over several million years."

A thousand vertical feet higher, just at the knife ridge between Big Cottonwood Canyon and Park City, we come upon several raucous Clark's nutcrackers (*Nucifraga columbiana*) picking at limber pine cones (*Pinus flexilis*), harvesting seeds for the coming barren time. One of these busy guys can bury thirty thousand pine seeds in a season—a prodigious feat. This allows them to nest and raise young next spring even before the snow leaves the mountains. Maybe Scott's got a point about the future of the world.

20 September, Great Western Trail, Mt. Timpanogos

A magpie scolds us as we top a hill on the lower part of the trail in the late afternoon. "Just about the only birds we have seen or heard for the past month," Scott notes. "Jays, magpies, and nutcrackers."

"Corvidae all," I reply. "Noisy, smart, and wonderful each. Confident tricksters having a good time." Scott notices a smallish raptor atop a scorched Gambel oak: a sharp-shinned hawk (*Accipiter striatus*). Sharp-shinned hawks have relatively short wings and beat them rapidly before a short glide. They are agile in dense trees and good hunters, taking birds up to the size of quail. Before the day is over, we see at least a half-dozen of these beautiful birds. They are moving south, and their migration suggests coming change on the last vernal equinox of the millennium.

Scott stops us on the way down, pointing to an explosion of black-and-white feathers on the trail. A magpie dinner for a sharp-shinned hawk?

26 September, Teasdale

On our way to Wayne County to hear our friend Susan Howe read this weekend for the fiftieth anniversary of the Bicknell Ladies Literary Club, Nancy and I see thirty-one Swainson's hawks (*Buteo swainsoni*) between Santaquin and Scipio— all facing south. My friend Clayton White, one of the world's experts on raptors, once mentioned that these birds migrate through Utah on their way to and from Argentina. A couple of years ago, maybe fifteen percent of the world's population of these birds were killed when they ate Argentine grasshoppers sprayed with a new pesticide. The loss is an unthinkable price for high-tech crop protection.

Gary Snyder, in the final line of a poem Susan reads to the ladies, recommends that we "stay together / learn the flowers / go light."

Fourteen

Lardass

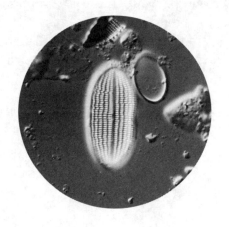

3 October, Mountain View Trail, Antelope Island

Nancy and I ride on Antelope Island this Sunday, the Mountain View Trail on the east shoreline. We have the trail to ourselves even though we drove to the island among hundreds of Sunday travelers. Ancient Lake Bonneville shows four shorelines on the island. We ride along the Stansbury Level, looking upward to the Provo and uppermost Bonneville Levels. We are in an interglacial time now, this afternoon and these millennia later. Water and ice will be back—count on it. Wish I could be around to see it.

We ride along at a civilized speed, in gentle and reflective conversation. Rounding a curve in the trail, we come upon an immense buffalo pelvis—sun-bleached and cradled in a patch of golden rabbit brush—a vision dear to Georgia O'Keefe. Oh my God, it is beautiful.

The shoreline is just a shout away. Thousands of shore birds float slowly out as we pass, not particularly concerned. Two Canadian geese honk, bringing us to a skidding stop. This sound vibrates in my bones, a primal memory that makes me sorry and ashamed for the male honker I killed thirty years ago, knowing now that its mate remained alone until she died. Holding this thought, riding behind Nancy in her black halter top across a thin, girlish back—a woman continuously alive to the moment and usually willing to overlook my assholery—I am deeply satisfied, if discomfited. Riding along with this woman I have been with since she was a girl leaves me filled with a fine satisfaction of memories both painful and inexplicably wonderful. I feel a deep companionship melded with a feeling of unknown pleasure for the years ahead. Makes me wonder what in hell I have been doing riding with Scott all these years. Makes me ponder how I could have been a better companion to this incomparable woman.

Makes me wonder how Scott is going to negotiate his version of this age-old story.

16 October, Great Western Trail, Thousand Lakes Mountain

It's just before noon and Nancy is driving Sam and me through Bicknell and north through Fremont. Alfalfa fields are lit by a brilliant sun that makes the white slashes of frost across the green grass all the more shocking. Gangly, big-wheeled irrigation pipes are rimed with gleaming white ice.

Hogan Pass on the Thousand Lake Mountain is high and exposed and windy and cold. We leave the car reluctantly to assemble our bikes, pull on our gloves, and draw our hoods tight amidst blowing ice crystals.

"You're making a big mistake," Nancy says, while surreptitiously tucking a bag of cheese curd into Sam's CamelBak (after having convinced him to add a bag of sunflower kernels and an emergency blanket).

"No question about it," Sam agrees.

We wave good-bye and head south on the Great Western Trail. Just below the pass, we stop to adjust our packs and fix an early flat. A moving shadow draws our gazes upward. A bird banks and sweeps and quarters into the wind, its white tail flared and white head brilliant against a dark body. A bald eagle (*Haliaeetus leucocephalus*). *Haliaeetus*, I discover later, is the Latin for sea eagle or osprey. *Leuco* is Greek for "white, light, bright" and is related to lux, luna, light, lightning, lumen, luster. *Leucocephalus*—white head.

"It's a good omen," I tell Sam.

We pedal south on what is supposedly a jeep road. I suppose that's true by Wayne County standards. The mountain ridge rises abruptly to the west. To the east, 3,500 feet below us, stand the buttes and spires and grotesque protuberances of Cathedral Valley. Sam points out Factory Butte at the north end of the Henry Mountains, whose peaks are half-veiled by dirty air courtesy of coal-burning power plants. We skirt the western edge of the mountain through sage scorched by a recent fire. A flock of mountain bluebirds rises and falls among the sage. The trail leads us down a steep jeep track into a grassy valley. Around one turn we find ourselves face-to-face with a corpulent elk hunter sitting on a rock next to his four-wheeler, a can of Bud Light in his paw.

"Sorry," I say, screeching to a surprised halt. "Didn't mean to screw up your hunt."

He answers with a hateful stare.

"Lardass," I mutter as we descend into the valley, shooting down the trail faster than I would have, had my mind been on the mechanics of the descent. My front tire loses traction and slides across a steep incline, and I hit the ground hard. I glance back quickly to see if the hunter can see me. He can't. I feel a little better, although I have ripped a hole in my new Gore-Tex shell.

"Hell," Sam says, riding up, "you do that on purpose?"

We hear motors. Two orange-clad elk hunters follow the trail out of the trees. They stop in front of us, a burly, burrheaded forty-five-year-old man and his father. We exchange pleasantries about how cold it is, about how riding a bike at least keeps your blood running, about the elk they have seen this morning, about the paucity of bulls. "Ah hell," the younger man says, "me and my dad hunt every year just for the chance to get out. On that scale, it's been a fine morning. Where are you coming from?" the younger man asks.

"Hogan's Pass," Sam answers.

They are surprised.

"Where you headed?"

"To Torrey."

"Torrey? You're riding to Torrey! Good luck! We'll report where we saw you last."

We've never ridden this trail. Now we're a bit spooked.

Tiring rapidly, we forge on, awed and sustained by the magnificent Water Pocket Fold stretching away to the south and by the fantastically colored Capital Reef now below us.

There is the final, sudden trail down from nine to seven thousand feet, what I call the Great Western Chute. It forces us to walk, making the tendons on the sides of my knees scream. The ride out, between magnificent white and red Navajo Sandstone walls, reminds Sam of a trip home from Disneyland. "Jed," he says, "two years old, wasn't overly impressed. On the way home, we drove through Zion National Park and Jed said, 'Now these are GREAT special effects.'"

Only a few miles to Torrey, along Sand Creek on a road so drifted with red sand that we have to fishtail our tired asses into town. We call Nancy from a pay phone and wait in gathering dusk for a blessed ride home. She too has had an adventurous day, we learn on the drive back to the cabin. After she dropped us off, she drove north off Hogan Pass and ended up at the Roosevelt Panel, famous for its abundant pictographs. She drove back to Teasdale, walked over to where her horse wanders free pastures, and rode bareback for a couple of hours. This country is good for the soul.

FIFTEEN

Agnostic Praying Mantis

25 October, Great Western Trail, Mt. Timpanogos

Sun-warmed, silicate-flared, cobalt-blue plums. The word "cobalt" comes from a German word for goblin. Sam and I stand in the sun and suck the flesh out of the tart-and-sweet, goblin-blue plums. Our hands measure the curved dense heft of warm fruit. Mountain avocados. "Avocado" means testicle in Nahuatl. "Sljiva" is the Serbo-Croatian word for plum. A year ago, I tell Sam, I sat with my friend Žarko in a sunny garden on the Drina River in Serbia and sipped juniper-flavored sljivovitz while eating heavy bread and soft cheese.

I tell Sam I am enjoying my new job. "I'm teaching an interdisciplinary course on the former Yugoslavia. Novels, films, history, politics, economics. I can bring a cup of coffee into class with me. I can describe the taste of sljivovitz. No administrator is going to try to fire me because I'm showing an R-rated film. I'm also teaching a course on philosophy and literature. Might do you some good to sit in some time."

"You can shove the philosophy up your ass," Sam says sweetly, "but I'd be happy to come to your Yugoslavia class and tell them that sljivovitz tastes suspiciously like turpentine."

27 October *(by email)*

Ok, Scott, round two of the fox story. Red foxes are an introduced species in North America, brought to the eastern United States more than two hundred years ago by fox hunters. Now, these years later, reds are all across the continent. On the surface, this doesn't seem to be much of a problem. Most people are as happy to see foxes in the wild as we are. Trouble is, as Barry Commoner states as his First Law of Ecology, everything is connected to everything else.

In the Strawberry country, as elsewhere, red foxes are hard on native sage grouse, which are in significant decline. Jerran Flinders, a wildlife biologist at BYU, has shown that the population of reds has increased substantially at Strawberry due to the continuing elimination of coyotes by the Wildlife Control folks. Coyotes are an important fox predator. Reds are excellent burrowers and climbers—Flinders has seen reds climb a tree to escape a predator. Once established, the smart and omnivorous foxes are hard to get rid of, even if the predators return. According to Flinders' student Kevin Bunnell, reds are taking dying kokanee salmon out of Strawberry Reservoir in the fall. The foxes stash these salmon and have a ready food supply all winter.

So, here is a case where a species was introduced in the east for sport, has expanded its range all over the west, increases substantially due to the elimination of a native predator, and gets a boost from an expanded food resource—yet another introduced species. In the spring, the foxes prey on sage grouse, pushing that species nearer to extinction. Like the man says, everything is connected to everything else.

The only solution is to rid the western United States of red foxes, likely impossible. But it is absolutely impossible if the feds and state keep poisoning and gunning coyotes. I actually had a coyote trapper / gunner / hater come into one of my classes a few years ago. He said, in a rare moment of candor, that he carried sheep wool in his pack so that when he killed a coyote he could plant wool in the gut of the often innocent animal. I find myself more in the camp of Ed Abbey, who noted that although ranchers were concerned by the number of sheep taken by coyotes, he himself was concerned that they didn't take enough.

29 October, Great Western Trail, Mt. Timpanogos

South wind blowing. Temperature in the sixties. Bright sun to the south. Black clouds swirl around the peaks of Mt. Timpanogos to the north. A single vertical lightning bolt shivers atop the mountain. Sam and I top the hill, our ascent aided by the south wind. By some sudden natural fiat, the wind reverses itself, gusting now from the north-west. The temperature drops twenty degrees. The sky spits cold rain. Raindrops pock the fox and raccoon tracks in the deep, grey flowerdust—thirty-eight days without rain—and we race down the hill, wind at our backs, exhilarated once again by our small places in this wild world.

On the knife-edge of the shifting front—that's where I have lived the last five years of my life. It's an uneasy locus, uncomfortable, challenging, and occasionally, as today, exhilarating. Having left a university that disappointed my hopes, having distanced myself from the religion that has marked my identity for five decades, and contemplating divorce after twenty-five years, occasionally exhilarating is sometimes enough to fend off despair.

Fourteen gunshots crack on the trail just above us, followed quickly by another twenty-three. One of our little bucks has happened into a shooting gallery. He's not going to come out again.

"I hunted deer for the first four years Nanc and I were married," Sam says. "I killed four deer with four bullets, often at very close range. I used all their meat, skinned them, and had their hides tanned, made cases, purses, slippers from their skins. And the meat was critical to our survival as graduate students."

I tell him about my own kill, my only kill: "I was hunting before the crack of dawn with my dad. When the deer came up from the La Plata River through the draw just as he predicted, Dad let me have first shot. I killed it all right, but I hit it in the butt and ruined half the meat. I still remember the scent of sage as I squatted on the hill that early morning, fifteen or sixteen years old."

30 October, Great Western Trail, Mt. Timpanogos

Headed off the hill, we turn down a route we haven't ridden in a month. I swing around a graveled turn, dip swiftly into a valley, rise to cross a dirt road, shoot precipitously off the road—or at least that's what I had in mind. Just as the trail leaves the road I sense something odd, a new texture, an unexpected flash—it happens too quickly to see clearly—and I'm airborne over my front wheel, my feet free of the pedals, my bike spinning behind me, and I'm tripping and running down the hill, upright and unhurt.

"Perfect landing!" Sam shouts. "It's a ten!"

I climb back up to find my bike in a freshly dug trench six feet across and five feet deep, backhoed into the trail just below the lip of the road. This trap is designed to be invisible to a rider. Someone, perhaps the owner of this land, has just tried to kill me.

Physically, I'm okay.

"We are careful riders," Sam notes with tight lips. "We never leave established trails. If the sociopath who tried to kill us were here, I'd return his favor."

31 October, Great Western Trail, Mt. Timpanogos

Sunday afternoon. A quick ride up the trail just to loosen up. We are nervous, riding while the deer hunt continues, and we stay mostly in the open and wear bright clothing. Hunters have been off-road everywhere. ORV trails zigzag up the mountainside randomly, crisscrossing at odd angles. It reminds us of the Alaskan congressman who claims he won't be happy until new roads in his state make a roadmap look like spaghetti.

We head off the mountain and end up behind two guys in a Ford Bronco bumping down a steep stretch toward a couple of hidden hollows. With no warning, the driver swerves off-road for two hundred yards through sage and cliff rose, making tracks that will remain for decades to come. I shout curses on their mothers.

"Jeez," Scott says. "Let's not get into a fight."

"Why not," I respond.

"Time, education, and demographics are on our side," Scott says. "There is a growing awareness about protecting public lands. It's a matter of time until the majority demands changes that will be more ecologically friendly."

"That may be true in principle," I respond, "but remember the four-hundred-pound woman who sneered at us during the Forest Service open house last spring when we suggested four-wheeler trails should be limited? 'It's my God-given right to be in the mountains,' she said, 'and with my asthma, an ORV is my God-given choice.'"

"When people actually see what four-wheelers do to the land," Scott replies, "they'll agree there should be more control."

"Where does this optimistic shit come from?" I ask. "You see the *Daily Herald* photo of Congressman Chris Cannon's yard-wide ass on his four-wheeler on the San Raphael Swell last week, saying how ridin' his machine gets him closer to God?"

"I did," Scott replies. "But I don't think Cannon and his boys have a future. His point of view is a throw-back to when people didn't understand the ecological damage of mismanagement."

"Could be. But ORV damage is bad now and getting worse. The whole issue is escalating and going to end up a constant confrontation in state and federal courts."

"So be it," Scott replies.

6 November, Great Western Trail, Mt. Timpanogos

The new *Catalyst* is out with our latest column. It lists Sam Rushforth as the sole author, and at the end says, "Scott Abbott, who usually co-writes this column. . . ."

"Sam," I say, after showing him the piece, "you mailed Greta our last column. Are you trying to ease me out of the picture here?"

"Actually not," Sam replies. "Greta must have thought this was our best column yet and assumed I wrote it alone."

"Does she know you type with two fingers?" I ask. "Does she realize that Nancy edits all your sentences?"

"This is a hitherto unknown and untoward side of you, Abbott," Sam retorts.

It must be eighty degrees Fahrenheit on the south-facing hill where we sit to repair multiple thorn wounds to my front and back tires. Goatheads. On the way down, I brake to a stop and call Sam back up the hill. A long, fat bullsnake (*Pituophis catenifer*) lies stretched out across the trail, its tawny skin marked from head to disappearing tail by a series of black diamonds. "You're beautiful," Sam tells the snake. "And if you want to live to see another summer, you had better get off this trail." It takes his advice.

Just down the hill, we stop to look back at the yellow grass shining against the deep blue sky. The blue heightens the brilliance of the yellow and the yellow deepens the blue. "See how the grass glistens in the slanting sun?" Sam asks. "The epidermis of grasses contains silicon that flashes the sunlight back at us."

How the hell does he know all this stuff?

7 November, Great Western Trail, Mt. Timpanogos

Brooding over my so-called marriage, I lead Sam on a double-time chase up the lower loop. We breathe hard and sweat and are glad to be outside under a partial overcast that constantly alters the light. Record November temperatures across the state this weekend, and well above seventy degrees today. Last year on this day, we had four inches of new snow. A combination of temperature and day length has tricked some plants into blooming. Cliff rose, for instance, sports new yellow blossoms among its few remaining leaves. Newly blossoming yellow flowers top some of the curlycup gumweed. Stalks of fresh green sweetclover are forcing yellow flowers.

"Whoa!" Sam calls out, and stops his bike. There's a huge neon-green praying mantis on the trail. "It only has one front leg," he observes.

"Must be agnostic," I suggest.

We ride on and Sam complains about how stiff and sore he has been. "At night, if I've been sitting on the floor reading the paper and start to get up, I hurt in all my joints. My muscles ache."

"If it's any comfort," I respond, "it's only going to get worse."

12 November, Great Western Trail, Mt. Timpanogos

Seventy degrees again today. We ride Frank for the first time in nearly two weeks. Or rather, Frank rides us. We're off our bikes more than we're on them, and when we are on them we're wheezing and coughing.

"You spit!" Sam shouts from behind me. "I've never seen you spit before. I didn't know you could spit. Maybe you're a man after all."

"Just got some snot in my mouth," I say. "Since I'm not inse-cure about my masculinity, there's no need for constant display."

"You're missing the point," Sam replies. "Spitting is a respected male ritual like talking about sports and beer and women and it's our job to carry on the tradition."

We stand at the top of the foothills, look across a hazy, pol-luted Utah Valley, and Sam becomes reflective. "I have always dreamed of sitting on a spit like this some thousands of years ago," he says. "What would it have been like to fish ancient Lake Bonneville for the *pisces du jour* while watching gators, giant turtles, and huge predators patrol the region?"

SIXTEEN

Little Column?

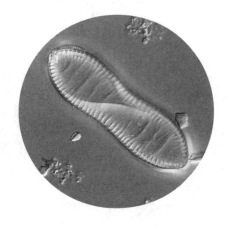

18 November, Great Western Trail, Mt. Timpanogos

We swing onto the asphalt of the Provo River Parkway Trail at the mouth of Provo Canyon. On the old railway bridge, we run into Lyn Bennett, a UVSC historian wearing her Kansas Jayhawk sweatshirt and out for what she says is her daily four-mile walk. "I won't keep you," she says after exchanging pleasantries. "I know you have to get up there to make your ride so you can write your little column."

Our little column? It's an important column for an important magazine! *Our little column*? First, Sam and Greta conspire to cut me out of the column. And now our friend Lyn refers to our work as a little column. Worse still, what if that was a double entendre?

22 November, Great Western Trail, Mt. Timpanogos

Two trees down between the trail and the river near the mouth of Provo Canyon, a couple of cottonwoods *(Populus fremontii)*, the largest maybe six inches in diameter. Hundreds of beautiful chisel marks ring their trunks. Kids with hatchets? No, beavers! *Castor canadensis*, our largest living rodent.

"Trying to dam the Provo?" I wonder.

"Repairing a dam on a branch of it maybe, or perhaps just intent on dining on the cottonwood bark," Sam says.

High on Frank, low on energy, we sit on a rock overlooking Utah Valley. "Tough time for you," Sam says. "How do you see the next months unfolding?"

"There's some anticipation," I say. "Some relief. It has to be done and I'm going to do it. But I have nightmares about losing contact with Ben, Sam, and Tim when I move out. I won't have those mundane, unplanned shared experiences with them. Will they be all right? Will I? Will we? It's the *we* I'm most fearful for. Will shared experiences structured by planned visits be enough? Shit!"

28 November, Great Western Trail

The fox scat on the trail has changed. During late spring and summer, the piles were exuberant—knotted and twisted, rich with seeds, insect parts, and mammal hair. Now they are tar-black and tapered to a point. No largess here, unless you count a surprising twist of orange plastic flagging one pile. During warm months, foot-high rocks on the trail were often adorned with scat—a message of the high-life from male rogues. Now, scat is dropped anywhere as though by tired travelers facing a long winter. A lack of concern for the message suggests plenty about the messenger. As if on cue, a magnificent bushy creature, broad-shouldered, golden and glowing in its winter coat, flying a glorious white-tipped tail, moves like a sine wave across the adjacent draw. And then it's gone.

29 November, Great Western Trail, Mt. Timpanogos

A biker bumps down the mountain toward us. It's our friend Paul Richards, former editor of the *Provo Daily Herald* and former public relations spokesman for BYU. His youthful face and strong legs belie his sixty-plus years.

"I've been meaning to ask you something," Paul says. "Every once in a while in your column you mention that you've ridden Frank without touching down. Can you really do that?"

"Of course," Sam says.

"Not often," I add.

Paul points down the road to the steep trailhead we usually ride down. "Can you ride up that?"

"Sometimes," Sam says. "When it's not too loose."

"And how about that steep rise just after the burned section?"

"No," I say. "That's impossible."

Paul is reassured. "So everything in the column isn't necessarily true?"

"Paul," I say, "everything we describe in our column is exactly and precisely and literally true."

He looks skeptical.

"The only exceptions," I continue, "are the statements about our potency. They, you should know, are always understated."

1 December, Great Western Trail, Mt. Timpanogos

We ride at noon today, trying to beat the front closing in from the northwest. Rain and snow predicted for this afternoon. Light and shadow play across the mountain's flank. With no breakfast to speak of, I'm feeling weak as we turn up Frank. Sam powers ahead while I try a new strategy: 1. you ride slowly, which saves energy, and 2. the slow tempo insures you will come off on steep parts so you can walk up, which saves more energy.

I'm implementing this strategy on the second chute (Sam is long gone) when I notice something moving up the hill across the draw. It's a herd of elk, cows and calves, flowing like a roiling river up a game trail. The leading cow is the largest, splendid in her black mantle and sleek brown sides. Fourteen of her sisters and their offspring follow. A sixteenth and solitary elk scrambles straight up the steep slope to the right of the game trail. He is silver-sided, heavily muscled, with a large, raked set of antlers that almost touch his back as he climbs. The elk flow over the top of the hill and disappear. I ride on up Frank to meet Sam, who has turned back to look for me.

"Thought you might have fallen on your head," he says.

We descend as the wind picks up out of the north—cold and harsh. We button and zip, pull hats over ears. Rain spatters Sam's glasses. "Hope we get offa here," Sam says. "Look at the mist on the mountain. Getting dark. Mountain hanging over us. Wind whipping up. We're insignificant here."

I shiver and agree.

"This mountain," Sam continues, "is comprised of rocks more than two hundred million years old with uplift begun more than sixty million years ago. I am grateful to be here at this moment, to see and partly understand the geology and biology of this mountain—to witness."

"Sam, I don't want to put words between us and the experience, but your response bears out Kant's theory of the sublime. Nature overwhelms us with sheer size or power, then reason moves us past fear to a fine mixed pleasure."

"No shit," Sam agrees thoughtfully.

5 December, Great Western Trail, Mt. Timpanogos

My friend and colleague Larry St.Clair has completed a wonderful book on lichens: *A Color Guidebook to Common Rocky Mountain Lichens.* This is what we have been waiting for. Book in backpack, we head for the Great Western.

Halfway up, Scott points at orange-golden lichens blazing on scrub oak trunks. We climb off our bikes for a closer look. Scott's field glasses turned backwards make fine magnifiers. The lichens show evident fruiting bodies (apothecia), making them *Xanthoria polycarpa.* Several are lighter in color, ranging to a greenish or even grey color. I assume these are another species and ask Larry about this the next day. He says it is the same species growing in less light.

At the top of our loop, a grey-green encrusting species is all over the quartzite—a *Lecanora.* Scott works on this species and thinks it's *L. novomexicana.* Larry suggests later it is actually *Lecanora muralis,* a close relative. We run into maples and oaks with the inch-wide, grey-green disks of *Physcia stellaris* clinging to their trunks. We see bright red lichens on limestone above us and we risk our lives on talus to clamber up and collect small fragments. It's *Caloplaca trachyphylla,* a common limestone dweller in our region. We find a bright orange species on quartzite along the trail. It's another *Caloplaca,* though it's young and we can't determine the species. "This is splendid!"

Scott says. "Something new to look for, another excuse to get our asses in the air and noses to the ground."

7 December, Great Western Trail, Mt. Timpanogos

Through binoculars, we examine the light-grey head and back and the swept-back black tuxedo markings of a Clark's nutcracker. Earlier in the year, we saw several of these high on the Wasatch Crest Trail, but this is the first we have seen on the lower reaches of Timpanogos.

Silhouetted against the western sky stand two mule deer—a doe and a four-point buck. The buck measures us intently. His neck is massive, pumped like a weight lifter's. "He's got his eye on us," I tell Sam. "Let's move on. He'll need his strength for the business at hand."

Later, I describe the buck to my colleague J.D. Davidson, an avid and knowledgeable hunter. "It's the time of year for the rut," J.D. says. "Hence the swollen neck. You were lucky to see a mule deer buck during the rutting season. Their courtship isn't based on showy displays by a dominant male, but rather on tending females serially. The less attention he can draw to himself and the doe the better."

8 December, Orem *(by email)*

Scott, here's the quiz of the day. What do Grizzly, Kodiak, Wolverine, Timberwolf, Badger, Big Bear and BearTracker have in common? Give up? They are all models of Yamaha off-road vehicles.

10 December, Great Western Trail, Mt. Timpanogos

I'm on the phone with Sam. "I've been thinking," he says. "It is snowing, but it's also cold. I bet we could make it up the trail." Thoughts of a comfy morning working in my study while listening to jazz evaporate.

Ruts have disappeared. Rocks are invisible. But we know this trail from hundreds or even thousands of rides and ease our way up the mountain. Heavy clouds veil Timpanogos. Slipping and scrambling, we climb into the clouds ourselves, standing finally at the top of the lower loop. "Glad you called," I say to Sam. "I'd hate to have missed this. It is magical."

We ride through four inches of snow toward the mouth of the canyon, a route that takes us past the trailhead of Frank. Full of bluff and bravado, Sam suggests that we turn up. I swing wide and scramble up the trail. The snow deepens as we climb, and by the C-turn we're done. Braking with wet pads on wet rims over a trail rendered invisible by snow is even harder than the climb, but when we leave Frank, we're both grinning at our audacity. In the falling snow, we follow deer tracks down the mountain. Our bikes are rimed and glazed and heavy with accretion. And still they carry us.

18 December, New York City *(by email)*

Nancy and I are in New York for a few days for Christmas. Shoppers in furs, limousines along every street. We exit the subway at 59th Street and enter Bloomingdale's. I head down a crowded hall toward the men's room. Several turns and the pissoir is nowhere to be seen. Left turn, straight ahead, I notice an old guy walking toward me. I jog right, he follows. I make fleeting eye contact, hoping to ward him off. I angle back left. He returns eye contact briefly and follows. The scruffy bastard continues toward me and I flush with adrenaline. WHACK. I run headlong into a ceiling-to-floor mirror at the end of the hall. My nose is flattened and for a moment I don't know what has happened. My instant response is to slug the guy who has just run into me. But with attending chuckles from a couple of onlookers, I damn quick figure it out.

Trying for nonchalance, I sidle into the men's room. I've

got a sore nose from the collision and acting cool at the urinal is something of a trick. Standing there disoriented, I can't get started—and I desperately need the comfort of a good piss. It's a shock, I tell you. How did I get here from there?

SEVENTEEN

Empty Sockets, Sardonic Grin

Christmas Eve, Great Western Trail, Mt. Timpanogos

Twenty-five degrees Fahrenheit. A cold wind blows out of the canyon. The trail is soft and slippery, the snow crusty and sand-like. Foxes have alternately played and hurried along the trail. A raccoon has left hand-tracks. Something smaller, perhaps a weasel, has left her mark lightly on top of the snow. Paramount is the spoor of a pair of cougars, abundant four-toed rounded tracks with no claw marks. We imagine the big cats angling quickly up a hillside, stopping to frolic. Farther along, their trails reticulate, leaving a playful record. We follow their signs for a mile or more, hoping for a sighting. For some reason, Scott lets me lead.

"I'd give your left nut to see these two," I tell Scott. "But you can bet our deer aren't keen to see them. An adult cougar can kill and eat as many as forty deer a year."

"That's why the Utah Wildlife Board continues to up the number of cougar permits," Scott replies. "They get a three-fer. First, they need to appease ranchers who hate cougars. Second, they are under pressure from deer hunters who want to up the number of available deer and who hate cougars. And third, they make a bunch of cougar hunters happy by expanding the hunt. What a bargain for the managers!"

Back at home, I look up the 1999 "Utah Cougar Management Plan" published by the Utah Division of Wildlife Resources. It estimates that hunters of *Felis concolor*, one of the most widely ranging mammals in our hemisphere, spent an estimated $2,143,899 in 1997-1998 in Utah. The report states that "no human ever has been killed by a cougar in Utah" and offers nearly sixty pages of definitions and regulations, including the following:

'Carcass' means the dead body of an animal or its parts.

'Cougar' means *Felis concolor*, commonly known as mountain lion, lion, puma, panther or catamount. 'Take' means to: hunt, pursue, harass, catch, capture, possess, angle, seine, trap or kill any protected wildlife. Legally obtained, tanned cougar hides may be purchased or sold. A person may not purchase, sell, offer for sale or barter a tooth, claw, paw or skull of any cougar. A person may not waste or permit to be wasted or spoiled any protected wildlife or their parts. The skinned carcass of a cougar may be left in the field and does not constitute waste of wildlife.

The "management plan" allows for a "harvest" of 647 cougars this year, including six in our "Wasatch Mountains Timpanogos" area (this will undoubtedly include the two cougars we were following) and six in the "Wasatch Mountains Cascade" area just across the canyon.

26 December, Great Western Trail, Mt. Timpanogos

Dense pollution, trapped by a temperature inversion, occludes the valley below. The stacks of Geneva Steel rise above the muck, their emissions rising, then flattening to join the stinking grey-brown mess. "I'm not riding back down into that," Scott says. "I've been breathing it for the past decade, but after reading Sandra Steingraber's *Living Downstream* it's beginning to make me jittery. And damn it, everyone I know is sick right now."

"I'm with you," I reply. "Our air is probably worse than we thought. We have high levels of PM2.5, the tiniest particulate matter. The EPA has presented new health standards for PM2.5 and they're being fought like crazy by industry right across the country. Senator Orin Hatch has joined the fight against the EPA on the grounds that the new standards will hurt business. Doesn't the SOB have a mother? When they're finally approved, we're going to have a hard time all along the Wasatch Front meeting the standards."

"I'm tired of my lungs being a high-tech pollution filtration system for industry," Scott states. "Wonder if the air will be any better in Midway? Next week I'm moving out of my house and into my sister's house there, empty while they spend another year in Beijing. Shit, never thought I'd be doing this."

"It's tough," I commiserate. "A few nights ago, Nanc and I were walking south in Salt Lake City along 4th West. Two young people, a man and a woman, were lying asleep on the cold sidewalk. We got a quilt from our car and covered the sleepers. Keep that in mind while you move into your sister's house."

"If we could look into the future, it would paralyze us," Scott says, still in his own world.

On the way down the mountain, we pass the stump-yard remains of last summer's orchard. Someone or something has dragged the skeleton of a red fox out of its grave. It is splayed out like a display—vertebrae, leg bones, the remains of its tail. Only a bit of dirty fur left on its head, which is turned to stare at us with empty sockets and a sardonic grin.

YEAR II

And not so much facts in themselves as the stories that are taken from them, that are brought up together, at the table, during special occasions or in the course of evening walks. This slow transformation of facts into stories which, like wine, improve with age, progressively abandoning insignificant details, tightening attention on essential words, inspiring the whole with a rhythm, a dramatic progression, a suspense, proper to enhance the value of the ending. So that, after some time, it is more a story elaborated in common and shared, exchanged many a time since then . . . rather than the faraway facts to which it alludes.

Jean Frémon, *The Botanical Garden*

EIGHTEEN

A Pretty Decent Fall

9 January, Teasdale

Time to get away from the Wasatch Front, the winter inversions, and flu. Nancy and I are spending a day or two in Teasdale.

Indian rice grass gleams in the late-afternoon sun, the Boulder sighs above us, shadows lengthen to the northwest. The wind gusts to forty miles per hour out of the north and the countryside bends with the wind. Later, Tchaikovsky's *Pathetique*, hot tea, a fine fire on the hearth, Orion crossing the black sky.

10 January, Midway, Utah *(by email)*

Sam—it's done. I moved out of our house. It is now her house. It felt like I was emigrating into some kind of exile. Standing in an aisle of a Heber City grocery store at 10 p.m. with a cheap coffee maker in my hands, I felt like I had embarked on a long and potentially dangerous voyage. I felt bereft, empty, alone. I shivered. It was absurd, this auspicious new beginning in the aisle of a grocery store in the dark of the night.

My sister's house—bless her generous heart—is good for my visiting boys, although the word "visiting" evokes plenty of anxieties. Here's a conversation from the weekend:

"Dad," Ben asks, "could I have five dollars for a field trip?"

"Sure," I reply, "anything for an educational experience. Where are you going?"

"To the state capitol building," he says.

"With your history class?" I ask.

"Not exactly," he answers. "I joined the Young Republicans."

"You did what?"

"I joined the Orem High School Young Republicans," he says, grinning.

"And you want me to pay for it!"

"Dad, don't get your shorts in a bunch. There's a girl I like in the club."

17 January, Great Western Trail, Mt. Timpanogos

The lower hill has dried and we're feeling good, so we turn up a ridge along one side of a deep gully. I'm half way up the steepest part when I hear Sam whoop behind me. The trail always pulls us to the left here, and I figure he's had to step off. Where the trail flattens, I step down and look back. No Sam to be seen. A movement at the bottom of the gully catches my eye. Far below me, Sam is trying to stand up. He falls back, unable to rise. His bike lies next to him.

When he gets his breath and hauls his bike back up to the trail, Sam shows me how gravity pulled him left and he tried to ride it out, swinging along below the trail till he thought he had it made. A rock made the thought moot and he found himself cartwheeling over and under his bike, down the precipitous but mostly soft slope. "I thought on the way down that this was an easy way to wrack up a pretty decent fall," Sam says. "Then came the rock in the ribs."

"It's a hundred feet to the bottom of the gully," I calculate, "which makes this a record for distance. You already held the record for severity—that time you tried to ride down through the boulder field and separated your shoulder. And you have the record for three falls in a hundred yards. I'm buying you a gyroscope."

30 January, Strawberry Peak

Nancy, Scott, his son Tom, and I ski up through aspen, spruce, and fir. The air is warm and sensuous; a gentle wind blows across the slopes. We break trail, feeling the work in our thighs. We have mixed feelings as we come to a snowmobile track leading up. Pristine snow is beautiful, but the track is certainly good for tired legs.

"I talked to Jerran Flinders yesterday," I report, "about his research on lynx in the Uintas. He says snomo tracks are a potentially serious problem for lynx. Coyotes range along the packed tracks deeper into the high Uintas than they could without them. They branch off the tracks to hunt snowshoe rabbits. Since these rabbits are important prey for lynx, snowmobiles most likely contribute to the loss of lynx populations. We live in a world of unintended consequences."

We lean back on skis thrust into the snow and enjoy a good lunch of peanut butter-and-honey sandwiches, juicy oranges, chocolate, and nuts. Our perch overlooks broad drainages to the east and west. Back on our skis, Telemark turns sweep or tumble us down a series of steep, narrow, unmarked meadows. Something explodes just inches in front of Scott's advancing ski, bursting up out of the snow to fly into a tall spruce. It leaves a single, delicate wing mark on the snow. A spruce grouse (*Falcipennis canadensis*), in all likelihood. Imagine the digestive prowess of a creature whose main winter diet consists of spruce needles!

7 February, Great Western Trail, Mt. Timpanogos

From where Scott and I stand, the sun yellow-golds the valley below and lights the hillsides with a warm memory of fall. The remaining autumn leaves of the oak and maple turn the slopes auburn in the evening slant. The color tugs at memory, melancholy and distant. I brush my mother's hair a hundred strokes on a windy childhood evening, a soothing tradition for both of us. Her hair is long and auburn, with a slight curl. I brush nightly for some years, acting also as the grey-and-white hair police, alert for any of the turning hairs, which must be pulled from the beautiful auburn mass. At some point, through some kind of pitiful masculine conditioning, I come to know that boys don't brush their mother's hair. What a shame. It may have been the most meaningful thing I ever did for her (and for me).

8 February, Great Western Trail, Mt. Timpanogos

Still warm. Scott spots *Phlox longifolia* in the middle of the trail in full bloom. Phlox! On the eighth of February—it's the damndest thing. Blossoms in every month of the year—the first time I can remember.

10 February, Salt Lake City

"Jeff," my daughter Sarah calls to her friend in the kitchen, "I'm reading this month's column and my dad fell down a hundred-foot drop still clipped onto his bike."

"Don't worry, Sarah," Jeff replies. "Keep reading. Your dad's tougher than that gully."

13 February, Wasatch Crest Trail, Big Cottonwood Canyon

Scott, Nancy and I ski to Scott's Pass for a second consecutive day. Two straight days of big storm—yesterday we skied down in a whiteout.

This morning we sweat and puff our way up the trail, breaking trail in three feet of soft powder. An hour into the ski, snow machines roar over the ridge above us. We jump off the trail as the infernal beasts race past. Rotund men dressed in black coveralls raise their hands in some sort of salute as they pass. Must be powerful machines to carry these bovine look-alikes up and down the trail.

They stink," Scott shouts, "but they're noisy."

The third in line hits a snow bank and sticks. He can't get his machine to move an inch—it roars and bellows and disgorges noxious vapors.

"Can't get this machine outta the snow," the guy shouts over his motor.

"I see that," Scott mutters. "Maybe with the spring thaw you'll have more luck."

The guide comes up, thigh-deep in powder, and apologizes

for compromising our trek. "Damn snow machines are a nui-sance—wish I was with you today."

We understand the need to make a buck. When he said he was sorry, we said no sweat—we were too damned tired to break trail any farther anyway and it was going to be nice to use his trail and thanks for mentioning it and maybe we'll see you around somewhere.

Nineteen

Mistletoe Birds

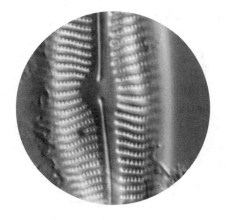

5 March, Great Western Trail, Mt. Timpanogos

In a plowed cornfield near the first hill, hundreds of European starlings (*Sturnus vulgaris*) fly together in a noisy vortex—a flock of individuals with a single control center. They are blue-black in the late afternoon sun, speckled on their breasts and backs. They flash metallic green.

We ride on up the hill and I tell Scott, "Some outfit called the American Acclimatization Society brought sixty starlings to Central Park in New York City in 1890. I think they wanted to bring to America every species mentioned by Shakespeare in his plays. Starlings did so well that they are now an immediate threat to some hole-dwelling birds in the west, including mountain bluebirds."

"So, the decline of bluebirds in Utah is caused by a mention of starlings in Shakespeare?" Scott asks.

"Henry IV," I answer. "Written over four centuries ago. I should add that merlins (*Falco columbarius*) are increasing due to the numerous and tasty starlings. I like merlins as much as I dislike starlings. It's a trade-off."

"Speaking of trade-offs," Scott says. "It's not easy to adjust to the new rhythms of living alone. I wake up in the night and wonder what the hell I have done. It's not the empty bed. I slept alone on a futon in the basement for most of the last decade. It's the absence of sound. Nobody flushes the toilet. There's no one talking in their sleep. There is no one happy I have made breakfast."

"You're describing an anxiety I deal with every day of my life," I reply. "Leaving behind the tried and true patterns is next to impossible for me. I've spent most of my life at the same university. We live in the same house we bought thirty years ago. I am OCD. Nanc and I are still together and in love, that's the good side. But it has its definite low points. You've got balls, man."

"It's got nothing to do with balls," Scott says. "It's fear. I got spooked as I contemplated a bleak and lonely future. I felt like I was dying, emotionally wasting away. And now here I am complaining about feeling lonely. What a whiner!"

"Hell," I say, "all you need is a girlfriend."

6 March, Great Western Trail, Mt. Timpanogos

The second day of riding after several days of cooling our heels. Since our regular trails are muddy, we again ride the particularly steep trail with the gully below. This is costly and we both pay—gasping and struggling on the hardest parts, sweating and swearing between.

"Maybe we ought to switch to writing about golf," Scott suggests. "No near-death climbs, no equipment failures, no falls off the trail."

"But I don't know how to golf," I protest.

"You know how to golf as well as you know how to ride a bike," Scott counters.

10 March, The Coffee Garden, Salt Lake City

To: The Editor, *Catalyst Magazine*

Subject: Auburn

I live in Loa. Since September's seasonal closing of the Robber's Roost in Torrey, I have been deprived of the Catalyst. *Today I'm in Salt Lake on my way to color my hair, but stop at the Coffee Garden first to see if they have a copy. I score!*

I grab the paper, order a double caramel latte grande, and sit down to browse. I immediately find what I'm looking for—"Biking and Botanizing the Great Western Trail." I settle in to read of Sam's and Scott's adventures.

I read about birds, wing prints in the snow, cat tracks, coyotes and snomo tracks. I come to the entry made February seven—the day my sisters and I headed for San Francisco, just the three of us.

I am the oldest and my hair is prematurely grey, although I usually color it purple.

As I read my dad's entry, I am seven years old, sitting at the oak table in my grandmother's kitchen. The smell of coffee, green peppers, and pipe tobacco comfort me. Sitting on the edge of the chair, I swing my legs, too short to touch the ground.

"Oh sugar!" My grandmother exhales from in front of the salmon-colored refrigerator.

I look over. Her hair is grey now, but I have seen pictures of her when it was auburn—the way it would have looked to my father as he brushed it one hundred strokes each night when he was seven.

I look up from the column, tears on my face. I am sitting in a coffeehouse and I am thirty-two years old. I stand to leave. Eighteen years after her death, I have encountered my grandmother, through my father's words, as the color auburn. Cheeks still wet, I walk out of the coffee shop. I decide not to color my hair today.
    Marie Rushforth

12 March, Strawberry Peak

I drive up Daniels Canyon, snow falling steadily, early Bob Dylan blaring from the tape deck: "Talkin' John Birch Society Blues," "I'm in the Mood for You," and a foreign song punctuated by a yodel he claims he learned in Utah, "Talkin' Hava Nagila." Sam's busy, my boys are with their mother, and I've got an appointment with my therapist.

By 8:00 I'm climbing through new snow with the rising sun at my back. Over the course of five hours, I hear the distant dentist's-drill whine of two snomos and the motors of a small airplane. Otherwise, there are only natural sounds and profound solitude. The powder deepens as I climb, and it's not long till I head for south-facing slopes where a solid crust under the new snow makes breaking trail a bit easier. The rhythm of skis and poles. The glow of my sweating body. The occasional chatter of birds. Hoar frost on aspens. Icicles hanging from conifers. The snowshoe tracks of hares. A squirrel's scolding. Erotic folds of snow where a stream peeks out of a sinuous valley.

The wind-blown snow at the top of the ridge is like powdered sugar. Clouds brush the ridge. Whiteouts alternate with sudden, sunlit openings that reveal an immense landscape stretching from Mt. Timpanogos to the Uintas, a vast and splendid mountainous expanse. I rip the skins from my skis, eat an orange—the brilliant color shocking in the white and blue landscape—gulp the last of my water, and shove off through aspens in swinging, bent-kneed turns that burn my legs and ease my mind. "Don't think twice," my therapist suggests. "It's all right."

16 March, Great Western Trail, Mt. Timpanogos

Dear Mr. Abbott, of the *Catalyst*:

I am taking the time this afternoon to write you a letter concerning the article you wrote about your son's joining the Teenage Republicans. I must admit, I found it rather amusing, but to be quite frank, on an intellectual level, I found it to be lacking. Please allow me to take this opportunity to inform you about the wonderful opportunities that the Teenage Republicans and the GOP have for all those "who have an ear to hear . . ."

Sincerely,

Chairman, Utah Teenage Republicans "An advocate of family values and the Republican way of life."

We're chuckling about the earnest teenage Repug as we wheeze our way up the mountain. "We're reaching a wider readership than we thought," I suggest, and Sam responds that soon we'll be up to double digits.

"By the way," Sam says later, as we roll off the mountain, "Greta just wrote and said the April issue will focus on recycling and gardening. She wondered if we could address the theme in this month's column."

"Riding up this damn hill again and again ought to count as recycling," I answer.

19 March, Great Western Trail, Teasdale

"Look at the mistletoe infestation." I point to a dense stand of Utah junipers as we top the hill. "It's on nearly every tree. Dwarf mistletoe is an important parasite on some trees and shrubs in Utah and is quite host specific. The species we see here are probably *Phoradendron juniperinum*, juniper mistletoe. Mistletoes can cause substantial damage to their hosts, but I'm fascinated by the evolutionary connection between specific mistletoes, their hosts, and associated mistletoe birds. Some mistletoe species occur only on one species of tree and their fruits are eaten mostly by mistletoe birds that inhabit the same trees. The fruits are laxative and the birds get the runs. They have evolved a startling behavior you can't believe. They squat, shit, step up-branch, squat, shit, step up-branch in a repeating pattern, planting mistletoe seeds in a row as they go. And the really interesting deal is that the shape of these birds is slightly different from that of a typical bird. They are more upright, so that when they shit they hit the branch rather than pooping off the edge into the forest."

"Sounds like a crock of shit to me," Scott opines.

"It's the god's truth," I say.

"It's Darwin's truth," Scott corrects me. "But the best part of the story was the little dance you did while describing a mistletoe bird pooping up a limb. I hadn't much figured you for a squat-shit-step dancer."

TWENTY

Ecstatic Phenomenon

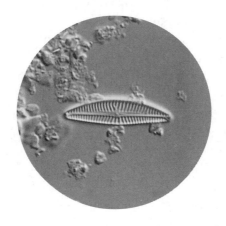

1 April, Great Western Trail, Mt. Timpanogos

Two magpies fly up from the winter-matted yellow grass on the hill just above us. Motion at an adjacent spot turns out to be a rusty-chested fox. No, it's too large to be a fox, and its tail isn't bushy like a fox's. A coyote. But the bright red chest throws us off. We watch it zigzag through leafless scrub oak on the way to the ridge top, from which it eyes us closely.

The coyote has left behind a fresh kill, a yearling mule deer, its flaccid tongue dangling from a closed mouth. The eyes are not yet glazed. Beneath my touch, the still-warm ribs are a washboard—not much fat left at the end of the animal's first and last winter. Sam finds a wound in the deer's neck that explains the coyote's red bib—a severed artery would have pumped blood in spurts while the coyote hung on for a final wild ride. The grass beneath the young deer's throat is stained red with the last of its life. Our thoughts swing back to the coyote.

"Hope the coyote comes back for its breakfast," I say. "Don't want this life and death to be wasted."

"She'll be back before we round the next corner," Sam says.

3 April, Orem *(by email)*

Scott—Talked with Jerran Flinders this morning about Saturday's deer kill. I told him we had found a yearling doe kill. He said to go back and look again. Jerran says nearly all the yearling kills he sees are males. This seems to occur since mothers keep young does closer than bucks. In fact, he thinks does with fawns actually encourage young bucks to drift away from them and to some extent from the herd. So, yearling males are often at the edge of herds, with the potential to get separated or cut out by predators. The loss of a doe means the loss of offspring potential for the herd, but the loss of a buck is probably not so important since a single male can fertilize many females. Furthermore, young bucks at the edge of the herd have to be smart and strong to survive—maybe some sort of evolutionary testing ground.

Been wondering whether two or more coyotes were working together. Jerran suggests the deer we found may have been taken by a pair of coyotes, one hazing the buck toward another waiting in ambush. But if I had to lay down my money, the strut of that sassy coyote leaving the kill was the walk of a confident and accomplished single mom bringing home the bacon.

4 April, Great Western Trail, Mt. Timpanogos

Two days after finding the coyote and its kill, we return to the scene. Just below the ridge, we step off our bikes.

Brilliant ruby light rises from the yellow grasses where the small deer lay, an ecstatic phenomenon that makes no immediate sense.

Then it comes clear: the late-afternoon sunlight blazes through blood-stained membranes in the ribcage. They curve up from the backbone like a stained-glass vault. Only the tough membranes between ribs remain. Not a scrap of muscle or skin. The skull has been stripped clean and white, leaving empty sockets where the eyeballs were still moist two days ago. As Jerran suggested, there are tiny antler buds on the skull. Most of the deer's bones and fur are scattered about. The lower bowel is intact, stuffed with half-digested browse—unappetizing to every mammal and bird that has fed here. Even magpies won't eat this shit.

6 April, Albuquerque, New Mexico *(by email)*

Sam—this bright New Mexican sky takes me back to my childhood near the Four Corners where we learned the words to "Oh fair New Mexico" at Farmington's Ladera Elementary School and at home watched the Channel 5 cowboy sing "Ridin' down the trail to Albuquerque, saddlebags filled with beans and jerky."

The Philosophical Association meetings are pretty interesting, but the interviews with prospective new philosophers for our department at UVSC are even better. Over lunch, we talked philosophy with a candidate named Hugh McDonald from the New School for Social Research in NYC. In passing, he mentioned that he's an expert on the sego lily, *Calochortus nuttallii*. He asked if I've ever seen a magenta sego lily. When I admitted I hadn't, he suggested I go to the reservoir near Enterprise, Utah for an extraordinary sight. "But don't tell anybody."

7 April, Midway *(by email)*

Sam—PBS's Religion and Ethics Newsweekly just aired its program on the Mormon Church. You remember that Lucky Severson and his camera crew showed up at UVSC a few months ago to ask me some questions about academic freedom and BYU. While they were setting up the lighting equipment, Lucky made sure he had my credentials right: "So, in 1981 you moved from a lectureship at Princeton to a tenure-track job at Vanderbilt. After being tenured there, you moved to BYU, and after eleven years moved to UVSC. Is that correct?"

"It is," I said.

"I've never seen an academic career in such precipitous decline," he said.

"Fair enough," I told him, "but you should know that each step was carefully taken."

They filmed me saying something about how disappointing it was to leave a promising university that had lost its nerve. Then they hurried off for their next interview, the important one, with quarterback Steve Young.

It left me thinking about choice, Sam. Which led to questions about truth. Conservative thinkers like Gertrude Himmelfarb are fond of quoting Nietzsche's "Nothing is true; everything is permitted." Mormons, including Himmelfarb's plagiarizing admirer at BYU, make the same point with a Dostoevsky quote: "If God does not exist, everything is permitted." They conclude from this that truth and God must be defended at any cost. On this model, atheists and their epistemologically relativist friends are immoral (or at least amoral).

But what if you look at Nietzsche's and Ivan Karamazov's claims through a less conservative lens? What if "truth" and "god" are human inventions, human definitions (*de-finis*, boundary, limit), human constructions meant to fence in and to control? And what if "permitting everything" is a prerequisite for freedom? And what if that freedom makes choices possible, fosters innovation, and catalyzes change?

The conservative sees only bad choices in this scenario. A pragmatist like Richard Rorty figures that we are better off making choices on the basis of what we think will work than we are when we claim to be making those choices because they are true or because god told us so. You remember when people used to stand up in testimony meeting and say, "I know the gospel is true"? We would have seemed like aliens if we had stood there and said something like "Best as I can tell, the gospel is pretty good for me and my family." If I were to bear testimony today, I'd say that despite its role in making me who I am, for the most part the Mormon emphasis on obedience and absolute truth and its narrow definition of the natural family is no longer working for me."

14 April, Great Western Trail, Mt. Timpanogos

Hard work up the steepest hill after a few days off the bikes. At the top, we step off to admire the view. A couple of pheasants exchange invective, staking their territories. Two grouse explode from some oak brush, spooked by our presence. Though we don't get a great look at them, they're likely blue grouse, *Dendragapus obscurus*.

"You been following the sage grouse deal the past few months?" I ask Scott.

"A bit," he answers. "Isn't there a new western species?"

"That's right. Sage grouse populations in Colorado and southeastern Utah are different from populations elsewhere."

"And isn't the sage grouse about to be listed as an endangered species?" Scott asks. "And doesn't that mean big trouble for managing federal lands in the west?"

"Hell yes it means trouble. Some land managers and ranchers are starting to call the sage grouse the 'spotted owl of the west.' A bunch of people are pretty nervous about this. Personally, I think it's the best thing for public land management in a long while. It will force us to look at the way we've been managing, see what we've been doing wrong, and decide what we may be able to do to fix things. This is a big deal. The sage grouse decline is just one important indicator of a hundred-year-long failure of land stewardship.

"And get this. Some people are still advocating hunting seasons on both sage grouse species, the new species—the Gunnison—and the Greater Sage Grouse. That's as stupid as the hunting season on trumpeter swans in Utah when we have just a few hundred total in the whole United States. The Fish and Wildlife folks say trumpeters are too hard to tell from tundra swans when they are flying and that there's support for a big tundra swan hunt in Utah. So, we are going to continue killing endangered trumpeters in order to please tundra hunters. Hell of a bad deal."

19 April, Utah Valley State College (*by email*)

Sam—the first cliff swallows showed up this morning outside my office window, back from their annual jaunt to Argentina. What stories they must have to tell!

And I've got a story to tell as well. I have been seeing our colleague Lyn Bennett for a couple of weeks now. Although she's a Jayhawk, and although she denigrated our column as "little" last fall, she's got great gear: two bikes, snowshoes, and a whole range of camping gear. Best of all, she seems to like me. Go figure.

Twenty-One

Sage Grouse Lek

26 April, New York City *(by email)*

Scott—I'm at McSorley's Old Ale House in the East Village. This place, reputed to be New York City's second oldest drinking establishment, opened its doors in 1857, though for women the starting date was 1972. Half an inch of sawdust on the floor, peanut shells in the sawdust, a barkeep who has been here for thirty-three years tending the tradition, and a beer list comprised solely of McSorley's light and McSorley's dark.

While Nancy and Kristin worked on their clam chowder and I cut the purple onion and block of cheddar that was my lunch, I met a guy from Buffalo who was two-and-a-half sheets to the wind. Bob is a middle-school teacher from Buffalo, in the city to visit his daughter who lives nineteen blocks up Third Avenue. Bob retires next year and is feeling at loose ends. He has done his work, apparently well, for many years and wonders who he will be next. He had walked down 3rd while his wife and daughter did their womanly bonding thing. He's going to have a harder time walking back. I buy him another brew and offer to pay for a cab back to his hotel. "Nah," he says. "I like New York and I need to think."

As we talked, I noticed a magnificently filthy light fixture over the bar. What appeared to be wishbones hung along a metal bar of some sort. I asked Bob about this and we struck up a conversation with Peter, the bartender. He said that on a December night in the early 1940s, several GIs and British soldiers met in McSorley's for an heroic drinking session the night before they shipped out. As the evening wore on, they drank pint after pint after pint of McSorley's dark and ate whole chickens. Each of them hung their wishbone on the light as they hoped to god to survive the violence of the war and idiocy of the world leaders and vowed to come back to the East Village to reclaim their talismans. Goddammit, so many wishbones still on the light, dusty with the years those boys have been in the ground.

9 May, Great Western Trail, Mt. Timpanogos

We chug up the trail, a day after a muddy ride that left Sam's derailleur in shreds and sent him to see Randy at Mad Dog. Wildflowers aplenty today: evening primrose in both fresh white and day-after pink incarnations, cliff rose blooming their yellow hearts out, matte-orange globe mallow, purple sweet vetch, yellow Dalmatian toadflax, yellow prince's plume, the hanging white fingers of chokecherry, and my favorite—deep-blue flax.

We grumble and curse and spit at the freshly graded and widened fire road, and we're fit to be tied at the sight of another Bureau of Wrecklamation drilling rig at work near the trail.

Still, nature continues her seasonal parade. A spotted to-whee sings from the oak brush, its triple note followed by a long *chrrrr*. We stop to look for the bird, but are distracted by a flash of blue. The first lazuli bunting of the year! Our initial sighting last year was May 14th, and the year before we saw the first one on the 17th. The multi-colored beauties are back a little early. Are we seeing the leading edge of global climate change (warming in many places, cooling in others)? Or is this simply the kind of variation that happens year to year?

10 May, Orem, Utah

I'll be go to hell! Sam has just been offered the job as Dean of Science and Health at UVSC. By fortuitous accident, I am the owner of a beautiful cake produced by the college's culinary arts people. I take it over and present it to Sam and Nancy. As a toast, I repeat what my friend Diana told her husband, Steven, when he was fired from his job as a professor of American religious history at BYU: "Now we can be Americans again!"

Six years ago, Sam suggested that we apply for two dean positions open at UVSC. "Sam," I told him, "we hate deans."

Maybe Sam will put the lie to that. If not, I'll have to remind him of the California Brain Transplant Clinic where professors' brains are $10,000, department chairs' brains are $100,000, and deans' brains are a cool million. A potential patient says he understands differences in quality—but a million for a dean's brain? The doctor answers with a question: Do you know how many deans it takes to make a brain?

May 11, Great Western Trail, Mt. Timpanogos

Late afternoon ride up the back hills. The sun flashes paintbrush under sage.

"You know," Sam says, "I've been at BYU for thirty years. Thirty years! I don't see how that's possible. And, by damn, it's long enough. I'm looking forward to the UVSC job. The folks at the state school have made me feel deeply welcomed. BYU was relieved that I was going and offered a decent severance package. I argued for a full year's salary as you did, but got less, I guess because they weren't as anxious to see my back as they were yours. Nancy, who has been teaching as an adjunct instructor of English at BYU, was with me through the negotiations and let the bastards have it. The university benefits office had figured the payout sixty-three cents higher than the Academic Vice President's office and the Vice President argued for a reduction in the offer. Nancy told him he was a penurious SOB. Okay, the noun is mine, but the adjective was definitely hers."

"It will save you the ten-percent tithing BYU requires," I point out. "You won't get fired for drinking a cup of coffee, and you can reveal whether you drank McSorley's light or dark. Good news all around."

"It was the dark," Sam admits.

23 May, Strawberry Reservoir, 5:30 a.m.

First faint light emerges in the east as we launch a flat-bottomed aluminum boat on the mirror-smooth reservoir. Kevin

Bunnel, a graduate student in wildlife biology at BYU, and his advisor, Jerran Flinders, are taking Sam, Nancy, Lyn, and me out to a sage grouse lek. "Lek" comes from Swedish, short for *lekställe*, mating ground, and is used by biologists to indicate an assembly area where animals carry on display and courtship behavior. The population of sage grouse (*Centrocercus urophasianus*) in this area has declined precipitously in recent decades and the two biologists have been conducting a study to find the cause and possible solutions.

"There they are," Kevin says, easing back the quiet, four-cycle, forty-horse Honda outboard. Jerran is already counting the grouse through his binoculars ("seventeen on that sweep") by the time I see the first bird. I'm not sure what I expected, but it wasn't these big (very big!) upright birds fronted by white chest sacs and backed by spiky fanned tails. The cocks strut along a stretch of shoreline, separated from each other by some agreed-upon distance.

"If we're quiet," Kevin says, "they'll start popping."

It is an odd sound—somewhere between a hoot and a breathy pop—that bursts from chest sacs that rise and fall like waves in a storm. When two hens walk onto the lek, the real storm begins. The cocks redouble their efforts, puffing and popping and fanning tails and strutting to prove their fitness.

"It's amazing—they'll do this every morning for several months," Jerran says quietly, "just on the faint hope…"

One of the cocks struts into the space of another, and they face off, a bit of chest bumping, until one backs down. "Typically male," Lyn and Nancy say simultaneously.

The sun is up now, and we sit back to watch the continuing strut. "Kevin," Sam asks, "what is the history of grouse on the Strawberry?"

"My research indicates that sage grouse here have declined more than ninety percent in the past sixty years," Kevin replies.

"A great deal of the loss seems to be due to fox predation."

"Are these birds doomed?" I ask.

Jerran replies, "Twenty years ago, I visited many leks in Utah that are gone now—not a single bird left. I have watched leks on cold sun-ups in Wyoming with three hundred birds on them. They're largely decimated now. The birds we're watching this morning are going to disappear. I'm afraid it's a runaway train."

"What about the Endangered Species Act?" Sam asks. "Isn't the sage grouse threatened and thus protected?"

"It's been petitioned," Kevin answers. "Chances are it will be listed. It'll be a big deal and will rile up a bunch of private western landowners. We've been involved in one Freedom of Information Action with the Natural Resources Conservation Service and learned that they treated a critical sage grouse habitat for a private landowner who didn't want a threatened species on his land. Collusion between governmental entities and private landowners is an old and sordid story."

"What does 'treated' mean?" I ask.

"They eliminated the sage with an herbicide. The NRCS wouldn't release the details to us and we had to fight them clear to Washington to get the information. We're thinking we're going to get more and more of this. The future doesn't look good for the sage grouse."

Kevin pilots the boat around a point, carefully beaches the craft, and we climb a sage-covered ridge behind the lek. "The birds will soon leave the lek and fly up here," he says. At that moment, one of the males skims our heads, a heavy lumbering flight that makes me think of a cargo plane.

"Are there other limiting factors besides foxes?" Sam asks.

"Yes," Kevin explains, "habitat questions are just as important, if not more so. Elimination of sage, as I said, and the introduction over the last decades of smooth brome, a grass that was meant to improve grazing. But the brome displaces native forbes—mustards, phlox, skeleton weed, flax, and the like—that sage grouse chicks need. The birds are under attack from all sides."

"Look at this," Jerran says, pointing with his boot. A slick, tarry deposit the size of a silver dollar shines on a piece of rock. "From a sage grouse," he says. "Night feces. It gathers in the bird's double cecum and then is eliminated during the night. They eliminate more normal pellets at other times."

Of all the sights and sounds of the morning, this shiny black substance feels like the center of the event. We see it only because of Jerran's experience, his focused attention over years, his concern for this declining bird. He's a biologist with a deep concern for wildlife, with a sharp eye born of a life of curiosity. Will his work make a difference? "Look at the fox!" Jerran calls, and points to the next ridge. Close to where a sage grouse has come in for a landing, a red fox dances up the ridge. We cross the ravine and find a honeycomb of fox dens on the ridge. Jerran shakes his head. "This is worse than I feared."

TWENTY-TWO

Oblanceolate to Spatulate

7 June, Great Western Trail, Mt. Timpanogos

Sam is busy today, but I'm anxious to work myself back into shape after a vicious viral infection.

I see another rider several hundred yards ahead.

"I'll catch him," I think. Then I think, "You've been sick for two weeks. You lost ten pounds." Then, "Ten pounds less to haul up the hill. I'll just up my cadence a little and see what happens." I round a corner—I've made up some of the distance. The rider sees me. He speeds up. I match him. I draw closer. As the hill steepens for the last long stretch, I catch him and, passing, ask him calmly, "How ya' doin'?" "Fine," he grunts. I hope he can see the grey hair curling out from under my do-rag. Then I'm past. I keep my cadence. He fades immediately. At the top, I watch him turn slowly onto a lower track. There are long-term benefits of having to keep up with Sam.

8 June, Great Western Trail, Mt. Timpanogos

Same trail as yesterday. I point ahead and show Sam where the guy was when I started to gain on him.

"I know the guy," Sam says. "He had a stroke last month, he recently lost a lung to cancer, and he's got one prosthetic leg."

11 June, Great Western Trail, Mt. Timpanogos

A panoply of sights and sounds this morning. Before we even leave the asphalt, a three-foot rattlesnake buzzes us past. He's the thickest snake we have seen in a couple of years, nearly two inches in diameter, with a wedge-shaped head to match. He's got an attitude and we pass with care.

Climbing the first hill we are met by the familiar song of a robin, which soon gives way to the quick, high-pitched songs of two lazuli buntings. The auralscape remains lively as we ride slowly through oak and box elder. At the top of the hill, we hear the distinctive calls of a chukar (*Alectoris chukar*) among the staccato songs of maybe a dozen towhees. A large redtail perching in a burned oak leans forward and drops out of the tree, catching herself with outstretched wings. Her tail flashes copper-red in the sun.

Ten thousand fruiting heads of goat's beard dot the hillside at the bottom of the trail, round puffs of smoke in the sage.

After the ride, Sam and I drink pints of a cold ale he has brewed—he's finally using his chemistry for something useful—and I ask him about the chukar call. "Do you have your *Peterson Guide* CD?" I ask. "I'd like to listen to the call."

"Better than that," he says, and opens a drawer in the hall. He rummages around and pulls out a three-inch wood tube. He punches it into his palm to produce a series of throaty squawks. Sam throws me the P. S. Olt chukar call, model 500, made in Pekin, Illinois forty years ago—red-stained maple with a red double-jointed rubber accordion boot.

"Thirty years ago," Sam explains, "well before I became a vegetarian, hunting on the Idaho border, I used the call to locate the birds, then blew an owl call to freeze them in place. I shot the hell out of 'em before they figured out I wasn't an owl."

13 June, Great Western Trail, Mt. Timpanogos

Sam and I find ourselves riding up Frank the back way, a steadier, more forgiving approach than the usual ridge. The unmistakably varied calls of a yellow-breasted chat bring us to a standstill. What an aural showoff. *The Peterson Guide* says that chats, unlike any other warbler, will hold their food, insects and berries, in one foot while eating. I'd like to see that—but the Guide also says the chat is reclusive, so the chances aren't good.

The meadow at the top of Frank greets us with a sea of yellow, green, and blue—the yellow, spurred flowers of Dalmatian toadflax, bright blue upturned flowers of silver lupine (*Lupinus argenteus*), the stalks already heavy with hairy green pea-like seed pods.

At home, I look up lupine in Stan Welsh's *A Utah Flora*. When I'm most proud of how closely I'm observing something, it's always instructive to see a real scientist (other than Sam, of course) at work:

> **Silvery Lupine.** Plants perennial, 18-90 cm tall, from a superficial caudex, puberulent to strigose on stems and petioles; leaves mainly cauline; petioles 1.5-8 cm long; leaflets 6-9, 7-95 mm long, 2-22 mm wide, oblanceolate to spatulate or almost linear, flat or folded, strigulose to strigose on both surfaces or almost or quite glabrous above ... flowers (5-7) 8.5-16 mm long, blue purple, blue, white, or rarely other hues. ...

It's the off-putting language of a heartless classifier, I think defensively. Not a mention of how deeply moving that blue is as it rises from the silver-green fans of leaves. Then I correct myself. It's our job to gush and quiver. It's Welsh's job to see the lupine through the language of precision.

TWENTY-THREE

Wicked Concoction

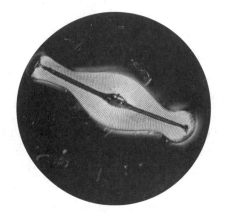

24 June, Great Western Trail, Mt. Timpanogos

After the initial wild scramble up over our nemesis—the quartzite-strewn curve just above Canyon Glen—we stop for breath in Johnson's Hole, protected by a ridge from the canyon's traffic noise. A flash of yellow and black makes us forget our distressed lungs.

"An American goldfinch," Sam says. "*Carduelis tristis.*" The black-capped beauty sits atop a thistle. On another clump of thistles is his less showy mate. They flit away with avian breast-strokes when we approach.

We've never paid much attention to thistles, but the finches make us wonder about their food source. The flowers are bright purple with a flat top and protrude from spiny receptacles. Spiny leaves alternate down the three-foot stem. The undersides of the leaves are slightly woolly. Nearby, a similar thistle has a larger and looser bundle of lighter lavender flowers. "I'll look these babies up when I get home," Sam says. "Thistles have always given me fits. We have maybe twenty species in the state and they often hybridize. I think the two we have seen commonly in the past few years are Canada and bull thistle, probably the only two members of our thistle flora that are introduced."

"Look at this," I tell Sam. An inch-long cross between a micro-wasted wasp and a praying mantis moves delicately on four legs across one of the thistle flowers. To cross over to the next flower, it stretches out double-folded legs that have been clasped against its head in what looks like prayer. "I'll look this one up," I say.

Another flower holds a beetle with an orange head and darker orange body. In fact, there are a lot of the shiny little beetles. "People generally see thistles as noxious weeds," Sam says, "but they host a bunch of beautiful creatures, don't they? And, by the way, did you know that one-fourth of all life forms on Earth are species of beetles?"

I ponder this as we ride along, noting mid-summer flora: blue flax, morning lily (actually an evening primrose), pale evening primrose, a tiny *Erigeron* (one of the more than fifty in Utah), skeleton weed, milk vetch, tar weed, lupine, toadflax, mullein, purple penstemon, and goat's beard.

29 June, Great Western Trail, Mt. Timpanogos

We're riding the fire road when Sam pulls us up short. "These are fine early sunflowers!" Three of the yellow-and-brown beauties nod their heads at us. "*Helianthus annuus*," Sam says. "Helianthus because they trace the sun across the sky."

I point out they are facing north, east, and west, respectively. "They're young and untrained," Sam counters. "By the way," he continues, "I looked up the thistles. Those were Canada thistles, *Cirsium arvense*. The hairy underleaf distinguishes them from the bull thistles also common around here. The variance we noticed in the flower heads was because they are unisexual and the males are more showy."

"Good work," I say. "And I looked up the wasp we saw on the thistle. It was difficult and painstaking work, but I can say for sure that that wasp is one of the approximately twenty-five hundred species of wasps in the order *Hymenoptera*."

5 July, San Francisco, Golden Gate Park *(by email)*

Sam—Lyn and I spent the morning in the Strybing Arboretum and Botanical Gardens in San Francisco's Golden Gate Park. It made me want to take up botany. And it made me wonder about what inspired you to be a botanist.

In the "Garden of Fragrance," I sniffed salvia, rosemary, lemon verbena, lavender, Grecian laurel, and a variety of sages, including *Artemisia absinthium*, the sage used by the makers of absinthe, the wicked concoction that fired the imaginations of so many French writers and artists.

I've tucked away a leaf for you.

6 July, Provo *(by email)*

Scott—I'll be lookin' for the leaf. I haven't smelled absinthe sage for 25 years. And absinthe liquor has always interested me. Some suggest it is the stuff of the gods—others the stuff of death. The ingredient in *Artemisia absinthium* that makes absinthe potent (lethal) is a neurotoxin, thujone. You up for cookin' this?

Why did I become a botanist? I had completed all my general education and math courses and had to choose a major. Took a class in plant taxonomy one spring semester and fell in love with the spring flora—the same flora we see on our rides. One thing led to another and I took a major's worth of courses in a semester and a half. Got a BYU fellowship for a year that stretched into 34 years and, by god, with no real planning here I am.

How about you? How did a boy from red-neck Farmington, New Mexico decide to be a scholar of German literature?

6 July, Napa Valley, California *(by email)*

Sure, Sam. Let's cook up a pot of absinthe. Maybe Greta will give us a raise if we start sounding like Rimbaud.

As for my becoming a *soi disant* scholar of German, it happened about the same time I learned that French way of saying "self-proclaimed" while reading e. e. cummings. Here's how I describe it in my "Immortal For Quite Some Time":

> German poetry has caught my fancy, so much so that I changed my major from pre-med to German literature. The literary ideas and forms and passions accompany me deep into the night and across weekends in ways calculus and chemistry and even zoology never did. By November I

know more about the works we're studying than the professor, who regards poetry as a pedantic game. Another student in the class, Thales Smith, a mandolin player, shares my interest in relationships between form and content. We often skip class to discuss the poetry ourselves. One day we walk into class together (we have calculated how many classes we can miss before losing credit) and Thales moves to sit down in the standard-issue wood-and-steel desk. He jumps up as if he has sat on a rattlesnake and points at the thick wooden seat, molded for a human butt. What is it? I ask. Birdseye maple, he whispers. The bastards have used birdseye maple. It's rare. It's unpredictable. You can't tell until you've cut into the tree that it has birdseyes. It's expensive. And only a half-witted sonofabitch would use it for a school desk. My best mandolin is made of birdseye maple!

7 July, Rio Dell, California, Ruby's Café *(by email)*

Sam—we are having breakfast in a little logging town on Highway 89 on the east side of the Sierras in California. A mural covering an entire wall features an engine pulling a dozen flatcars over a trestle, each bearing a section of a giant redwood tree. The engineer waves cheerfully across a stream where three lumberjacks are cutting another 2000-year-old *Sequoia sempervirens*.

8 July, Provo *(by email)*

Scott—Nancy and I are teaching a class this fall dealing with the impact of art on the American perception of wilderness. Your mural is pretty interesting. It promotes the view that nature is here for us and for us alone and that any human use of the land is progress. Furthermore, "using" nature is divinely mandated—just read your Bible, brother.

It's always been an uphill battle to suggest that humans are a part of nature and don't have the right to destroy it. I'm still interested in the idea of "legal standing" for non-human living beings such as redwood trees. Where did we get the idea it was acceptable for us to simply walk up to a redwood tree that has been alive for a couple of millennia, look it up and down, estimate its worth, and then kill it for our use?

17 July, Great Western Trail, Mt. Timpanogos

The heat today seems a physical pressure on our bodies. We're happy to step off our bikes near the mouth of the canyon at the remnant of a century-old homestead. Two half-dead apple trees stand near flourishing plums and a variety of shade trees—all reflecting someone's hard work and dreams. Why did they leave? What happened to them?

I will make plum jam this fall with these plums. And I will brew a plum ale. As I work, I will conjure these people with a sense of solidarity and respect for their ephemeral lives and dreams. Maybe they would be happy to know someone is thinking of them and is cheered by their plums.

On our way down the hill, Scott says he's been reading about legal standing for trees. "In medieval Germany there was something called *Baumfrevel*. 'Baum' means tree. 'Frevel' is a strong word that means outrage or sacrilege or wantonness. If you were caught destroying someone's fruit tree or stripping birch trees of their new spring growth to feed your animals, they cut off your hands or put out your eyes or cut a hole in your abdomen and pulled out your intestines—*Entdärmung*, de-intestining, evisceration. So there have been times when trees *were* protected from wanton destruction. Not exactly legal standing, but carefully protected property."

"'Wantonness' is a powerful word," I say. "The problem in a nutshell."

23 July, Great Western Trail, Mt. Timpanogos

Eight a.m. Already heating up. In the "cool" of the morning, we find open blazing stars, their thin yellow sepals separating five sharp, narrow, yellow petals. A mass of long yellow stamens bristles up from the center. Each of the large plants bears dozens of flowers in various stages of development and decline. They are named after a seventeenth-century German botanist, C. Mentzel—*Mentzelia laevicaulis*.

Sam points out a rangy, wispy plant bearing a few yellow flowers. "Prickly lettuce," he says. "*Lactuca serriola*. Pick a bit of a stem to see where the name comes from." I do so and trace a thin, white, milky line of latex across my finger.

The fox shit on the trail is another revelation, loose with pits of the same small, golden plums we like so much.

With the waning half-moon sharp white above us, we gaze up at Frank. "After the C-turn," I predict, "after the chutes, where the ridge rises after the major climbs, we're going feel like we've been hit in the chest by a sledgehammer."

"Yup," Sam grunts, and up he rides.

Neither of us flops dead from a heart attack, and in thirty minutes we stand in the meadow at the top of Frank. We're flushed, hammered, beat, worked over—but at the top one more time.

25 July, Great Western Trail, Mt. Timpanogos

Another early morning ride to beat the heat. From the ridge we see a plume of black smoke rising from Geneva's coke ovens and spreading north. "Full of benzo[a]pyrene," Sam says. "An epidemiologist from the University of Utah did a study of cancer in the areas surrounding Geneva and when the numbers showed only an 80% higher chance of getting cancer there than elsewhere, he went with the statisticians who like 95-99% probabilities, and declared there was no increased risk of cancer."

Blazing yellow sunflowers greet us around a corner. A gold-finch feeds on one of the heads, its yellow and black plumage a perfect match for the flowers, most of which, Sam points out, face the sun.

TWENTY-FOUR

Mr. Nice Dick

29 July, Heber City Rodeo Grounds *(by email)*

The world is changing, Sam. Even in rural Heber Valley. This final week before I move into the house I bought in Provo, I took my boys to the annual Heber City demolition derby, hoping to broaden their cultural horizons. They loved the chases and crashes and fires and rollovers. I was more entertained by the dinosaur of an announcer.

"We've got a $1500 prize for the winner," he announced sonorously. "And for the winners of the grudge matches, there's $150 apiece. And, of course, there's $125 for the powder puff winner." Five minutes later, his surprised voice reported that "a little lady just dropped by our booth with $25 to bring the powder puff winner up with the grudge match winners. Ain't that cute!" Almost immediately he had an update: "Well I'll be. Two little girls just delivered two dollars for the powder puff winner. And ladies in the west stands collected $70. Whoaaaa! You ladies in the powder puff had better put on some show for all this money!" Before the five women involved finally accelerated into the ring, $700 above the original $125 had been donated, and the tight-sphinctered announcer's voice could no longer be described as sonorous.

Who says we're not making progress?

30 July, Great Western Trail, Mt. Timpanogos

"You ready?" Scott asks on the phone at 6:30 in the morning.

"Whaddya talkin' about," I hear myself mutter. "Ready for what?"

"Our Sunday morning ride," Scott replies cheerfully. "We talked about this last night."

"Right," I reply. "But this is still last night. Call me when it's tomorrow."

Thirty minutes later, we're on the trail in the early-morning heat.

Thick smoke from local fires fills the valley, reflecting orange and blue in the early sunlight. It's a surrealistic apocalyptic scene. But the truth is, much of the western United States is a set of fire-driven ecosystems. Fires must burn for the health of the forest. In the long term, fires increase the health of watersheds substantially and they are critical for renewing wildlife habitat. But they're certainly not good for lungs. Nor for houses built up onto brushy foothills.

12 August, Orem *(by email)*

Scott—a surprising letter just reprinted in the *Atlantic Monthly*. He pays attention to this Utah landscape like we do, but I shudder at the thought of the not-too-athletic author in nothing but shorts and tennis shoes.

> We are living in wild eagle country, terribly far from everything, terribly high up. There used to be mines here, five thousand miners, shootings in bars. . . . Now there is no one, a rocky remoteness, a "ski" hotel on an open slope (8600 feet high), the grey ripple of aspens amid black firs, bears crossing the roads, mint, saffron crocus, lupin flowering, Uinta ground squirrels (a kind of suslik) stand upright beside their burrows, and from morning till night I collect the rarest butterflies and flies for my museum.... The climate here is harsh, icy winds, loud thunder, and as soon as the sun beats down, painful black flies stick to one—which they especially enjoy when you go dressed as I do in nothing but shorts and tennis shoes; but the collecting here is magnificent, and I have rarely felt so good.
>
> Vladimir Nabokov, Sandy Utah
> August 6, 1943

If he'd come around a few decades later, we could have traded high-altitude mountain-bike lessons for some writing tips.

13 August, Provo *(by email)*

Sam—my neighbor Lillian Hayes just gave me two boxes heavy with the "1990 Utah BLM Statewide Wilderness Final Environmental Impact Statement." You know the document well, but I'd never seen the actual books and accompanying maps. The overview volume begins with color photos of some of the proposed sites, reminders of the rugged beauty of our state. They also remind me of that infamous telephone interview radio journalist Kat Snow had with Congressman Jim Hansen during which he asserted that the areas under consideration were nothing but rocks and sagebrush. When she said she thought they were beautiful, he told her to go to hell and hung up.

As opposed to the environmental blindness demonstrated by the dis-Honorable Mr. Hansen, the impact statement pays meticulous attention to a variety of rare plants, insects, arachnids, and reptiles. These names make me smile: Gumbo milkvetch, pavement milkvetch, Coral Pink Sand Dunes tiger beetle, Higgins biscuitroot, sand-loving wild-buckwheat, Rabbit Valley gilia, Stella's pepper-grass, bladderpod, sand-loving beardtongue, last-chance Townsendia.

18 August, Great Western Trail, Mt. Timpanogos

Early morning and we're riding after the first thundershowers in god knows how long. It's so fresh and cool that we turn up Frank, a thought without a forethought, and before we know it we're standing in a meadow high up on the flank of the mountain. "A ride to make me forget I'm a dean," Sam says. "Last night at dinner the dog came up and wanted my attention. I told him to 'beat it' and told Nancy even Kiva knows I'm the dean and wants attention."

"Hell," I respond, "you're having to do a full day's work for the first time in twenty years and all you can do is whine."

"At this stage I'm not thrilled with what I'm doing. Life's short and my ass ain't nailed to the dean's chair. It's ironic that we're both administrators now—something neither of us ever wanted or expected. You figure the damned officials at BYU who were so anxious to see us go got the last laugh after all?"

"Don't confuse a department chair with a dean," I counter. "Remember how many deans it takes to make a brain."

19 August, Orem *(by email)*

Scott—Damndest thing last night. I been havin' a bit of "crotch rot" lately from all our sweaty riding and so I've been puttin' some athlete's foot salve on the fungal spots on my groin. Middle of last night I get outta bed with the itch and think I will use a bit of the cream. Trouble is, several years ago one of our kids had some stage blood they were using for a play at Orem High School. The damn stuff was in the same drawer as my crotch-rot stuff and it was dark.

Well, you can see where this is going. I slathered stage blood all over my balls in the dark thinking I was putting a hurt on the crotch-rot fungus. When I woke up the next morning I took an unsuspecting look, although I can hardly see my belt buckle any more for my tumescent belly, and thought things were about over for me. You can imagine I was pretty relieved to find out the fresh "blood" was out of a tube and not the result of some below-the-belly-button catastrophe. When the final curtain isn't too far away, something like this makes a guy wonder and whisper a little prayer of thanks for the safety of his testicles.

21 August, Provo *(by email)*

Sam—in and out of a dream last night I came close to transcendent knowledge. A phrase kept flitting through my mind that I sensed encompassed the secrets of the universe: "The coyote, evidently, will do anything to have a gloam sister." That's it! I thought. That's the answer I've been searching for. But what's a gloam sister? I went round and round with that question, knowing its answer would reveal everything. So close. Oh so close.

23 August, Great Western Trail, Mt. Timpanogos

Sprinkling lightly when we ride away from Sam's house. A fat doe eyes us from under the plum trees. A red-tailed hawk floats over us, curious, and she hangs there in the wind blowing down the canyon, her reddish tail feathers spread, her head swiveling as she turns to follow our progress. It starts to rain. We're soaked in seconds, but keep riding until black clouds blow over us, rumbling thunder. Sam crouches down next to and partly under the big green pipe ("a rattlesnake is going to bite me in the ass!" he hollers) and I crouch under some dripping scrub oak.

The threat of lightning gone, we climb back on the bikes, happy for the warmth of pumping blood. Near the top of the first climb, swinging around a pipe-gate someone has built to keep jeeps from coming that way, we smell fresh urine. A hundred yards later, approaching a second gate, we smell it again, pungent as kerosene. Something big marking its territory. We stand at the second gate to catch our breath. On the top pipe, a congratulatory message is written neatly in caps in yellow paint—"THIS IS A REAL NICE GATE, MR. NICE DICK!" A two-headed arrow points to a weld and to the words: "NICE WELDS!"

We start along the jeep road to get to the next trailhead. Around the first corner, not twenty feet in front of us, stands a badger—low to the ground, its stomach flat, its back and shoulders rounded with heavy muscle, its legs short and powerful, its small head and powerful jaws turned to us. We brake. The badger moves in short spurts, looking for a way up the steep embankment. We follow, keeping our distance. The badger stops and swings its head pugnaciously in our direction. It continues up the road. Awestruck, we follow. It turns at us repeatedly, ready to fight. Finally, it scrambles up the slope and disappears.

"That," Sam declares, "was a gloam sister."

TWENTY-FIVE

Evolutionary Theater

26 August, Robber's Roost Bookstore, Torrey

Invited by Frank McEntire of the Entrada Institute, sponsored by Steve Peterson, uplifted by the new paintings Kathy Peterson has just unveiled, and eased into the reading by Larry Harper's riotous autoharp, Sam and I begin our first public reading from "Wild Rides, Wildflowers." The bookstore is packed with friends and curious residents of the little town, and as we read about mountain bikes, flowers, and our crusty old selves, they seem to like it. Sam has practiced saying "Goethe" all afternoon, so when he gets to that point he reads the name flawlessly. I haven't practiced the Latin names—*Poecile atricapillus*, for example—and stumble again and again.

Without planning to, we have given Sam the most personal sections to read, and I have the most comic entries. Sam seems uncomfortable, especially when he reads about his father, but as I watch our listeners, his are the stories that move them most deeply.

After the euphoria of the evening wears off, I think about Sam's discomfort, about how intensely private he is and about how easily I display my private life. I'm interrupted in those thoughts by a sharp inner voice: "That's how you like to think of yourself." Disconcerted, I run my mind back through our column. There are a good many memorable moments when Sam writes about himself and his life-long relationship with Nancy, about family members, about his fears and obsessions, about deep-seated feelings of many kinds. Less so with me. It was no accident that Sam read about his inner life and I read about bike crashes. Biking has helped me avoid some lurking demons, but it can't be good psychological strategy to sublimate what will, at some point, demand its due.

Still, any kind of writing is better than not writing at all. Writing and riding (you have to say the words carefully to make a distinction) with Sam makes him my gear-headed, botanical

169

therapist. Although I'd prefer a full Freudian analysis, this is what I've got.

27 August, Torrey *(by email)*

Scott—Our reading last night at Robber's Roost was terrible for me! I will never again stand in front of people and read this stuff. I'm, by god, too private for that. I couldn't make eye contact with a single person in the room, not even Nancy. What in hell was I thinkin' to read with you? A short reading career for me—that's for certain.

8 September, Great Western Trail, Mt. Timpanogos

Magpies fly up just inside Provo Canyon, their long, graduated tails spread formally after them. The little flock squawks raucously and Sam remembers something that makes him grin: "Nancy's mom, Vera," he says, "was stressed one day with the noise and demands of children and with the constant worries about the farm and how to make ends meet and by the bushels of tomatoes that demanded canning that very morning. Outside the kitchen, a magpie screeched and squawked through the entire morning, enough to drive her crazy. 'This is a problem I can solve,' she thought. She drug out Dick's shotgun, loaded a single shell, stepped out into the yard, and blew the noisy sonofabitch into next year."

Two scrub jays, blue as the Utah sky, squawk along with the magpies, their close relatives in the Family *Corvidae*. We see white flashes from an occasional towhee tail and the shadow of a low-flying northern harrier and the ever-present, tail-bobbing kestrels and swallows and sparrows aplenty—and robins and yellow warblers down by the river and starlings and chickadees. Who says August and September are bad months for birds?

Sunday, 17 September, Great Western Trail, Mt. Timpanogos

I see a snake stretched out full length across my path. I hit the brakes and jump the bike sideways to miss it. The snake is unfazed.

"Scott, check this guy out." We walk up to the eighteen-inch-long, brown-and-white reptile.

"It's a bull snake," Scott says. "I grew up with these in New Mexico."

"It's what I've always called a blow snake," I reply. "And I think people around here also know them as gopher snakes."

I touch the snake and it shakes its tail like a rattlesnake. I touch the tail and the snake coils lightning-fast, all the while shaking its tail, striking at me twice. It's only by my own youthful, lightning reflexes that I pull my hand away fast enough to avoid the sure bite. The snake pulls back and flattens its head—all part of the show to make a predator think it's a death-dealing pit viper.

"Scott," I say, "I know as well as I am standing here that that snake is a blow snake. But for me, when it coiled and struck, it was a rattlesnake plain and simple."

"I have a hard time trying to figure out how this sort of thing happens," Scott says. "How did that snake figure out how to mimic a rattlesnake?"

"It's one of the interesting evolutionary questions of the past century," I respond. "It works by natural selection. By mutation, some snakes have traits that mimic rattlesnakes and they tend to survive a bit better than those that don't. Across the generations, the rattler look-alikes leave more offspring and the commonness of their traits increases."

"I get that," Scott answers, "but it seems a bit thin to me. I figure that snake took one look at us and decided it had a couple of greenhorns here and could scare the bejeezus out of us by pretending to be a rattler."

"Well," I agree, "it did."

24 September, Great Western Trail, Mt. Timpanogos

Plums and elderberries (*Sambucus racemosa*)—silvered-blue skins breaking open between our teeth to sweetness and high-country tartness, make this ride a success before it has begun.

Up and over the quartzite we scramble, pleased that we can still ride this technical stretch now and then. We stop for breath in Johnson's Hole, where the late-afternoon sun features hundreds of back-lit plumes we haven't seen before. The snaky inflorescences are made up of dozens of six-petaled flowers. "I took it for a mustard," Sam says, "but it's got six petals. Don't know what this might be. This is surprising."

"Doesn't surprise me," I chime in.

"It's hard to be surprised when all your blood has drained to your ass," Sam opines.

Purple asters (*Aster integrifolius*) are bright among the fall's yellow grasses—individual flowers topping curly, spined cups, maybe twenty flowers on vigorous stalks.

"Ok, Sam, over the last year I've learned that monocots—sego lilies, for example, or death camas—have three petals, mustards four, and most dicots five. How many petals does an aster have?"

"That's not an easy question," he answers, predictably. "But at least it will make me rethink your brain capacity. As you know, asters are composites, members of the sunflower family. Each of the purple ray flowers you see arrayed around that aster 'flower' face is really an individual flower with five separate petals that have fused into one. So the answer is five times whatever you see, maybe seventy, eighty, a hundred—but five per flower. And that's just the beginning. The face of the 'flower' is actually a cluster of flowers, lots of them, and each one of the disk flowers also has five fused petals."

"Why so many petals on a single flower? And while we're on the subject, do other flowers, like this Dalmatian toadflax that looks like a snapdragon, have any petals at all?"

"The three-dimensional toadflax flower," Sam says, "is really a flower with five petals that have evolved into that very specialized shape to attract specialized and smart pollinators, and smart pollinators, largely bees and wasps, show a high degree of fidelity to their flower types. The composites, on the other hand, have evolved to attract generalist pollinators, insects that may tromp all over a bunch of disk and ray flowers arrayed as a flat surface. But here's a really odd part of the story. After the aster had evolved to its fivemerous state, it evolved again to fuse the five petals so they would appear to be a single petal with a lot of other 'single' petals surrounding a host of disk flowers. Ain't the world grand?"

I pluck a handful of boxelder fruits, "helicopters" we played with as children, and fling handfuls up against a late-afternoon sun.

Bunched red fruits of sumac glow like crushed velvet among green leaves. Bluish-purple flowers, some sort of borage, shine from the end of a twisted stalk that has borne flowers all the way up. Bright yellow matchweed or snakeweed (*Gutierrezia sarothrae*) lights up entire hillsides. A wispy little mustard defies the late-summer heat and dryness. Sunflowers and curlycup gumweed add more yellow to the afternoon's color.

Sam turns up a grass-lined trail and raises dust from the dried grass. The scent takes me back to some forgotten childhood scene for the second time in minutes. Proust was right about the evocative power of scent.

Sage blossoms rise above three-toothed leaves, heavy and ready to open. "Sages are related to sunflowers," Sam notes, "as is rabbit brush (*Chrysothamnus nauseosus*). The plentiful flowers of both these plants have often showered us with golden pollen."

"This feels marvelous today," I tell Sam. "We've slowed down and are seeing things again. The last couple of months have slipped by with us mostly in our heads."

25 September, Orem *(by email)*

Scott—Been thinkin' about loss and gain today. Fall's a time that does that to me. I suppose on the gain side has to be the autumnal foliage, the thickening and golding of the light, the cooler air, the increased value of sunlight, sage and rabbit brush in blossom, maybe a narrowing but deepening focus, thoughts of friends and time passing, a cold bed drawing Nancy near.

But I by god rue a world without my sister Anne, the loss of the light, the absence of birds, the tight muscles in my neck, my age, long-gone friends, my lessening passion for political fights. And finally, I both rue and celebrate my children in the difficult spots where they belong.

25 September, Orem *(by email)*

Sam—you have touched a melancholy chord in me. Your sister Anne is gone. I will always regret not traveling with you to her funeral. My brother John is gone too, and has been gone for almost ten years. You know I'm still trying to come to terms with that loss, writing almost every day about him and about our family and about myself in what I've started to call "fraternal meditations." The book's title will be "Immortal For Quite Some Time," a phrase that gets at the glorious and brutally short nature of human existence. John died of causes related to AIDS and he died alone—estranged from our Mormon family, separated from me by my tight and ambitious focus on education and career and growing family. I stood looking at his corpse hours after the autopsy and knew I had to live differently. My writing has been a halting but steady exploration of the possibilities for change.

Our fights for academic freedom at BYU were fights for a critically important principle. But, at least for me, they were also battles for people who were being shouldered aside by powerful, self-righteous forces because they were different. They were battles, in my subconscious at least, for my brother. When colleagues told us we were brave to take on the university administration, I was always surprised. It's not brave to fight for your brother. It's human.

John's death triggered a reexamination of a lot of things for me. And here I'll turn back to the melancholy that you mentioned and that I've been feeling too. I've made some big changes, drastic changes even, and with those kinds of decisions come accompanying doubts. I left the religion whose practices and precepts had structured much of my life. I ended a marriage of twenty-five years that was as rich with joy as it was with trouble, at least during the early years, a marriage that produced the seven children who are as dear to me as anything in my life. I abandoned the university for which I had been so hopeful and for whose well-being I had worked so hard. In short, I left people and institutions and beliefs that had been good for me, for the most part, for a long time. So what now?

I ride my bike with you and write about what we experience. I work on the old house I bought—the fine new deck on the back will be a good place for friends to gather. I try to be a good father, especially for the three boys still at home. I explore the relationship with Lyn, hoping it continues to develop. I look for stories that work better for me than the Mormon stories I grew up with. Poems and novels and essays that are less certain of their truth than are the scriptures have become my moral guides. I work hard at my new job, knowing the satisfaction of good, hard work.

And often, in the night, I wonder what the fuck I have done.

25 September, Orem *(by email)*

Scott—battles for your brother, battles for my sister. That strikes a chord in me. And what the fuck you've done is try to save your life.

One thing I have never told you, and have not told many people, about Anne: She was in her last days at the hospital. The end was near. It had been terrible for my sister and still the nurses were coming in all night to poke and prod her and take her goddamned dying blood pressure. Our family gathered on her last night in the hospital and asked the nurses to give her her meds all at once while we were there rather than through the night. They did so, and Anne's blood pressure fell and she became less responsive.

Almost immediately, a nurse came in. He quietly asked my sister-in-law who was the biologist in the room and she nodded in my direction. He stuck around in a corner. I stepped out for a minute or two and came back into the room to find Anne was seizing. I held her, trying to calm her, but the seizures went on for some time. She calmed after an hour or so and we all decided to leave, hoping she would rest through the night.

As we drove home, I asked Nanc for some details and gradually realized that bastard nurse had waited for me to leave and then stepped forward and injected Anne with a strong dose of some stimulant so she wouldn't die on his watch. If I had known what was occurring at the time I swear I would have thrown the rotten sonofabitch out of the 6th floor window with no regret. I failed my sister and am haunted still.

TWENTY-SIX

Jesus is the Answer

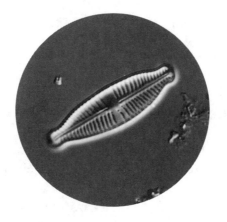

1 October, Highway 126, Val Verde, California *(by email)*
Scott—On the way back over the mountain from the Pacific to Val Verde and Sarah's home—California 126—we tune into PBS and find Ira Glass' "This American Life." The voice we hear is Scott Carrier, our pal from Salt Lake City. Scott is talking about amnesia, what it feels like to lose yourself.

Nancy, Sarah and I shoot knowing glances at each other— hell, we all know what it feels like to be lost. This seems a natural piece for us—plausible, biographical. But, here's the twist, and I swear it's true. As Scott talks about amnesia, a voice breaks in: "…come to Jesus Christ to find yourself…COME TO JESUS."

So, here we are crossing from California 1 to Val Verde with Scott Carrier asking what happens when you lose yourself to amnesia, and some Christian guy breaks in through static to assert "JESUS CHRIST...*crackle, snap, crackle*...Jesus Christ... Jesus Christ...fade out, *hissssss, crackle*...Jesus is the answer, friends, Jesus is YOUR answer...find your way with JESUS... Jesus..."

The hypnotist is removing Carrier's memory when the Christian voice fades. Scott wakes and talks to her about what it feels like to lose your memory. We hear, "What's your name … *fade out, crackle, hiss, loud static* … I can't remember … fade out, sputter, crack* … Jesus Christ … Jesus ..… Jesus saves …… in a dark world, friend ……. *crackle* ……….*hissssssss*…"

At first we think this whole thing is part of Scott's piece—a colossal send-up. But we figure fast it is something else. We are at the mercy of the ether, receiving unsolicited messages from the airwaves: Jesus Christ, Jesus friend….Jesus….will save…Jesus… Jesus … Jesus. None of us is disrespectful, though all of us doubt the accepted Christian religion. But this sends us over the edge. We have to pull off the highway to laugh ourselves out.

2 October, Great Western Trail, Mt. Timpanogos

Golden sunshine on this late afternoon. Just inside Provo Canyon, the folded blue limestone juts out of the north end of Cascade Mountain, lit doubly by the sun and by the sun's reflection off the brilliant red maples running like a river up the fold of Pole Canyon. We round a corner to surprise a huge bird, much larger than the pair of big redtails we often see at the canyon mouth.

"It's a golden eagle," Sam exclaims. "*Aquila chrysaetos.* Probably this year's chick."

"Good lord," I reply as the magnificent raptor hunts along the ridge. "How could anything that size be a chick?"

Steller's jays (*Cyanocitta stelleri*) and magpies greet us raucously.

"Why," I ask Sam, "are we seeing Steller's jays here where we've usually seen scrub jays?"

"Good question," he answers.

We swing up over the tricky quartzite, past Johnson's Hole, up the rocky ridge, to the top where we snake through shoulder-high oak brush.

"Is that a cicada?" I ask.

"Sounds like it."

"That reminds me of Galileo."

"What?"

"My son Ben just loaned me Sobel's new book, *Galileo's Daughter.* Sobel recounts Galileo's story about a 'man endowed by Nature with extraordinary curiosity and a very penetrating mind' who tries to figure out how a cicada makes its sound and ends up killing it with the needle he's using to observe it."

"That's always been a problem for me," Sam says. "I even have a hard time collecting algae from streams for the same reason. It hurts my heart to kill and preserve these tiny and alive organisms, though I may be the only member of my profession to even think about this. But, by damn, sampling aside, it is interesting and fine for me that we're on this mountain, this day, asking the same kinds of questions Galileo and others asked five hundred years ago. That's a fine connection. Do you suppose anyone will be here in another half-millennium wondering about the same kinds of things?"

6 October, Great Western Trail, Mt. Timpanogos

"Look how the light slants in, now the sun is moving south," Sam says.

"Galileo described wine as light held together by moisture," I note.

We round a bend in the trail and ride into a sea of tall, golden, malodorous rabbit brush, *Chrysothamnus nauseosus*. *Chryso—* golden; *anthemon—*flower; *nauseosus—* that's the malodorous part. A poor man's chrysanthemum. We lay down our bikes and wade into chest-high plants. Sam wears a black muscle shirt that draws golden pollen like a magnet. The flowers swarm with pairs of orange-and-black striped beetles, hundreds of copulating pairs.

"One kind of pollination leads to another," I suggest. "I'd rename this plant *Chrysothamnus aphrodisius*. By the way, I've been meaning to ask you about the diatoms you mentioned the other day. So you collect them from streams and springs. Then what happens?"

"To prepare the diatoms for identification, I boil them in nitric acid, wash them half-a-dozen times with distilled water, and mount them in an expensive, specially prepared mountant. Then I examine them under the microscope, one with specialized optics. Diatoms 'prefer' different kinds of habitats, so you can tell a lot about the environment by identifying which ones are present or absent. For the people concerned about water quality in Utah, for instance, I examine samples for changes in diatoms over time and can tell whether mitigation efforts are working."

"Impressive," I say. "My disciplinary skills are in constant demand as well. I consult for a wide range of people who have questions about the new poetic forms in eighteenth-century German literature."

12 October, Great Western Trail, Mt. Timpanogos

As we swing up the trail, I mention to Sam that my son Tom has just headed east in a two-hundred dollar Honda to take up residence in New York City.

"Twenty-one years old and itching for adventure," Sam says. "Those were the days!"

"The last thing he showed me before pulling out," I say, "was a supply of horse-tail or smooth scouring rush, *Equisetum laevigatum*, their jointed hollow stems rough with silica and perfect for sanding his saxophone reeds." 'No telling if I'll be able to find these in the city,' he said, and off he drove."

"You're proud of him," Sam comments, "and nervous as hell."

"That sums it up," I say.

"Damn kids'll be the death of us," Sam says. "Last summer, kicking around Venezuela and Brazil, our son Jed ended up with malaria. I've never seen anyone much sicker. Made him something of a medical celebrity. None of his Salt Lake doctors had ever seen a case. While Jed was suffering the horrible chills and fever and sweating of malaria, his roommate Chad's black wolf, Dimmer, hung out with Jed for a week, lying on his feet and mothering him. Dimmer was killed by a car the day after Jed was up and about. That damned wolf broke my heart."

15 October, Great Western Trail, Mt. Timpanogos

Plums again, sweet and tart like the October sun on a brisk Sunday morning. We ride on, noting the remaining wildflowers: a few sunflowers, the remains of the rabbitbrush, scattered purple asters and yellow toadflax, a couple of pale thistle blossoms, a little buckwheat. From the steep hill above us, a raptor drops off a snag and catches the canyon breeze.

"A redtail?" Sam wonders.

"I don't think so," I answer. "The wings have black tips and are light underneath. See the black bars on both sides of the head? But then again, look how the sun catches the top of the tail—there's a hint of copper." The bird swings by just over our heads and we head on up the trail.

"I'm interested in why it's so important for us to classify things," Sam muses.

"We've often poked fun at ourselves for this penchant," I remember, "worried that the naming inhibits our ability to see. But I'm wondering now if something more important isn't at work. Correctly classifying a snake or a mushroom or fellow human can save our lives. Maybe our compulsion to classify is a biological adaptation."

Sam agrees. "If you have categories and your categories can distinguish between safe and not-safe, the world's an easier, more navigable place. But the interesting issue for me is how easily this can slop over into trouble. Obsessive-compulsive disorder—my major day-by-day nemesis—may stem from something like an exaggerated need to classify. And don't you think xenophobia originates from the same tendency?"

"That's got to be one reason why we invent religions," I suggest. "Explanations for the inexplicable ease our minds in a dangerous, complex, and ambiguous world."

"Maybe," Sam replies. "As I've aged and given up so many of my early beliefs I'm less and less comfortable—though I sometimes feel more authentic, whatever that means. But I wonder occasionally what it would be like to go back. Sometimes the comfort of an ordered world seems so damned enticing."

"I'd choose Scott Carrier over Jesus any day," I say.

19 October, Great Western Trail, Mt. Timpanogos

"Nancy and I went to Mozart's comic opera *The Magic Flute* last night," I tell Scott as we head for the first difficult climb. "I must say I've always liked the music to this opera, but I didn't care for the opera itself."

"*The Magic Flute* is no comic opera," Scott states flatly. "It's part of the classical cannon and a major work of art based on Freemasonic rituals. You're an uncouth botanist riding Nancy's coattails."

"It's true about Nancy," I reply, "and *The Magic Flute* is certainly a major work of art. But if you had any brains you'd know that *The Magic Flute* is most accurately classified as a Singspiel. What's this 'uncouth' shit?"

"Here we go again," Scott says, not willing to admit I'm right. "We're caught up in classification. It's what we do as creatures of language. Words of any kind work as definition, and getting the best words is important. Herder, one of Goethe's mentors and friends, argued that we don't speak language but that language speaks us. We get caught in the webs of clichés and assumptions and traditions and mistakes and discoveries and wisdom and collective stupidities that have fossilized into languages. When we speak or write, we're just regurgitating the processed words and sentences. When you say, as you often do, that there are too many words and ask why we should add to the surplus, you're responding to that, I suppose."

"That's part of it," I say. "The other part is my thought that the good writers we know will read this and know what they already suspected: we're just a couple of semi-ambitious half-wits."

"We've got one advantage," Scott reminds me. "We know we're not as smart as we wish we were and we're not trying to hide that—so what's to lose?"

TWENTY-SEVEN

Horny Goat Weed

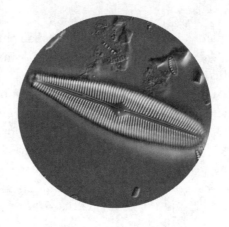

29 October, Phone call from Provo to Orem

"Hi Sam, how 'bout a ride?"

"It's raining. The hills are still swarming with anxious hunters. Are you nuts?"

"Probably. But rain and hunters never kept you from calling me. What's going on?"

"Woke up in the night and had the Northern Lights flashing across my eyes. Then this morning I had so many floaters I thought I was looking through my moustache. Until I see my doc tomorrow, I'm not gonna ride."

"Flashing lights? Isn't that a side effect of Viagra?"

"No, those are blue flashes. These were white."

"Sounds like you've had both experiences."

"That's enough from you, you schmuck—and you know I'm using schmuck in the Yiddish sense: limp dick."

"I don't mean to push this," I counter, "but that glossy pamphlet about 'horny goat weed' I found on your counter has had me wondering about you. It points out elegantly that 'low testosterone is not like a car engine that's low on oil' and that 'not feeling like a man and having less to live for creates an overall negativeness in our attitude.'"

"Overall negativeness pretty well describes me on most days," Sam says.

30 October, Great Western Trail, Mt. Timpanogos

Light rain and mist—but we chance a quick afternoon ride anyway. On the way down, we see four horses approaching from below. Scott and I step our bikes off the trail to let the riders pass.

As far as we can tell, they constitute a small family—husband, wife, and two boys, maybe eight and ten years old. We exchange smiles and howdys. The man is at the end of the string and unresponsive, a bit distracted perhaps. He draws even and we see he is on a cell phone.

"Ma'am," he says, "yours is the only house where the siding blew off. It's an act of God. What am I supposed to do about it? Aluminum siding does not last forever!" A pause as he rides past. The sound diminishes as he distances. "I told you, it's an act of God. It's not my fault and I am not going to replace it…"

Reminds us of the Woody Allen line about the man in hell who, when asked, "What did you do to get here?" answered, "I invented aluminum siding."

8 November, UVSC

Our friends Jim and Melinda Harris have published a second edition of their *Plant Identification Terminology: An Illustrated Glossary*. Melinda's illustrations, over two thousand of them, are beautiful and exact, perfect companions to Jim's descriptions. When Jim writes, for example, "Orthotropous ovule. An ovule which is straight and erect," we're glad to have Melinda's figure #811 so we can see what the hell Jim's talking about. But without Jim's description, the illustrations would make little sense.

The second part of the book, "Terminology by Category," provides an education in systematic observation. Plants have roots, stems, leaves, surfaces, inflorescences, flowers, and fruits, as we already knew, but if we are looking at leaves, for instance, the book says we should pay attention to parts, shapes, bases, apices, division, venation, margins, attachment, and arrangement. Leaf arrangement, to take just the one case, may be alternate, basal, bilateral, cauline, decussate, dextrorse, distichous, equitant, opposite, ranked, rosette, rosulate, sinistrorse, verticulate, or whorled.

9 November, Great Western Trail, Mount Timpanogos

It's snowing lightly when Sam and I head out. The ground is wet as we turn off the asphalt, in places downright muddy.

Predictably, at the first real climb, my chain sucks.

"Shit," I say calmly.

The wet chain binds again, and again I emit a carefully reasoned sentence: "Son of a bitch yellow shitty bastard."

"That's odd syntax," Sam says. "You aren't a native swearer, are you?"

"Nope," I say. "I grew up in a monolingual Mormon family and came to the second language late. I was twenty-two and working my first summer as a roughneck on a drilling rig before I was really introduced to the vocabulary. And obviously I'm still not comfortable with the grammar."

The chain sucks again.

"Jesus H. Christ!"

We've climbed high enough on the mountain that I don't have much breath, so I foreswear any more obscenities, jump off my bike, and push it to the top, where a pair of spotted and masked kestrels turns my mind away from what my old friend Walter Fuhrman called "the absolute depravity of all inanimate objects."

10 November, Provo *(by email)*

Scott—Just got a call from Starr, who is working on my diatom collection for mailing to the Cal Academy of Sciences. This is a much bigger deal for me than I had thought. It's 30 years of work and collections.

I am happy my work will be accessible for study across the years by students and professors from around the world. But I wasn't prepared for the emotional jolt. I sent off nearly 20,000 microscopic slides, 3,000 pellet samples, my library of more than 20,000 papers and books—most of a life's work.

When I got the call they had been shipped, I sat in my office staring out the window wondering what in hell does a man's life come to in the end—a few specimens, a wall of books, maybe four dogs, five if you are lucky, a few friends, and with any kind of luck, someone like Nancy who helps make sense of it all. But finally it's a slim enough legacy even for the best of us. No wonder people choose to believe in some sort of an afterlife and perform strange rituals to honor the gods and even engage in the bizarre behavior of begetting and nurturing children.

10 November, Provo *(by email)*

Sam—speaking of diatoms, I just took a look at a remarkable little book published by J. Cramer in the "Bibliotheca Diatomologica" series. The book has two halves: 1. "The Diatom Flora of Blue Lake Warm Spring, Utah, U.S.A. and 2. "A Contribution to the Freshwater Diatom Flora of the Hawaiian Islands." Both parts of the book list you as a co-author. Vaduz, Liechtenstein is the publisher's home and the book is printed in Germany. Next time you pooh-pooh my work in the German Enlightenment, I'll remind you that had there been no German science inspired by the Enlightenment, there would have been no German scientific publisher and you'd have no book.

That aside, I loved this glimpse into your science. In the Blue Lake Warm Spring (which Lyn and I recently visited on our way from Wendover to Ely), you found 136 taxa of diatoms. You and your co-author describe them and organize them into "four distinct floristic elements." But what I most enjoyed were the microscopic photos of all 136 diatoms. They are beautiful little plants I never knew existed till I met you.

17 November, Great Western Trail, Mt. Timpanogos

It's cold. We wear layer over layer over layer. My face aches with the wind chill.

"Tom's moved again," Scott says. "He's still in Brooklyn somewhere, but has moved to a place where he says he can pay the rent daily. No phone, and the letter he sent has two addresses."

"Ah hell," I respond. "I'm sorry."

"I know a guy's gotta let go of his kids," Scott says. "And I'm happy for Tom to have a chance to play jazz in New York City, but this is not easy for me in the late hours of the night."

19 November, Great Western Trail, Mt. Timpanogos

We climb up a steep, snow-covered trail this morning, surprised at how high we finally get. Turning around, we are met with an unnerving sight: a lake of silver-grey pollution shimmers in the sunlight just at the level of the ancient Lake Bonneville.

"We're going to have to ride back down into that crap!" Scott says.

"Yup," I reply. "And that's not the half of it. Sorry—I'm headed into my diatribe mode."

"Fire away," Scott says.

"You probably know the American Trucking Association has a case before the Supreme Court to limit the power of the Environmental Protection Agency to regulate clean air. This is a big deal. A bunch of new studies in the past few years have shown the impact of small particles on human health. In fact, one of my friend Arden Pope's recent studies shows that living in the polluted parts of Utah costs a person better than three years of their life on average as compared to less-polluted Utah environs.

"If the truckers and their allies are successful, we will see a substantial dirtying of our air and water. I can't tell you how strongly I feel about this. We simply have to hold polluting industry accountable for their goddamned crimes and allow the EPA to do their work."

20 November, Mount Timpanogos

Sunday morning, bright enough for sunglasses, cold enough for tights and wicking underwear and fleece and shells and gloves and stocking caps and balaclavas. There's too much snow for our normal ride, so we head past the water-treatment plant and on up the dirt road that takes us to the mouth of the canyon. Standing there, blowing and sweating after a climb exacerbated by four or five inches of snow, we gaze at the polluted valley with dismay.

On up the canyon we ride, slipping and sliding along a trail broken in the snow by a horse, a runner, several deer, and dozens of big-footed elk.

"I finished J. M. Coetzee's *Disgrace*," Sam says, "and like you said, it's devastating."

"The first sentence," I puff, "made me sit up and pay attention. 'For a man of his age, fifty-two, divorced, he has, to his mind, solved the problem of sex rather well.' Then, however, we find that this Wordsworth and Byron scholar, employed by what has become a technical college, has sunk to teaching a subject he hates to indifferent students. 'Month after month he sets, collects, reads, and annotates their assignments, correcting lapses in punctuation, spelling and usage, interrogating weak arguments, appending to each paper a brief, considered critique.'"

"I have strong affinity with the man. That's where I've lived all my life," Sam says. "In constant fear that I'm nobody, a clown."

"But you'll remember the story progresses," I point out. "After a lot of character development precipitated by an ambiguous affair with a student who gets him fired from his job, he ends up practicing true human kindness as he euthanizes and incinerates stray dogs."

"It was the wrong story for me to read as the winter darkness thickens," Sam mutters from where he now stands, looking up a hill tracked by dozens of elk.

We leave our bikes standing in the stiff snow and climb the steep hill on foot. Where Earth shows through the snow in the bright sunlight, little green leaves shine fresh and juicy. "*Erodi-*

um cicutarium," Sam says. "Storksbill, ready to burst into bloom at the first hint of spring."

I trip over something and lean over to pick up a cupped piece of rusted metal the size of my palm. Although I've never seen one without a leather covering, I know immediately what it is. "Sam, look at this steel toe cap. It's from a right-footed boot. I left my last pair of these in a doghouse locker on a drilling rig in northwestern New Mexico in 1974."

We never get high enough to see the elk herd, lying contentedly on some south-facing hillside soaking up this morning's sun. But we lurch and slide our way back down the canyon with an expansive sense that we've been in their territory, that we've shared their space, that we've soaked up the same Sunday sun.

TWENTY-EIGHT

As Common as Paradox,
As Odd as Love

21 November, Orem *(by email)*

Sam—trust a poet to get to the heart of the matter in a few words. Our dear friend Laura Hamblin read last night at UVSC, opening with a series of her October/November poems. These lines from the first poem captured everything we've been trying to say for two years now: "as common as paradox, / as odd as love, when / black air snaps with cold."

11 December, Great Western Trail, Mt. Timpanogos

After a week of trails dry enough for us to ride, after the high-lung burn and leaden legs of Monday and Tuesday and Wednesday, we finally have the lungs and legs to try the steep Great Western Trail again. There's the initial scramble, an anaerobic sprint, then the trail flattens to an almost forgiving climb.

"I like the way you slow down and gather yourself before the next climb," Sam says from behind me.

"What's the alternative," I gasp as I start up the second rocky climb.

We stand on a knoll overlooking Utah Valley, its skies swept clean by the storm blowing in from the north.

"Tom called yesterday," I tell Sam.

"From New York? What did he say?"

"Lots of mundane things, details that ease a father's anxious mind. He's getting mail now, including my last letter. He's earning enough playing his saxophone on subway platforms to pay his rent and buy food. He's got some friends. He had a gig last night at the French Consulate, he said, and when he finished his first solo he looked up and saw Lionel Hampton at the nearest table, applauding him."

"So you can breathe a little easier," Sam says.

"Well, yes, until he told me about the night he helped his friend Brian Thurber carry drums to his practice space. Police vans screeched up, a swat team burst out shouting for everyone to freeze. They broke down a door and tossed in a smoke grenade. When Tom and Brian started crawling away on elbows and knees, the cops grabbed them, cuffed them, and made them kneel against a wall for half an hour. Nothing to really worry about, I guess."

"I hear you. This has been standard fare in our family. The blue gang is made up of jerks. Every damned one of them except for a few of my pals."

12 December, Great Western Trail, Mt. Timpanogos

In response to the Supreme Court's decision to stop the counting of Florida ballots and declare George Bush president, a spokesperson for the Democrats, Mr. Malaprop, is reported to have said that the action "cast a pail over the legitimacy of the election."

"That's pretty much how I see it," Sam says as we survey Utah Valley from our perch at the mouth of the canyon. "An enormous, shitass pail that cheapens democracy in our country. I have been wondering lately whether we will survive as a functional democracy or whether we will become an aged and wealthy oligarchy."

"It reminds me," I chime in, "of the Republican during the Clinton impeachment hearings who said that the whole thing was out of control like a runaway train in uncharted waters."

"Yeah," Sam says, "but all the senators got their votes counted and Dubbya wasn't at the helm of the train before it capsized off the track."

17 December, Provo

The ringing phone drags me out of a warm bed.

"Hello?"

"Hello," Sam says defensively. "Don't get me wrong. I'm not trying to get out of riding, but up here at the mouth of the canyon it's blowing like hell. Forty-five-mph winds. I don't think we could even make headway."

"Ah!" I reply. "What a shame to have to crawl back into warm beds on a Sunday morning."

"That's true. I'll call you if there's a change."

Thirty minutes later, the phone rings again

"The wind is still blowing, and now it's snowing like crazy. I'd ride now, but you probably don't have the balls for it."

"See you in ten minutes."

In a near whiteout, against gale-force winds, I drive from the vintage 1927 house the bank and I now own in Provo to Sam's house in Orem. Trying to sort out whose fault this is, we wheel our bikes onto the street and head north into a bitter, snow-spitting wind. We can scarcely see. Our joints set up an arthritic chorus.

"Only an idiot would be on a bike in this weather," Sam says.

A huge yellow dog sniffs the snow at the street corner. The shaggy animal glances up and does a double take. It starts running like hell, keeping a keen eye on us all the while.

Just as we start to climb the flank of Timpanogos, snow abating and cloud cover breaking up, a fox bursts from cover and ghosts up the steep incline ahead of us. The switchback brings us to where it crossed the trail and we stop to admire the round little tracks. Below us, a second fox, red-gold in the morning sun, sails down the hill, flies over a fifteen-foot ditch, hits an icy rim, and skids out as it turns, bushy tail hanging in the air like an apostrophe.

The snow lies deeper on the trail now, grabbing at our wheels. We round a corner to enter a protected valley. Dozens of deer stand up from beds under the scrub oak, ears rimed with snow, backs snowy. They shake off the snow with twitching hides and eye us warily. The trail takes us away from the deer into snow that finally stops us cold. We throw our bikes into the snow, making splendid bike angels. We admire the clear valley below, the wind-troubled lake, the snow-blown darkness to the south, the light breaking through to the northwest. We call it a day.

22 December, Great Western Trail, Mt. Timpanogos

"This is a bad idea," I tell Sam as we ride into the nine a.m. sun. "It's thirty-one degrees, the trail will be muddy where the sun hits it and snowy where it doesn't. Plus, we haven't ridden for a week."

"Yeah, yeah," he says.

Yesterday was the winter solstice, and we celebrated with the mead Sam brewed last Christmas. The Potawatomi plums we picked along the trail in September flavored the mead so fragrantly that just swirling the precious liquid in a glass made us smile.

"You're an alchemist," I told Sam.

"Two months ago," he reminded me, "you tasted this and complimented me on the turpentine aftertaste."

On the trail, the slick film of mud on top of the frozen earth gums up our tires, the snow slows us, the ice makes us slide, and our aging bodies complain.

"I'm getting hammered," I gasp.

Sam keeps riding.

At the top, bent double, sucking air, wondering if it would be easier to just die, I try to explain what has happened. "Sam, it's never been this hard on us. The trail is simply steeper today. I think we're witnessing the geological upthrust that has formed the canyon."

"Sure thing," Sam says. "We're old enough now to understand geologic time."

YEAR III

It's not expensive to pay attention to the phases of the moon, to transplant lemon lilies and watch a garter snake birthing forty babies and a catbird grabbing some, or listen to the itchy-britches of the Canada geese as autumn waxes. We will be motes in the ocean again soon, leached out of the soil of some graveyard, and everlastingly rocking.

That is my sense of an afterlife and my comfort. The hurly-burly of streambed turmoil will be our last rush-hour traffic—thocketing through boulders, past perch pools and drift logs. Enough, we will say, reaching tidewater. We saw enough.

Edward Hoagland, *Sex and the River Styx*

TWENTY-NINE

Strange Behaviors

1 January, Great Western Trail, Mt. Timpanogos

Morning ride while the trail is frozen. Both of us feeling sluggish: two old men chugging up the hill at the start of a new year. "Sam," I say, "you know how I've been worrying about my son Tom in New York? I told you how cold it's been, about how he starts playing on a subway platform dressed in layers of clothes and then, as he warms up from the playing, doffs layer after layer. Remember the night he got arrested with his friend Brian? Remember all my letters that came back stamped UN-DELIVERABLE? Well, that vision changed radically last night. Imagine this: New Year's Eve, Salt Lake City, Hotel Monaco's chic Bambara Restaurant, seventy-five-dollars-a-plate-dinner. And there, in the center of the restaurant—the two miscreants, Tom and Brian, with Josh Payne on guitar and an elegant Japanese-American on bass, all of them suited, silk-shirted, playing the coolest jazz on the planet for a sophisticated and appreciative audience! With that lucrative gig booked, Tom bought a round-trip ticket and came home for three weeks. Let's go hear him next Thursday in Park City."

"Good for him," Sam says. "Good for you. Count me in."

"What are your best memories from the last year?" I ask Sam.

"Hard to answer," Sam says. "So many nice things. But high on the list would be the home-made card from Alex, our fourth grade pal from Oak Dale School who reads our column. She says she thinks we're funny. Drivin' home from Mexico with Nancy in a pickup truck after droppin' off wheelchairs in Chihuahua. Readin' Terry's *Leap* aloud for hours arguing about what in hell she meant and what our leap was to be. Meetin' the fine new men in our daughters' lives. Knowing Jed is in his last class at the U before he graduates. Three totaled cars by three kids without a single serious injury. Twelve geese honking over us low in blowing November snow in Sigurd. Lying awake next to Nanc last night listening to her sleep."

"Leaving BYU doesn't make your list?" I ask.

"Funny deal," Sam responds. "Except for a few friends, BYU has faded out of my consciousness. It's an anachronism, a dying institution, dedicated now to propaganda rather than inquiry. I really don't give a shit about it."

4 January, Mother Urban's Ratskeller, Park City

It's colder than a well-digger's ass tonight, but when Sam and Nancy and Lyn and I walk up to the door of Mother Urban's (formerly a brothel) and see the sign—TONIGHT: THE TOM ABBOTT QUARTET—I don't feel nearly so cold. Tom's happy we've come and, as his quartet heats up the place, so are we.

An hour into the first set, I'm lost in the solo Tom constructs over the chords and rhythms of his rhythm section when my mind's eye mistakes Tom's face for my brother John's. Then it's Tom again, and I notice for the first time the jaw that Tom and John and I share, the long face, the deep-set eyes.

"Sam," I say, "you know I've written a whole book manuscript to keep John's memory from fading. Look at Tom. He's the spitting image."

21 January, Great Western Trail, Mt. Timpanogos

Twenty-three degrees, Sam reports as we ride off on this Sunday morning, right after Nancy has stepped outside to hug me. "I just had to give you a hug," she said. "If you weren't riding with him in this cold, I'd have to."

"You're a lucky man, Sam," I say as we ride against the cold canyon wind.

"Don't think I don't know it," he replies.

"How long have you been married?"

"Thirty-five years," Sam says.

"You and Nancy will still be holding hands in the old-folks home," I predict. "Unless, of course, she comes to her senses. It's been a year now since the end of my marriage. I guess the thing that most surprises me is how hard it is to create new patterns of living, productive patterns. I'm living alone for the first time in my fifty years and keep finding myself engaged in strange behaviors."

"You had plenty of those while you were still married," Sam chuckles. "You were the paragon of strange behaviors."

"Yeah, yeah," I reply. "But I didn't sit for hours—five hours, six hours—playing solitaire on my laptop. I didn't flip through the fuzzy channels of my old TV looking for something to dull my thoughts on a sunny Sunday afternoon. I didn't drive to Wendover to shove a hundred bucks into the nickel slots in hopes of a sudden clear ordering of the world in the form of accidentally lined-up double diamonds. I didn't stop my car in traffic when the odometer read 1111111. I didn't watch license plates for patterns, three licenses in a row from states that begin with 'W'—Wyoming, Washington, West Virginia."

"This is something I didn't know about you," Sam says. "It's tough. Subconsciously, at least, you're looking for messages in numbers and letters, just as I've found myself wishing for salvation in lost rituals. I dreamed the other night Nanc was dying and I couldn't go with her. Our ways were parting after these years and I was heartsick. I tell you, when I woke I would have believed anything, done any ritual, danced any dance, paid any price to go with her. But nothing was there. It left me in an indescribable state for days. I just wanted to believe! But I simply can't bring myself to believe the unbelievable."

A small herd of deer moves warily, easily, up the hill away from us. Most of them are does, with one heavily muscled buck carrying broad, thick antlers. "He won't make it through the next hunting season," Sam says.

"Not a chance," I agree. "But look at that herd of pregnant does. He has already conceived his seminal ideas. Maybe there's a lesson there for us."

27 January, Great Western Trail, Mt. Timpanogos

It could be tricky today, forty-one degrees after new snow this week. We're likely to mud up. "Why are we riding today?" I ask Sam.

"Because neither of us is psychologically stable enough to live with a lard ass," he answers. We turn a corner into a gust of cold wind blowing out of the canyon. The trail is frozen solid, snowed over, slick as Sam's old back tire. We slip and slide and duck the swirling wind. "This is pitiful," I shout over the wind.

"It is beautiful," Sam shouts back. "Look at the fall gold where the wind has swept away the snow."

We make our way to the top of the hill where the wind whistles and howls. Pulling our caps tighter around our ears, we dive off the mountain. Ice abets gravity and before I know it, I'm flying over my handlebars. Sam's brakes won't work, so he uses his legs like outriggers. At the bottom, we laugh and hoot and Sam says, "Our best ride in months!"

3 February, Great Western Trail, Mt. Timpanogos

Feeling slow and blue, I agree to a mid-day ride. I need the work and the sweat. Halfway up the first steep stretch, Scott says, "Damned *Catalyst* didn't even bother to print our column last month. Suppose it had anything to do with us being three days late?"

"Horseshit," I respond. "You think the presses don't wait for Philip Roth or Norman Mailer? They're sending us a message. We've run ourselves out of ideas and this is their way of tellin' us."

"Could be," Scott replies. "But you watch. We'll be able to count on our bright and literate reading public. We know they'll come through for us by the thousands and force our editor to realize the gravity of her mistake."

"You ain't helpin' here and you're not funny," I respond. "We worked our asses off on that column and had a few things we wanted to say. The hell with it, I'm not climbing this damned hill any more if Greta's not printing our column."

10 February, Great Western Trail, Mt. Timpanogos

"We'll make it up that hill today if it kills us," Sam says as we wheel our bikes out of his garage, still caked with mud from our last ride.

"Spoken like the appropriately socialized American male," I reply.

Dark clouds cloak Timp. To the south, Utah Valley shines clear and bright. The mud on the trail is frozen, perfect for winter riding. We ease our way up the mountain, exchanging our usual litany of complaints.

"How's your first grandkid?" Sam asks.

"Doing great, and so is Maren. What a shock that was, walking into the hospital room Thursday night to find a spanking new person in my little girl's arms."

"How does it make you feel?" Sam asks. "Does it make your back crawl with worry for the new kid? Have you been wondering if there's any chance she'll be able to make a decent life for herself?"

"No, I just looked at her and at her parents' beaming faces and felt more hopeful than I have in a long time."

"Your basic disposition is antithetical to mine," Sam wheezes as he fights to make his back tire grip the ice. "I look at a baby or a kid and see a dark future. Not a chance in hell kids are gonna grow up in a world worth living in. You're so damned optimistic."

"In high school," I pant—the pace isn't quite as leisurely as I thought—"I won second prize in an essay contest sponsored by the Optimists Club. Fifty bucks and a free lunch at the club meeting, where I read the essay."

"Now that's sweet," Sam says. "If there had been a cynics

club at Davis High when I was in school, I would have won first prize."

"The Greek root for cynic means dog," I say. "It fits you like a glove. You're also sentimental as hell. A sentimental cynic. But back to the baby. There's got to be a biological imperative at work. All animals must feel a surge of hope at the birth of one of their kind."

"Could be," Sam says. "But remember the incident that knocked Darwin off his pins a century and a half ago? He was gathering specimens in Patagonia, when he saw a native boy drop and break an egg he was carrying. His father turned and killed him, banging his head against the rocks. This is no benign and predictable world. This is no place where family ties automatically bind and make safe."

We stop and blow and then head down a steep side trail. From a copse of scrub oak, a herd of mule deer keeps a nervous watch on us, but we're quickly past without spooking them.

I hear something behind me and turn to see Sam in the air above his handlebars. It's an awkward fall, and he lies immobile for a second. He rolls over and grimaces. "Maybe there's a biological imperative we're ignoring when we ride downhill on two wheels," I suggest.

Thirty

Elderberry Melancholy

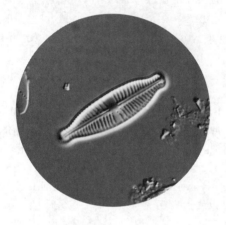

1 March, Great Western Trail, Mt. Timpanogos

Late afternoon meetings for both of us. Even so, the days are lengthening and we sneak away from campus a bit before 5:00. If we hurry, we can get a fast up-and-back and beat the dark.

"How much do you worry about your job?" I ask Scott as we start up the first steep stretch.

"Not too much," Scott responds. "I don't think I'm as anxious about it as you are. It disappoints me when my students don't do their work, but I don't lie awake thinking about it."

"That's what I thought," I respond. "I seem to have antennae out that most of my friends don't even own. I can monitor five conversations in a room at once and I seem to worry about everything equally—a very bad strategy, especially when much of it is trivial. You know I don't sleep much, and when I'm awake I'm as apt to worry about problems with our Institutional Review Board as I am with problems of poverty and social justice. Why the hell can't Human Resources keep their noses out of my attempts to hire good faculty? How can we keep the grounds crew from knocking down cliff swallow nests this spring? What will my new faculty do without lab space?"

We're at the top of the hill and Scott admonishes me: "Sam! There's a kestrel floating at the edge of that cliff. How the hell can we talk about work in the face of a sight like that? How many more times in our life are we going to see that? Jesus, man—get a grip."

3 March, Mad Dog Cycles, Orem, Utah

Labor Tune-Up Plus:	$39.00
Cable Brake and Derail Wire:	$5.97
Housing Derail and Brake:	$5.97
Brake Pad V Sh Xtr Severe Cond:	$23.98
Chain Sh HG92PD: $34.99	
Labor Shock Overhaul:	$10.00

Tire 26 Sp Team Mast Spt 1.9:	$24.99
Small and Middle Chain Rings:	$35.99
Lube Pedro's Extra Dry 12OZ:	$10.99
Total:	$191.88

Minus 10% discount, Plus tax

"Thanks for the discount, Randy," I tell the young manager standing in front of a photo of his little son. "And thanks for cleaning off the winter's grime. The bike looks beautiful."

"What have you been greasing that old chain with?" Randy asks.

"I used Pedro's till it ran out. Then I had a can of TriFlo. When that ran out I just used WD-40."

"Yeah, it looked like it. You might want to be more careful with this new one."

"I will," I promise. "By the way, last time I put on a new chain I also had to change the rear cassette. Don't they wear together?"

"I checked that," Randy says. "I think you're okay."

4 March, Mad Dog Cycles, Orem, Utah
| Rear Cassette, SP: | $78.99 |

Minus 10%, Plus tax.

Later, on the trail, I point out to Sam that the grand total was nearly $300. "That's what I paid for my first mountain bike."

"Quit whining," Sam says, sympathetically. "You'll take it off your taxes as a business loss. You make $250 a year writing the column. You pay Randy $500 a year to keep your bike in shape. That's a business loss of $250. Some guys have to pay lawyers big money to figure out tax shelters like that. But here's the more important question: How many cogs on your low gear?"

"I don't know," I say. I compare my pedal speed to Sam's as we climb the hill. We're both in granny gear and he's pedaling faster than I am.

At the top of the hill, we tip up our bikes and count cogs. Sam's got thirty-four. I've got thirty-two. "You've got a lower gear," I point out. "Your bike weighs five pounds less than mine. I hope you remember that when I whup your ass on Frank."

March 2001, *Catalyst Magazine*, Letters to the Editor

Dear Editor: I am one of those unfortunate souls who live in Utah Valley and do not have direct access to *Catalyst*. I have a friend who commutes to SLC every day and he picks up a copy for me each month. I was saddened this month to discover that my favorite column, "Wild Rides, Wildflowers," does not appear in this issue. Surely you have not discontinued this piece. As a female reader of *Catalyst*, I have enjoyed this honest glimpse into the male psyche. Scott and Sam, in their self-deprecating and ironic voices, offer rare insight into the macho male mind and reveal a tenderness that most of us have always hoped lay hidden there. Gender and gender identification are at the heart of many of our most pressing problems. This column provides much more than botanical information and a daily chronicle of the adventures of aging bikers. I pray nothing has happened to our boys. But I wonder why else their column would so suddenly disappear from your pages. Surely you know that this column is the "best of" *Catalyst*.

I hope to find the originality, insight and humor of "Wild Rides" in your March issue.

—MaryAnne Evans
Provo, Utah

Dear Editor: I'm an avid reader of your monthly magazine and look forward to your contributors' comments on Utah society ranging from politics to the environment. So it was with great disappointment that when I finally made my way to REI to pick up the February edition I realized that one of my favorite columns, "Wild Rides, Wildflowers, Biking and Botanizing the Great Western Trail" had mysteriously disappeared.

I wondered perhaps if the authors had decided to call it quits, spend their earnings on new cycles, and head off to bike paths unknown? Or maybe they had met an untimely end defending the last edges of wilderness against ATV or ORV bullies? But then I imagined that these two bikers, no doubt fit but "getting along" in years, may have sucked in their final breaths climbing Frank, collapsed by the wayside, and have been feeding the animal community ever since?

Could you end the suspense?

—L.E. Bennett
(real and vicarious biker)

5 March, Great Western Trail, Mt. Timpanogos

"Sam," I ask as we pedal our beautifully clean and mostly new bikes up a muddy trail, "did you see the new *Catalyst*?"

"Sure did. Greta printed our column along with letters from both of our readers."

"That's not fair," I argue. "We read it too, which makes four. But here's what I'm getting at—with all the stuff Greta prints, the feng shui, the new-age health, the yoga and Zen, where do we fit in?"

"I don't know about you, Abbott, but I'm a holistically balanced, newly aged Zen Meister."

"That's what worries me," I say. "Let me ask you about that Zicam gel you gave me yesterday for my cold. It says on the box that it's homeopathic medicine. In my experience living with Anthroposophists at the University of Tübingen, that means that the active ingredient is mixed one part to a hundred with an inert agent. Then one part of the new mixture is mixed with a hundred parts of the inert agent. That's repeated, with careful attention to the rhythms of the mixing, until the active ingredient all but disappears. My German friends seem otherwise intelligent, but treating an illness with an absence strikes me as nuts. You're a card-carrying scientist. How can you fall for snake oil like that?"

"Slow down, pardner," Sam says. "There really is an active ingredient in Zicam, and there's an interesting idea behind the medicine. The zinc in this nasal delivery is thought to hook onto viral receptors in nasal passage cells and block the attachment and multiplication of viral particles."

"We've got viral receptors?" I ask incredulously. "What kind of intelligent design is that?"

"They're likely cellular receptors for other things as well," Sam explains patiently. "But they can also be used by viruses."

"So what else does the zinc block besides viruses? The Zicam won't affect my libidinal or ethanol or biking receptors, will it? You haven't sabotaged me, have you?"

"That's the trouble with your lazy approach to science," Sam answers. "You're dependent on a blow-hard scientific crank like me for important information. You'll just have to sweat this one out."

21 March, Orem *(by email)*
Scott, I'm making a solstice mead for a new year—Elderberry Melancholy. This honey brew will be ready for the spring solstice a year from now. Somehow this commitment to making something beautiful to drink is cheering to me.

All in all, meads are pretty simple affairs. I heat 12 pounds of honey in 2 gallons of water to 170F and keep it there for maybe 40 minutes. I then cool it to room temperature and siphon it into a 6-gallon bucket, adding enough water to bring the incipient brew, known as "must," to 5 gallons. Finally, I add a French champagne yeast and seal the bucket with an airlock in place.

Most of the fermentation will occur over a week or two and I'll transfer the young must into a glass carboy, leaving behind some of the remnants of fermentation and impurities in the honey. I'll do this again three or four times through the spring and summer. I use glass carboys so I can enjoy the color and clarity changes. By summer, the must will be pretty clear and a light-to-medium amber color. Depending on the yeast, temperature, and water conditions, the young mead could have quite unusual flavors by this time. If it is too acid and dry, I will add a cup of honey once a week until it is pleasing. If it is too sweet, I will add an alcohol-tolerant yeast and try to get it to ferment a bit more.

When the time is right—perhaps the equinox in September—you and I will harvest some elderberries from bushes we know on a cliff edge high on the trail. I'll try for maybe five pounds of elderberries and we'll carry them down the hill in our sweaty shirts and that evening I'll pasteurize, squeeze, and add them to the aging must. Maybe another couple of months and another transfer or two, maybe some more adjustment by adding honey and I'll bottle the new mead. It will still be a bit young, but we'll gather dear friends and toast the spring equinox with elderberry mead.

It seems a long time and a lot of work to make something we won't drink for more than a year. But it's important to me. It's a connection with people who did this 20,000 years ago and, more important, it's a promise to the future. It is my way of saying that even though this is such a short trip and we can never know what might happen, we'll be here while we can and we'll gather friends for a while and we'll celebrate the beauty and ephemeral nature of our lives with a fine and ancient drink and maybe, for a while, it will be enough.

22 March, Provo *(by email)*

Sam, your description of the hows and whys of making mead is educational. But don't you think our readers deserve to know the rest of the story?

The honey you used has a history of its own, blending politics and religion in a bizarre way. Back during the Cold War, Mormon apostle Ezra Benson was Eisenhower's Secretary of Agriculture. Benson was also influential in the John Birch Society. He and other Mormon leaders told their followers to put up a two-year supply for the coming Armageddon. You and Nancy faithfully followed that council and hoarded wheat and honey and who knows what else. Now, three decades later, cut loose from religiously tinged conspiracy theories, you find you've got a mead-mine in your basement. We'll have to toast old Ezra when the mead matures.

And finally, our readers ought to know that a Celtic custom links drinking mead during the first month of marriage to the conception of a male child. That's why we call that month a honeymoon.

Thirty-One

Do You Believe in Love?

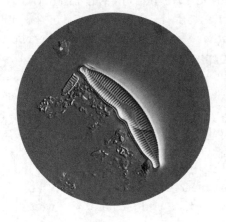

24 March, Great Western Trail, Mt. Timpanogos

"In the rush to send Greta last month's column," I tell Sam as we head up the mountain on a mild Saturday morning, "we forgot to mention the first flower of the year, *Cymopterus longipes* (Longfoot spring parsley), sighted in mid-March."

"We sure did," Sam huffs, looking along the trail for the unassuming umble, its tiny yellow flowers arrayed in what look like upturned umbrellas atop stems that elongate into pseudoscapes to crane the flowers up to vertical heights of an inch or two.

After a week of almost daily rides, Sam feels relatively good today, while I'm still fighting the tail-end of a cold. Sam rounds a corner and continues up the mountain. "We ought to see storksbill, *Erodium cicutarium*, shortly."

Two minutes later, I spot a flash of purple and stop my bike. "Sam, you're a prophet."

By the time we're done admiring the patch of fivemerous flowers, a branch of the Geranium family also called Redstem filaree, I've got my lungs back and agree, against my better judgment, to follow Sam up Frankie, a short but abrupt trail that intersects one arm of Frank. Horses in mud have chopped up the trail, and despite our new rear tires, we both spin out early and have to push the bikes up most of the trail. As we get back on, higher on the mountain than we've been since October, I have a question for Sam.

"Do you believe in love?"

"What in hell are you talking about?" he responds delicately.

"Our philosophy students just read their prize-winning essays on love," I explain, "and in the ensuing discussion I argued against any kind of 'pure' love, against 'true' love, against any Platonic absolute. One of the students quoted bell hooks to the effect that love shouldn't be a noun but a verb. I guess my point was that, noun or verb, at least in part love feels to me like something I do or feel for biological reasons. I 'love' a woman because of a biological need to propagate myself. I 'love' my children because it increases their chance for survival. I 'love' my relatives and friends because it enhances our chances for prosperity."

"You've become an even worse cynic than I thought," Sam says. "But since you raise the question, I never have thought about love in any sort of clichéd sense. I love to share experiences. I am nearly always pleased to know someone's stories. It has always been a delight for me to come to know someone because they want me to. But all kinds of nuances exist. And ego and rejection can certainly get mixed up in the deal. Many men confuse intimacy with sex. For me they are not the same, though when the two converge it can make the best possible relationship. And perhaps best of all is when two people make a story together while being very attracted to one another. I don't think I see this much. It is what Nanc and I have tried our best to do over these decades together."

"I don't mean to downplay the importance of love in my life," I counter. "I love Lyn and my children dearly. But I get tied into knots if I start wondering about 'true' love. It's like wondering about God—just a potentially dangerous dead end."

"Okay," Sam agrees. "Enough simpering. We get paid to be botanical bikers, not to write a column for the lovelorn."

25 March, Provo

On my way to Sam's for an early ride, I think again about love, make a wrong turn, and find myself in front of what used to be my house before the divorce. I had meant—after the ride—to drop off a movie for Ben and Sam and Tim, but there I am, so I get out and knock on the door. When no one answers, I leave the movie by the door and jump off the high porch with some exuberance. I find myself, inexplicably, lying in the grass clutching a collapsed knee. I don't do well with pain, but neither do I do well with humiliation. My first thought is to look around to see if any of my ex-neighbors are looking. None is, as far as I can tell, so despite the pain I get up and hobble to my car and drive the few blocks to Sam and Nancy's.

"What the hell's that limp for?" Sam greets me.

"My knee collapsed," I tell him, "on Sunday morning in front of all my ex-neighbors who I'm sure think of me as a dead-beat. *Schadenfreude* lit up the neighborhood."

"Joy at someone else's pain," Sam says. "You'll note that I know more German than the brewer's terms I use. I bet you looked swell flying through the air like a superhero and then biting the dust as if your powers had failed, which, by the way, they have. Just a second. I'll get you some ibuprofen and a knee brace and we can do our ride."

I take the pill and put on the brace and limp my way toward the garage.

"You can't get on your bike," Nancy orders. "Go home and put ice on that knee."

And so I do.

10 April, Provo

My phone rings. It's Sam.

"Hey, what did the orthopedist say? Not that I care how well you can fake a knee injury so you don't have to ride today, but Nancy said I had to call and ask."

"That's sweet of you," I reply. "He said that since last Thanksgiving when I hurt my knee playing football with my boys, I've had a Grade III Complete Tear of the Anterior Cruciate Ligament (acute) of the left knee. I fell the other day because I have no internal ligament to hold the top and bottom parts of the knee in place."

"Yeah, yeah. You also fell because of the trouble in your head. So, can you ride today?"

"Sure can. He said that my left quadricep had atrophied and

that I needed to ride a bike every day until the operation."

"Does he know you're riding the Great Western?"

"Not exactly. But here's the good news. I've been beating you up the mountain with one leg."

"You've got nothing on me," Sam says. "My right kneecap is badly damaged, as you know. I've been riding for years using my left leg. Maybe we ought to get a tandem mountain bike. You can pedal with your right leg, and I'll use my left."

15 April, Great Western Trail, Mt. Timpanogos

"The neighborhood's empty," Sam notes as we head up the hill. "Everyone's in church singing about resurrection. Doesn't truth matter?"

"The cynic triumphs over the lurking sentimentalist!" I note. "The Easter story is a good metaphor. Look at the death camas sprouting from the bulbs buried for the winter."

"I love the metaphor," Sam asserts. "But we're headed to see the resurrection live and in living color. Forget the metaphor. It reminds me of the time my corpulent bishop called me in to ask if I would be the fitness director for the ward. I had been out on a run and so had stopped by in my sweats. He made the ask, but said there were caveats: I had to pay a full ten percent of my salary to the Mormon Church in perpetuity. And I had to attend all my Sunday meetings and be civil (three full hours' worth of civil meetings—is there such a thing?). I told him (civilly) that his ass was too big and that he ought to obey the laws of health and maybe he oughta be the fitness guru himself. I kissed him goodnight and finished my run."

Ahead of us, a golden marmot slips off a rock and slips her fat body into a crevice. We cycle past a couple of little white butterflies, then a sulfur, and later a mourning cloak. Above us, two redtails turn lazy circles. A golden-red fox with a white-tipped tail bounds up a rocky hillside like a sine wave. Box elders hang heavy with blossoms. A meadowlark warbles ahead of us. Two rufous-sided towhees exchange their staccato trills. As we return to the Provo River, we hear a birdcall that reminds us of the towhees, but deeper. We're surprised to see a Steller's jay, with its black crest. Where's the usual crow-like screeching? Is this a mating call? Fun to be surprised by nature!

Thirty-Two

Just the Stuff About Your Virility

30 April, Great Western Trail, Mt. Timpanogos

A meadowlark sings us up the steepest part of our afternoon climb. There is something charming, warm, and welcoming about this natural music.

I tell Scott that yesterday morning we spent half an hour in Teasdale listening to a bird none of us could immediately recognize. Jim and Melinda suggested the song was a meadowlark, but it was sustained and rhythmically odd, not what any of the rest of us were familiar with.

"This morning," I say, "I got an e-mail from Jim suggesting our unidentified bird was indeed a Western meadowlark. He and Melinda checked the song against their new recordings of North American birds. This is heady stuff to me. Thinking all along you know something pretty well and finding out things are different than you thought. I checked on the Western meadowlark in the *Sibley Guide to Birds*: 'Voice may be the most reliable clue in identifying meadowlarks, but individual birds can learn the 'wrong' song. Listen for details of pitch and for repertoire size (Eastern male sings 50-100 songs, Western fewer than 10). A bird usually gives the same song several times before switching to another one, so extended listening is required.'"

"Seems to me like this is a pretty good framework for most situations in life," Scott responds to my long account. "You may be wrong, and extended listening is required."

5 May, Great Western Trail, Mt. Timpanogos

Sam's gone to Teasdale for the weekend. The ACL operation is coming up on the ninth. So on this sunny Saturday morning I head up the trail, hoping for the first (and last) extended ride of the spring, anticipating silence, focus, rhythm, and beauty.

Just above the Provo River, I hear a familiar high-pitched Mozartian trill and thrill to a flash of iridescent blue. Last year we saw the first lazuli bunting on May ninth, and the previous year we didn't see one till the fourteenth. I'll miss much of this spring's flora and fauna, but because he's a bit early, I won't miss this showy little blue and orange and white and black songbird. I ride steadily, easily, intent on two things: observing everything and riding as high on the mountain as I can. Trailing along the green pipe, I'm rewarded with a second sight I thought I would miss this year, the yellow blossoms of bitterbrush or cliff rose—whichever these are.

After the difficult ride over the quartzite, I'm rewarded by a second flash of blue: flax, with its stringy stems (*Linum lewisii*), named after Captain Meriwether Lewis. In Johnson's Hole, death camas bloom white on their single stalks. The ridge is steep and long, but this morning I feel like I belong here, in this smoothly working body, on this bike, on this trail. Over the hillside behind me the sun catches the mottled red-brown and green of the scrub oak—the red-brown from leaves that have just begun to open, the green shining from the tender, fully opened leaves. I try to summon a few lines from Gerard Manley Hopkins' "In Praise of Dappled Things," but it has been too long.

Painted ladies by the hundreds flit colorfully in the meadow at the top of Frank. I sit on a chunk of blue limestone and look down into Provo Canyon and farther into Utah Valley and even farther to the mountains receding in dark rows to the west.

Given my gimpy knee and the fact that I'm riding alone, I'm very careful on the way down. There is one little butt smasher when I look too long at a doe and her fawn and hit a rock with my front wheel, but before I know it I'm overlooking the mouth of the canyon.

Just above the last switchback, above what used to be an orchard, I see a fox lying on the top of a rise, sunning herself, watching the approaching bicyclist. A flash of red-gold and she's gone. When I top the rise, a sharp bark startles me. Another bark—the fox springs up onto a shelf of limestone. She barks again, and then again. With each bark, her ears flatten against her head. I bark back. The fox looks at me quizzically, barks again. I bark twice, nearly matching the high pitch, but I can't make my ears flatten. The fox climbs to a new place on the hillside and barks and barks. I bark and bark. We converse for a good while and then I leave what must be the proximity of her den to cycle back to my own den.

7 May, Great Western Trail, Mt. Timpanogos

An unexpected ride with my son Ben while Sam works late. Ben's sixteen-year-old legs and lungs give him a distinct advantage, but my plan is to keep him slow as long as I can, to take advantage of the technical sections, to underplay the advantages of my clipless pedals and fully sprung bike, and to pay plenty of attention to the flora and fauna.

Ben's a blooming biologist/geologist and a deeply curious young man, so I see the familiar trail with new eyes. I name the larkspur and flax and wallflower for him, he points out coral in the limestone for me.

After a strong ride up the initial stretches, we turn up Frank. I ride the C-turn and the chutes better than Ben (ten years of mountain-biking experience count for something), but when we pedal into the meadow at the top of Frank and I compliment Ben on how he has done, he suggests we keep going.

"Aren't your legs tired? Your lungs?" I ask.

"No," he answers.

So on we ride. This is new territory for me this year, and we're rewarded by a new set of flowers: the low, ball-headed waterleaf, the yellow flowers of arrowleaf balsamroot and, in the quiet maple grove, masses of bluebells. Finally we're high enough for the yellow Nuttall's violet and even a delicate white woodland star.

Traversing an open space almost as high as the saddle between Little Baldy and Timpanogos, I stop, legs shaking, and suggest to Ben that I've had enough. "Aren't you feeling this altitude?" I ask.

"Not really," Ben says, "but I sure enjoy riding with you. None of my friends are this good."

"You know how to make an old man happy," I say.

Down we ride, Ben twice as fast as I. At one juncture, I try to explain to him the need for caution.

"Sure Dad," he says. "I read your column."

"You don't believe all that stuff, do you?" I ask.

"Just the stuff about your virility," he says.

8 May, Great Western Trail, Mt. Timpanogos

Scott has tired legs from a long ride yesterday with his son Ben. And both of us are feeling lazy, though we agree to ride Frank.

"Get the doc to use Versed," I say to Scott as we ride along the trail among the deep blue flax. "You remember last year when I had my wisdom teeth out? The doc used Versed rather than a local and I'll be damned if it wasn't a pleasure. He inserted the tube into my arm and began counting backward. Nothing happened and I remember thinking he had administered the wrong dose. Next thing I know, Nanc is walking into the room—I swear I thought she was an angel and the most amazing feeling swept over me. I asked her if I had 'passed on.' After she assured me I was just fine, I asked her when they were going to get rid of my teeth."

"They're long gone," Nanc replied. "You've been cut open, teeth pulled out, and you don't remember a thing."

"I'll ask about it," Scott replies. "But I think they have something else in mind."

"Yup," I reply. "They're goin' to open your knee and get after it with a mini Mixmaster. And you're goin' to whine about it for months and lay off your bike as long as you can."

We approach Frank and both of us ride past without comment. This is not a trail we want to ride this afternoon.

9 May, TOSH (The Orthopedic Specialty Clinic), SLC

I nearly panic when I walk into the operating room. I feel perfectly healthy. I don't want to lay myself down on that table. I don't like the strap someone tightens over my torso. And then I'm fighting my way back to consciousness and Lyn drives me home and the recovery begins.

10 May, Provo

Dizzy with pain pills, I feel like I've been in a fight I didn't witness. Fifty-one years of good health haven't prepared me for this. Any and every shriveled, hip-replacement, geriatric case can do this better than I can. In a brace from my ankle to my groin, I have to keep the knee raised and well-iced. I'm allowed to crutch my way to the bathroom a couple of times a day.

11 May, Provo

Visits by Lyn, Sam and Nancy, my daughter Maren, my mother, and Lillian Hayes the highlights of this painful day. What the hell did they do to my shin?

12 May, Provo

Tim, Sam, Ben, and I view a videotape of the operation, taken through the arthroscopic camera the surgeon used. The drill breaks through the bone! There's my hamstring being pulled through the center of the knee, where it will serve as my new anterior cruciate ligament. The whole operation is a monument to human ingenuity. The breaks in the tape are ominous, however, like the ones in the Nixon tapes. What did the doctors edit out?

18 May, Great Western Trail, Mt. Timpanogos
Quick up and back by myself. Sweat and mood work, but no chatter with Scott. Who in hell needs him anyway?

THIRTY-THREE

Mr. Feelgood

23 May, Provo, Physical Therapy *(by email)*

Sam—I'm back! On a bike! Two weeks to the day from my surgery! Okay, it's a stationary bike at the therapist's. The calorie counter says that after ten minutes I've used four calories. I'm nowhere near being able to turn the crank all the way around (90 degrees at most). But by damn I'm sitting on a bike.

25 May, Provo, Physical Therapy *(by email)*

Sam—Day two of therapy. After a regime of ultrasound and electroshock and a torture device called GENUFLEXION invented by officers of the Catholic Inquisition, I did another ten minutes on the bike. Back and forth, stopping front and back to push the knee to flex just another fraction, back and forth, wincing like a baby, running a cold sweat. By the time the therapist rescued me, I could rotate nearly 270 degrees.

29 May, Provo, Physical Therapy *(by email)*

Red-letter day, Sam. Enough range of motion in the knee today to turn that crank around and around and around. Twenty minutes at breakneck speed. Even a few spots of sweat on my T-shirt. Grease your chain, partner!

4 June, Squaw Peak Overlook Road, Provo Canyon

While we pump up tires and spray Pedro's lubricant onto our cleats, I tell Sam about the dream I woke from this morning. "I was riding my bike through a juniper and piñon landscape, down a single track, swinging from curve to curve, in tune with the world, body and mind united. The trail led me down toward a town, but before I got there, I turned around, headed back up the single track. Even climbing I could still coast! It was like flying, easy, effortless, utterly beautiful."

"You've been off your bike too long," Sam figures.

We leave Sam's house gingerly. At least, I move gingerly. This is no stationary bike. After a block or so, the knee warms and my confidence returns and my ankle-to-groin brace recedes from consciousness. Sam is uncharacteristically solicitous, suggesting by implication that I am a half-assed weakling.

"Shall we just ride up the jogging trail along the river? Are you sure you want to cross the highway? We'll stop this ride any time you want. Do you want to go down to K-Mart and ride their mechanical horse? Only costs a quarter. Are you sure about this?"

I'm not sure about anything as we switchback up the narrow, paved road that climbs the south flank of Provo Canyon and I test my string-of-a-leg. Not sure about anything, that is, except for the lifting claustrophobia. I haven't moved through nature like this for nearly four weeks.

We hear a lazuli bunting, then spot a colorful female Western tanager. Prince's plume rises yellow from the roadside. White sego lily cups dot open hillsides. Paintbrush rises red-orange next to silver-green sage. Yellow sweet clover wafts fragrance our way as we wend (slowly) past. Scarlet gilia blazes on delicate stems, and sweet vetch, purple and white, follows us up the mountain. There's yellow wallflower, yellow bitterbrush, bushes of wild roses, and even early pink geraniums.

"Sam," I say, "I have missed this more than you can know."

"Me too," he replies. "Is this high enough? You don't want to overdo your first ride. And if you get hurt, I am the bad guy."

"This is enough," I say, turning to head back. "More than enough."

8 June, Squaw Peak Overlook Road

Ride number two, one month since the operation. I don't even have to warm up today to crank my pedals.

"You're moving faster today," Sam observes.

"Feeling stronger and more limber," I say. "The physical therapy is going well. Range of motion yesterday from three degrees to one twenty."

A half-dozen partridges burst from a pine tree and sail down into the oak brush.

"Scott," Sam says as we climb on up the mountain, "I was really disappointed by our last conversation about love. Things went south and I didn't have a chance to tell you how full of shit you are."

"I need love as much as the next guy," I reply. "But as a scientist, you surely don't deny there's a strong biological component to what we call love."

"Of course there is," Sam responds. "In animals, sex resides in parts of the brain that are impulse driven. Sex seems to be an urge to satisfy and maybe not much more. It's as primal as anger, fear, hunger or domination. Human lovers have those urges too, but there's more, much more."

"Are you hinting at the spiritual? Why isn't biology enough?"

"I like to think we make choices about whom we love and why we love them and that often such choices are beyond mere chance or lust. And I think we have the capacity for enormous love uncoupled from other needs. Furthermore, healthy people filter their impulses through their cortical areas that modify urges, impulses, domination, and so forth."

"Come on," I counter. "Love is just an idea. We make it up to make ourselves feel noble."

"You really think that's all?"

"No, not really. You know I've always fought the fear I somehow don't have the capacity for love as you're describing it. My argument stems in part from that fear. But maybe that gives me a bit of realism you obviously lack, Mr. Feelgood."

"You see," Sam says, "whenever we approach this issue, you either change the subject or lean on me as having clouded vision. You need psychological help and an enema."

We're at the fork of the road near the top. I'm stronger than on our previous ride and try to goad Sam into a race up the last climb. He matches my feeble sprint, but won't pass me.

"You condescending sonofabitch," I pant. "Show me what we can do when we're healthy. It won't hurt me."

We stand at the top, breathing the sweet, yellow scent of cliff rose, overlooking all of Utah Valley. Then, before my knee stiffens, we swoop off the mountain.

12 June, Park City, Cooley and Rosenberg Clinic

"The knee looks good," Dr. Rosenberg says. "Have you been riding a bike?"

"Sure have," I answer.

"One with toe clips?" he asks. "So you can pull up as well as push down?"

"No, I ride Speedplay pedals, 'Frogs,' with cleats on my shoes."

"On your stationary bike?" he asks, eyebrows raised.

"No, on my mountain bike."

"You've been riding your mountain bike? We're only five weeks out from your operation. We don't encourage free-wheeling till three months."

I don't mention yesterday's off-road ride—or that I've been leaving my brace at home.

13 June, Great Western Trail, Mt. Timpanogos

I'm damned if Scott and I don't ride pretty fast and hard in substantial heat up the lower loop of the Great Western to the start of Frank. Not only that, Scott turns up Frank for a go at the technical and difficult upper trail.

"Scott," I suggest from my perch on the fire road, "don't you think you're pushing it here? I'm fine to ride this and will have at it if you insist, but I think you may be making a mistake."

He turns back, claiming it was a bluff.

Five weeks out of major knee surgery. He couldn't even walk three weeks ago. Doesn't bode well for me for the rest of the summer.

15 June, New York City *(by email)*

Scott—Spent most of the day today in the Frick Museum on Fifth Avenue and 70th Street. It was my first time there. Maybe my favorite museum in New York. I'll tell you I was simply rocked back on my heels by Vermeer's "Officer and Laughing Girl." It was all I could do not to bawl as I stood in front of this painting.

The laughing girl, or at least the model for her, was smiling and free and wholly alive 400 years ago with sunlight warming her face and human connection in her heart. She was present with someone she admired, maybe loved, those years ago and I am here to live this moment with her today. Vermeer is telling us four centuries later that this moment is all there is—this moment, now. But even in the midst of the breathless light and intimacy of this painting, shadows gather. And true to Vermeer's prophecy, these two are both 400 years dead. Did they share intimate conversation? Did they kiss? Did they remember this moment from time to time? Did they think of each other? Did they love?

16 June, New York City *(by email)*

Scott—Nanc and I went to the William Blake exhibit in the Met yesterday. It's funny how sometimes you're ready for something and you don't know it. All my life I have been aware of Blake and his work, but I had considered him to be some kind of aberration—a spiritual nut of some sort with a need to countermand the prevailing wisdom of the day. Well, in some ways, that's exactly what he was. But this exhibition showed him to be so much more.

I know I'm not telling you anything new here, but it's new for me. Blake worked against the confining and circumscribing religious and scientific views of his world. One of his predominant messages was to explore and question. He wanted to find his own way. And even though his way, in my opinion, turned out to be just as wrong-headed as the other religious world-views of his day, it was the exploration and daring that counted. The guy was alive and filled with questions. Would that I were the same.

18 June, Great Western Trail, Mt. Timpanogos

"Don't you think we ought to ride the road this afternoon? Aren't you afraid of going over and screwing up your knee?"

"We'll ride slowly and carefully. Any trouble and we'll turn back," Scott replies.

As we start up the first steep reach, I am instantly grateful for Scott's fortitude. The trail is wet and thousands of sulfur and cabbage butterflies enshroud us, form a living mist around us like a solstice blessing. We are giddy as kids. We are, in fact, the grown kids we are.

A couple of steep miles later, Scott still rides hard and well. As a reward, we are again surrounded in the steep light of late afternoon sun, this time by thousands of painted lady butterflies. Lazuli buntings, spotted towhees, and western meadowlarks sing us off the mountain in the midst of the shimmering butterfly escort. I go home and find that scene in *The Voyage of the Beagle* where Darwin and friends are off the coast of Patagonia: "Even by the aid of a telescope it was not possible to see a space free from butterflies. The seamen cried out 'it was snowing butterflies,' and such in fact was the appearance."

Such in fact was our ride.

19 June, Provo *(by email)*

Sam, I'm thinking about that amazing passage from Darwin's book. It struck my fancy and triggered a memory of a book I read while teaching a graduate course on German Romanticism— Robert Richards' *The Meaning of Evolution: The Morphological Construction and Ideological Reconstruction of Darwin's Theory.* He lays out Goethe's groundbreaking science of morphology— "Form is a moving, a becoming, a passing thing. The doctrine of forms is the doctrine of transformation. The doctrine of metamorphosis is the key to all signs of nature"—and then traces Darwin's use of Goethe's ideas in the section on morphology in *Origin of Species.*

That's interesting enough by itself. But here's what I've been thinking about. Goethe was Germany's Shakespeare, his poetry and plays and novels marvels as fine as anything ever written in any language. On top of that, he was a lifelong administrator in the Principality of Weimar— little tasks like overseeing mining, public roads, public celebrations, and the University of Jena. How was he able to do real science on top of it all?

Think about it. You're a botanist. You also read more widely than anyone I know—poetry, novels, history, politics, science. But could you be an important novelist and poet? That's unthinkable. I'm a decent literary critic and I love reading about science. But expect me to make a scientific breakthrough? Forget it. I know science is more specialized than it was at the end of the eighteenth century, but I don't think that's the whole story. It's also, surely, a matter of genius.

19 June, Orem *(by email)*

Scott, neither of us is a genius. And neither of us has become the world's expert in our respective discipline. I could have been a well-known botanist if I had concentrated on that and you could have done the same among Germanists, I suppose.

Instead, we have spread our attention more broadly. We're amateurs in the sense of doing what we love. You proved that when you left Vanderbilt and told the dean you missed the scent of sage. I proved it when I turned down the invitation to join the leadership of the Botanical Society of America. And finally—I bet Goethe was no good on a mountain bike.

By the way, Thomas Kuhn, in *The Structure of Scientific Revolutions*, argues that truly remarkable paradigm-changing ideas are very rare. Perhaps just a few a century. The rest of us do 'normal' scholarly work, which is also important but not Earth-shaking. I, for example, am a normal scientist. I certainly don't rue that fact, but I have never created a thought or piece of scholarly work that has changed the world. Almost none of us has.

THIRTY-FOUR

Death Defying Act of Defiance

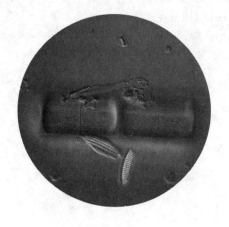

30 June, Salt Lake City *(by email)*

Sam—I just read your *Catalyst* column with Scott for last month and thought it was great. It's a pleasure to read what you guys are thinking about each month. I think you ought to change the title of your column to "Wild Rides, Wild Thoughts." David Keller

30 June, Salt Lake City *(by email)*

David—How nice of you to respond to Scott and me. I'm glad you sent your note to me which indicates you understand I am the primary writer here. I been tryin' to figure out how to get shed of Scott for a year in order to showcase my own writing abilities, but it's hard. After all, Scott's a friend of mine. But the most encouraging thing about your note was to let us know we have yet another reader. That brings us up to a total of five.

30 June, Salt Lake City *(by email)*

Sam—Your estimate of your readership is flawed. I was in the men's room at Einstein Bagels this afternoon and in one of the stalls was a copy of *Catalyst* folded open to your column. So you have at least one more reader than you thought.

30 June, Salt Lake City *(by email)*

David. They out of toilet paper at Einsteins?

8 July, Great Western Trail, Mt. Timpanogos

Our Sunday-morning ride begins just inside the mouth of Provo Canyon with a wild flurry of birdcalls, a half-dozen, loud-mouthed birds disputing the death penalty or the local ban on Sunday beer sales or the existence of God (three interrelated topics in Utah). One bird whistles three times, another caws like a magpie, another trills like a towhee, a fourth hammers like a woodpecker. The discussion is by turns harsh and sweet, loud and soft, but the exchanges are always clearly and respectfully spaced. "Maybe it's a meeting of a passerine UN," I suggest. Sam voices his own conclusion: "It's clearly a yellow-breasted chat, *Icteria virens*, that elusive and effusive warbler we first identified on this hill a couple of years ago."

The ride ends with a death-defying act of defiance. Just outside of Provo Canyon, on land that only a year ago was still an orchard, I watch Sam weave down between a behemoth backhoe, a bulldog bulldozer, a mantis-like grader, and a beerbelly water truck to plunge down a fifteen-foot slope of soft dirt, somersaulting beautifully over his handlebars. He picks himself up, dusts off his shorts, and rides off triumphantly. "Guess I showed those bastards!" he growls.

12 July, Great Western Trail, Mt. Timpanogos

Today's ride starts as a tour of yellow flowers: heavy-headed sunflowers, sticky curlycup gumweed, sharp-petaled blazing star, small-flowered buckwheat, dusky goldenrod, milky-sapped wild lettuce, and two little yellow daisies.

"The yellow flowers of mid-to-late summer make me melancholy like little else," Sam says, a refrain I have heard from him every summer for a decade.

"The thistles have gone to seed," I point out, "as have most of the grasses."

Approaching the steepest climb of this trail, Sam's mind slips from nature back to work. He tells a story of a department's intractable stupidity, of frustrated vision, of mendacity. Suddenly he accelerates up the mountain at unimaginable speed. Although I try valiantly to keep up, he gains a hundred yards on me.

"I'll curse the members of that department if I see them," I gasp at the top. My breath returns slowly and I return to the question of our work. "As frustrating as a university can be—it's a bureaucracy like every other bureaucracy, after all—I wouldn't want to work in any other profession. Did I ever tell you about my epiphany in Nassau Hall?"

"Nope," says Sam.

"You want to hear it?" I ask.

"Don't suppose I have much choice."

"That's right, you surly SOB. I had to chase your ass up the hill and now you're going to listen to my story. After I finished my graduate work, Princeton offered me a two-year lectureship. I vividly remember my first faculty meeting, held in Nassau Hall in a room that had been exposed to the elements by a British cannonball during the Revolutionary War. The University Chaplain opened the meeting with an invocation. When he asked God to 'Bless us who labor here at Thy University,' it made immediate sense to me. Any institution engaged in serious research and education is engaged in what amounts to holy work. At that moment I committed myself to the moral responsibility of good thinking and good teaching, and resolved to be an active citizen in the academy."

"Yup," Sam said. "And you were well rewarded for that at the other 'Lord's University.' Let's see if we can get down off this mountain."

13 July, Great Western Trail, Mt. Timpanogos

"I'm tired of the same route every day," I tell Sam as we ride along the green pipe. "Let's ride up over the quartzite today, along the ridge."

"You're not wearing your brace," he points out.

"And you're not wearing your helmet," I counter.

Sam leads the way up the narrow trail. I swing onto it just behind him, thinking how often we have fallen here, remembering the T-shirt I once shredded sliding down the gravelly decline on my back. Before I know it, I'm too far to the left and the trail disintegrates beneath my front tire. My left foot unlatches from the pedal (thank Speedplay for the life-saving cleats!)—but that's not the leg I want to be hopping on! Hop I do, however, awkwardly, dragging my bike till I swing over and slide the rest of the way on my left shoulder. I lie there for a moment, waiting for pain in my newly reconstructed knee, and am relieved to find pain only in my shoulder. Lucky for me, I'm wearing a tank top today and have ripped nothing but my flesh.

14 July, Great Western Trail, Mt. Timpanogos

"I've been readin' the damndest book," I tell Scott. A small reddish doe creeps along the side of the hill above us, thinking she is out of our sightline. She is graceful and slow, nodding deeply with each step. "Do you remember the *New Yorker* article by Andrew Solomon on depression? I think it was called 'Anatomy of Melancholy.' Now he has published a book-length version called *The Noonday Demon*."

"Hell yes, I remember the article," Scott replies. "It was a shock to me this guy could write like that while he feels the way he does—that he could write at all."

"If we get home today, I'll send you his first paragraph and you'll see what I mean."

Later that Afternoon *(by email)*

Scott—here it is:

Depression is the flaw in love. To be creatures who love, we must be creatures who can despair at what we lose, and depression is the mechanism of that despair. When it comes, it degrades one's self and ultimately eclipses the capacity to give or receive affection. It is the aloneness within us made manifest, and it destroys not only connection to others but also the ability to be peacefully alone with oneself. Love, though it is no prophylactic against depression, is what cushions the mind and protects it from itself. Medications and psychotherapy can renew that protection, making it easier to love and be loved, and that is why they work. In good spirits, some love themselves and some love others and some love work and some love God: any of these passions can furnish that vital sense of purpose that is the opposite of depression. Love forsakes us from time to time, and we forsake love. In depression, the meaninglessness of every enterprise and every emotion, the meaninglessness of life itself, becomes self-evident. The only feeling left in this loveless state is insignificance.

14 July, Provo *(by email)*
Sam, I'm on my way to the bookstore to pick up a copy of Solomon's book on the basis of the first paragraph alone. I think I could believe in a love that has depression as its flaw.

14 July, Provo *(by email)*
Scott—You know, reading this book is both a revelation and a memory for me. The lines written about the abortion rights attorney Janet Benshoof, for instance: "She is by any standards an impressive person—well read, articulate, attractive, funny and unpretentious…Utterly self-possessed, she spoke of the depressions that laid her impossibly low. 'My accomplishments are the whalebones in a corset that allows me to stand up; without them, I would be a heap on the floor.'"

I have had these feelings. I revel in this honesty. Jesus, man, I may not have her accomplishments, but I understand the sentiment completely. What is it that drives us like this? What is it that makes us need more and more and more? Where does a guy find the "LEMME OFF" button?

This book by Solomon is a treasure, though the pieces of gold are made of zinc. This book is a message I have been waiting for, though it is the wrong message. I want to know how to get past depression! I want to hear success stories. I want to LIVE like I have never been able to live. I want to BE. I am not afraid of death. I am afraid of insignificance and of being afraid. I am thrilled that Solomon's dad made it his life's work to save his son. Both of them have given us a great gift.

14 July, Provo *(by email)*

Sam, I've been reading Solomon, and the rest is as good as that first paragraph. When he writes about love as ameliorating depression, I'm almost willing to take back the nasty stuff I said about you as a simpering romantic. Your enthusiasms are antidotes to lurking depression. As for how to find the "LEMME OFF" button, you're asking the wrong guy.

Solomon has me thinking back over the last year. So many big changes. Despite the fact that I chose them all, depression lurks constantly as the grand prize. I don't know what the hell I would have done without our rides.

15 July, Great Western Trail, Mt. Timpanogos

Muttering something about my delicate knee, Sam won't ride the quartzite today, so we head up the fire road instead. A fox flashes red in front of us, not much more than the curved line of a body and a bushy tail at this distance. Just below us, a marmot chirps like crazy at the fox's proximity. The fox stops to listen to the marmot. A gunshot cracks from the firing range across the canyon and the fox jumps, whirls, and is gone.

16 July, Great Western Trail, Mt. Timpanogos

My son Ben rides with us today, lean and strong and young. Sam, no longer young, has been on clear liquids since noon in preparation for a colonoscopy tomorrow morning. Ben and I try to engage him in conversation, but it's not till he has beat us to the top, Ben by a few lengths, me by a hundred yards, that he'll reply.

"I can't let someone lean me over a sawhorse and thread a telescope up my ass," Sam complains. "Imagine the doc calling Marge and Sally over for a look."

"I guess at your age and with your family history," I say, "you've really got to do it. And think what a good story it will make for the column. By the way, Greta sent me an email after my surgery hoping my knee was okay."

"Sure, Abbott," Sam growls, "a guy gets sympathy for a torn ACL, but there's no such thing as a sympathy card from our editor saying HOPE YOUR ASSHOLE IS OKAY."

"True," Ben chimes in. "That's the card they send to your wife."

THIRTY-FIVE

Nurses

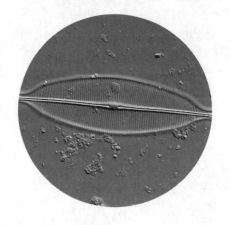

25 July, Fairbanks, Alaska *(by email)*

Sam—I'm visiting Lyn's sister and brother-in-law, Michele and David Light. They live on a beautiful ridge outside of Fairbanks. The nearly twenty hours of sunlight each day has given me plenty of time to contemplate geologic patience in the face of human exploitation.

The Chena River runs through Fairbanks, past Pike's Landing and the Pump House and other establishments on whose decks we sip Alaska's best and watch the afternoon slip by. But drive up any valley outside Fairbanks and you'll find entire fertile river bottoms pillaged and raped by gold dredges. There are thousands of massive, moribund, dead-end, water-filled trenches. Monstrous rows of fist-sized rocks stripped of every organic particle stretch fifteen feet high along the trenches for miles and miles and miles. Second-growth aspen and spruce now cover the surrounding hills, but photos only fifty years old show raw, clear-cut ridges in every direction.

How, Sam, did human beings justify this lasting violence?

The answer, I suppose, has to do with belief systems. Remember that statement by Alexis de Tocqueville I ran across in Vienna, that "When God decided not to give the capacity for civilization to the original inhabitants of America, he destined them to certain decline. The true owners of this continent are those who know how to use its riches." With this kind of "Christian" thinking, the dredging of Alaska was inevitable. The caption to a photo of a gold dredge in the Alaskaland museum states that "because gold lies between 8 and 200 feet below levels of frozen muck, moss and rock, dredges must be used..." I try to imagine another sentence: *Because gold lies below delicate tundra and ancient permafrost, we'll leave it there.*

And, it seems we haven't learned anything from the ruined landscape. Last winter, talking about oil potential in the Arctic National Wildlife Refuge, Alaskan Senator Frank Murkowski held up a blank sheet of paper and said, "This is what the Alaskan coastal plain looks like most of the year, not like the American Serengeti environmentalists portray."

28 July, Fairbanks, Alaska *(by email)*

Sam—We drove out to an old dredge this morning and David, who works for Caterpillar installing and repairing diesel engines and electrical turbines in villages all over the state, gave us an engineer's tour of the slowly disintegrating hulk. "Look at how carefully these wires have been bundled and hand-tied," he said, opening an electrical box. "These huge I-beams acted as pivots for the dredge. Ingenious, don't you think?" David had a comprehensive and historical picture in his mind of how all the levers and pulleys and belts and wheels and gears and buckets and drums worked to dredge up huge quantities of rock and mud and sift it for gold. "See how the rivets gradually give way to welding beads as welding became more reliable," David pointed out. "You can get a history of twentieth-century technology on this dredge."

It's the damndest thing, Sam. You have to admire the ingenuity of the men who designed and worked these monsters, men like David, whose minds can encompass big mechanical systems that serve practical purposes. But then your mind floats back to the natural calamity and you can't even comprehend that the U.S. Smelting, Refining, and Mining Company did all this damage for $125 million worth of gold.

A final warning, partner: I'm returning with even more belly than I left with. Michele has fed us red salmon (which she dipnetted the day before in the Chitna River), stir-fry with bear meat (traded for moose meat from David's bow hunt), clam linguini made from clams Michele dug, and all washed down with her cranberry wine. In her spare time, Michele is a full-time nurse. Do these long days make people superhuman?

2 August, Salt Lake City *(by email)*

Scott—OK, after your description of the wreck of an entire landscape, I'll describe the dredging of a single anal sphincter. I finally got a colonoscopy. After canceling my first two appointments at the last minute, I called the butt-telescope center and made another appointment, followed all of the requirements, took all of the preparatory "shit-your-intestines-out" stuff, and altogether acted like an adult. Clear liquid diet (it took me a while to find a couple of my homebrews I could see through). I've had worse suppers.

Showed up this morning bright and early after fasting, purging, and all of the other psychomedical demands. Met the in-charge nurse, who escorted me into a changing room and asked me to change into a hospital gown. I sat on the floor, pulled off my boots, dropped my Levis, put on the gown, and walked out into a room of nurses, all chuckling.

"Oh hon," one of the nurses chirped, "you've made our day, but your gown is too small and it's on backwards. It's supposed to open in the back."

"Well ma'am," I respond, "it must not take much to make your day, but I'm glad to have cheered some of you up. I'll go back in and get the damn thing on right."

Ten minutes later, I'm lying in a bed wondering how in hell I'm going to get back to campus for a 2:00 meeting.

First of all, they had the wrong scope set up. They were arranged to do a look down my throat and had the scope with "lips" ready. I allowed as how that might be interesting to use for the colonoscopy, but now that there's a Utah porn czar they might find themselves in terrible trouble if they used that device on the wrong end of a guy.

"We're not going to put you out," a nurse tells me. "The level of Versed we'll use will allow you to watch the whole procedure."

"Oh that's swell," I respond. "I've always wanted to look up my own butt."

She was right. I was awake throughout and watched on a monitor as they cut chunks of tissue out of my ass—a few polyps growing on my colon. As I watched, I thought, "This ought to hurt but I'll be damned if I can feel anything. I wonder if those little bastards are malignant."

Later, I spoke with the doc and the nurses and they thought everything looked pretty good. The pathologist's report was fine—no malignancy, no bleeding, no inflammation. So, no cancer of the colon—a disease that claimed my mother, vigorous and alive at age sixty-seven, twenty years ago.

So, pardner, go get a telescopic look up your ass. You're old enough and it isn't as bad as you think. But put your gown on the right way to start with. You most likely wouldn't get the same kind of fine reception I got.

11 August, Saint Mary's Hospital, Grand Junction, Colorado
(by email)

Sam—Lots of e-mails this month, and only a few rides. But I'm just back from a three-hour ride on the Tabeguache Trail just south of town and I thought you would be interested. My sister Carol was in a head-on collision between Green River and Price when a car drifted into her lane. I'm in Grand Junction with her for most of the week. The good news is that she didn't die. The bad news is that she looks like a giant bruise punctuated by tubes and pins and staples. She's got broken feet, kneecaps, pelvis, hip, and elbow. There's a long incision snaking up past her navel through which internal repairs were made, and she's got staples in her scalp. The good news is she will recover. The bad news is that a child in the other vehicle was killed.

Yesterday one of Carol's fine nurses told me about the Tabeguache Trail after I mentioned that my bike was in the back of my car (fortunate accident!). The trail stretches over 100 miles from Grand Junction to Montrose, Colorado, rising up out of the Colorado River Valley onto a plateau, knifing through canyons and climbing mountains. Today, while Carol's sons, Tyler and Dustin, played cards with her, I drove across the river, parked at the trailhead, and rode a piece of the trail.

After the cold and sterile hospital, the hot badlands I rode through at the beginning felt like paradise (the nurse said they were dotted with sego lilies in the spring). As I gained altitude, I entered a familiar piñon/juniper forest—familiar, I thought, from my childhood on the south end of this landscape in Farmington, New Mexico. On that cue, a rope-tailed, yellow-headed lizard ran from under my front tire, a collared lizard—we called them "mountain boomers" as kids.

I climbed for maybe an hour, utterly alone and my mind emptied, leaving only the rhythms of the bike and the difficulties of the trail. At the top of the bluff, overlooking a canyon stretching down to the west, I saw another trail. My water was almost gone, my knee a little shaky, but the trail called and down into the canyon I went. Two hours later, I wheeled up to my car, parched and tired and happy.

22 August, Great Western Trail, Mt. Timpanogos

Scott and I are both riding in our heads today. Chatter is about how to solve problems at the university. We nearly miss the first changing maple leaves across the canyon, just below an impressive outcropping of Great Blue Limestone.

We top our hard reach and hit a quick pace along a high fire road. We round a bend near our elderberry patch and it has been cleaned—not a single berry is left. The culprit is easily seen—a fat squirrel nearby has scurried out of the elderberries and up a bigtooth maple. It's her domain and we don't begrudge her the fruit. But damn, where are we going to get the elderberries for our winter mead?

23 August, Great Western Trail, Mt. Timpanogos

The trail is nearly silent now as summer ends, a cricket here or there, no bird songs, no cicadas. "The exuberance of summer is waning," I say.

"As is the exuberance of our lives," Sam opines.

THIRTY-SIX

Stories I'll Tell at Your Funeral

26 August, Great Western Trail, Mt. Timpanogos

"You can feel it," Sam says. "The first bite of cold that will soon have us thankful for tights and gloves." Just inside the canyon, we stop at the old homestead for a first taste of mouth-puckering-sour blue plums. How is it possible that something this sour can transform into sweetness?

"Woke up this morning thinking about our friend Gene England," Sam says as we continue up the mountain. "The memorial service yesterday was full of contradictions as big as Gene's life. Why, for instance, did he remain loyal to a church that despised his thinking? His mind and writing were way too big for the narrow and clogged waters of a more-and-more timid and confining religion."

"And now he's gone," I puff, fighting my way up a steep little hill. By this time, we're high on the fire road. My repaired knee feels strong and my lungs aren't scorched and the early sun glances in and out as we turn sharp corners. A final turn brings us to the overlook where Utah Valley stretches north and south far beneath us. Cars cluster around churches. The morning breeze out of the canyon tugs at our do-rags and shorts.

"I'm already thinking of the stories I'll tell at your funeral," I tell Sam just before we dive off the hill.

"I'll outlive you by ten years," Sam hollers over his shoulder. "And besides that, I am not going to have a funeral, and besides that, even if I did have a funeral, I would never let you speak!"

27 August, Great Western Trail, Mt. Timpanogos

Short and quick ride this afternoon after interminable meetings—meetings about planning future meetings, meetings to review past meetings. I got to campus this morning and my assistant had smothered my calendar, blocking out lost hours filled with appointments. Our rides this year feel more precious than ever—hours stolen from the duties of professional bullshitters.

"Scott," I say as we ride through the flour dust of the new development on the orchard ground, "does it sometimes feel to you like we are mired in minutia when life is so short and precious? Maybe that Cat driver over there has a better idea—work a shift, turn the sonofabitch off right where it stops at five p.m., and go home."

"Trouble is," Scott replies, "we like the people we work with. We like ideas and books. We can't live without good, strong argumentative colleagues and students pushing us with well-thought, experience-based conversation."

"Ok, I can see that," I reply, "but damn it, I have carpel tunnel today from signing endless forms and dead brain syndrome from meetings. I have taken to wearing a napkin tucked in my neck so I don't drool on my shirts and dark glasses so people can't see my glazed eyes."

2 September, Great Western Trail, Mt. Timpanogos

The new semester has upset our riding schedule, but here we are on another gorgeous Sunday morning, just before noon, scrambling up the loose, steep, oak brush-lined trail we call Frankie. That we are even attempting this is a testimony (it's Sunday morning, so I can use that word) to the strength of our riding this morning, fueled in part by warm, sweetening Potawatomi plums the size and shape of testicles—the root metaphor for "testimony."

Frankie's steepest chute wins this morning's contest, as usual. Pulling my bike and myself out of the embracing oak brush, I look up at a grassy patch and catch my breath. "What's that?" I ask my attendant botanist, pointing at a trinity of bright green, wispy plants as tall as I am and hung with bright red berries. "Did I hit my head? Is this an epiphany?"

"Well I'll be damned," Sam says, "it's asparagus. Sort of out of their habitat on this high dry slope. *Asparagus officinalis,* an introduction from Eurasia. It's a member of the Lily family, like the Sego Lily we see on this same slope in the spring. What a fine sight!"

What a sight indeed, I think as we soar up and down and along the narrow trail toward the mouth of the canyon. We ride the same trail week in, week out for ten years, and every time we discover some wonder, see some new slant of light.

7 September, Great Western Trail, Mt. Timpanogos

The taste of hot, sweet plums still in my mouth, I look down at something moving slowly across the trail. A large wasp, its body gleaming coal black, its single wing bright orange. The colors and forms are breathtaking, but what catches Sam's attention is the determination of the crippled creature.

"Born to fly. Big and dangerous. A glorious summer in its past. And here it is, one wing gone, moving purposefully along, even though it's easy pickin' for a dozen predators and likely won't last the afternoon."

Higher on the trail, overlooking Utah Valley, we stand and wait for our hearts to slow. Three black-and-white, narrow-winged birds slice above the oak brush fifty yards west of us. They circle once back over us, head north, and are gone in a heartbeat.

"White-throated swifts," Sam says. "*Aeronautes saxatalis*, likely the same birds we saw here two years ago—they tend to return to past nesting sites after wintering in Central America."

12 September, Great Western Trail, Mt. Timpanogos

Like everyone else, we are in awe at the events in New York and Washington yesterday. The public spectacle of disaster and horror is impossible to process. We ride fast and hard, seeing nothing, pushing our bodies to take the edge off the sights we have seen on television.

"Ideologies!" I spit at Scott when we stop for a blow. "The idea of being so tied to a belief system that you could kill *en masse* is incomprehensible to me."

"The terror, the fear, the helplessness," Scott replies, "remind me of the NATO stealth bombers blasting cruise missiles into my friend Žarko's mother's apartment complex in Belgrade."

"The frenzy will build until there's a groundswell demand to respond with violence and damn the consequences. And hatred for Islam will increase in our country. Wish we could consider a more thoughtful response, trying to understand, and search for causes. Don't suppose W and Cheney will take that route."

"It's a shitty deal," Scott adds. "I don't know what will come of it, but you can be sure it will be bad." He points at the flowering rabbit brush. "Fertile and hopeful and golden and pungent as hell. That's my ideology."

16 September, Great Western Trail, Mt. Timpanogos

We have other stuff to do today but neither of us wants to pass a Sunday ride, another chance to work off some of the effects of this past week's events.

Across the canyon, a massive exposure of Great Blue Limestone shaped like an upturned woman's breast (a telling identification for Dr. Rorschach!) is mostly black, backlit in the coming light. Misty light streams down both sides, highlighting the red maples in Pole Canyon. The sun tips the limestone with a blazing nipple and slides above the horizon to fill the canyon with light.

"Damn!" Scott whispers. "And look how the color of the limestone changes from black to grey to blue as the sun spills down the slope."

"It's enough to give a guy religion," I suggest quietly.

19 September, Great Western Trail, Mt. Timpanogos

"Look at the blue limestone this evening," I tell Sam. "The light is beginning to slant in from the south, the maples are fading from red to rust, and the limestone has taken on a grey-brown cast. It couldn't be more different from Sunday morning."

"That's true," Sam replies. "This time of year, the light takes on a different texture for me—makes me feel loss, brings on my autumn melancholia, reminds me of all my lost friends, my foibles, and the coming darkness."

"These colors," I say as we snap our cleats back onto the pedals and head on up the trail, "the ever-changing light on the limestone, cheers me. After the nineteen red, white, and-blue flags we passed on your block alone, after the jingoistic patriotism you simply can't escape right now, the geological solidity and beauty and grandeur of that fold of limestone in the shifting light eases my soul."

23 September, Great Western Trail, Mt. Timpanogos

"The bull thistles," Sam says, "blasted and torn and gone to seed, are still putting on a new purple flower here and there. Life's not necessarily over for an old guy."

"The Dalmatian toadflax are sporting a few new flowers too," I add. "And we're still seeing buckwheat, several little yellow composites, a bright purple 'daisy,' a few wisps of yellow sweet clover, remnants of curlycup gumweed, and sunflowers. The yellow matchweed is bright and new for fall, just before it turns cold. I love this time of year."

"Hey," Sam says, "look at the tumbleweed! Russian thistle (*Salsola kali*)."

I look down at the familiar spiny branches, look back at Sam, and ask, "So what?"

"So what? Look at the flowers."

"I don't see any flowers."

"The pink. Look closely. Little solitary pink flowers in the leaf axils, protected by sharp spines."

When I look more closely (isn't this always the case?) a whole world opens up. Tucked into branches are hundreds of the tiny flowers that give the tumbleweeds a colorful pink cast.

"Each of those plants will produce up to 200,000 seeds," Sam tells me, "which it will then deposit all over creation, tumbling in the wind. These weren't even introduced from Eurasia till the late nineteenth century, and already they are everywhere."

"As are patriotic European Americans," I note as we ride off into an earlier sunset than we've been used to.

THIRTY-SEVEN

Transcendental Balance

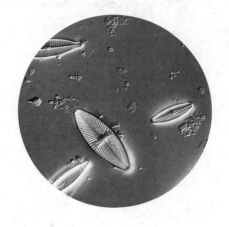

30 September, Great Western Trail, Mt. Timpanogos

On the last Sunday in September, we enter the mouth of Provo Canyon and turn up the trail to the north. We're looking forward to the tart taste of plums on our tongues, but when we leave our bikes and walk over to the line of trees we find not a trace of the cobalt-blue beauties that were still bending branches the last time we were here. Grinning at us from a high branch is a fat squirrel.

"Little bastard," Sam spits. "First the elderberries, now the plums!" He picks up a pebble and flips it toward the squirrel. "Who invited you to the banquet?"

Plum out of luck, we head up the trail. I tell Sam about Lyn's and my trip to Great Basin National Park, about the dense, smooth wood of the ancient bristlecones (*Pinus longaeva*) and the sharp wind arcing out of the Nevada basins across the ridge leading up to Wheeler Peak.

"But the real revelation," I say, "came at the Border Inn just before we reentered Utah. After feeding coins into an old slot machine for who knows how long, hypnotized by the turning cylinders, I watched a fat seven drop into place, then a second, and finally a third. Three red sevens across the line, as pretty as you please. The machine went crazy announcing my luck – *ding ding ding ding ding ding*. I sat there, happy as a medieval philosopher experiencing time standing still, the proverbial *nunc stans*, the 'now standing,' a moment of perfection, eternity carved out of ephemeral temporality."

"I'll be a son-of-a-temporal-bitch," Sam replies. "So how much was the jackpot?"

"Sixty dimes," I answer as we swing up over the quartzite. "Put in fifteen dollars and got back six—and a revelation of order and meaning."

"I'd spend nine bucks to get that," Sam replies. "But you gotta watch those endorphin rushes. You could get hooked on this kind of magic."

Sam climbs ahead, through loose rock, past a protruding root, up and over a big rock onto the tricky slide. My back tire slips in the scree, then again, and a third time. With no forward momentum, with no grasp of the trail, I come to a standstill. Somehow, miraculously, I'm balanced perfectly—absolutely still, unmoving, suspended. My tire catches a firm piece of trail and lurches me forward onto the protruding root and over onto my back in the oak brush, bike still attached to my cleats, rising, wheels first, into the blue sky. "I achieved transcendental balance," I shout to Sam. "Unfortunately, it's not compatible with mountain biking."

"Haul your ass out of the brush if you can," Sam says. "You've obviously hit your head."

"Sam," I say as we swing up the ridge skirting Johnson's Hole, "remember our disagreement about Gao Xingjian's novel *Soul Mountain*?"

"Sure," Sam answers. "We argued about the wandering narrator's string of erotic encounters. You thought his risking those relationships, however short they were, was an attempt at hopeful intimacy. I saw the same encounters as proof of failed intimacy. But why are you thinking about that now?"

"I was thinking about how productive it is to bring two perspectives to bear on an issue, how revealing dialogue is, how fun it has been to see this trail for a decade through your eyes as well as mine."

"Yup," Sam replies.

7 October, Great Western Trail, Mt. Timpanogos

A beautiful Sunday morning, streets traffic-free, trails empty, the sun bright and warm—all anyone could want in an early autumn morning. God bless those church-going Mormons.

The maples are marvelous in red after a late season drought—

a few red leaves color the trail that is still an inch thick in fine dust. The oaks remain green, though golden and orange tints tip the leaves in some patches. Golden box elders, one of our three Utah native maples, snake brilliantly up some of the draws.

We ride up over our old nemesis, the steep quartzite. It still shocks me Scott is able to ride like he does a couple of months after his surgery. He makes the ride with seeming ease, though I know the cost. I'm off early, try again, off again, try again, off again. The trail owns me.

"Damn," I blow as I catch up to Scott, "how'd you do that? You looked so smooth."

"I'll pay for it the rest of the day," Scott replies.

We continue along the trail and turn up Frank—our first attempt since Scott's knee work.

"We likely can't do this," Scott says, "but let's give it a try."

"I think we ought to wait a while longer," I shout as Scott disappears around the first curve. So it's a matter of playing catch-up again.

It's a deep pleasure to be on this trail. We both ride better than we expect and climb past our usual meadow stop to an overlook we named "Nude Knob" after surprising sun worshipers there a few years ago. We pass a tall lupine, green as June and in full flower among its dry and fruiting peers—showy, hopeful, and brash.

Scott pries open one of the lupine fruits. "Mmmm," he says. "Smells like fresh peas."

"Lupine is mildly poisonous," I add, touching my tongue gingerly to the inside of the pod, "and it doesn't taste like peas!"

Pleased with ourselves, we set our sweaty butts into the dry, yellow grasses and look over the valley. We notice only four distinct sounds: the wind in the drying maple leaves, a lone chickadee, a cricket, and a single cicada song.

14 October, Great Western Trail, Mt. Timpanogos

Mostly sunny today, but clouds create shadows that change the light continually as we climb. The maples are gorgeous and the oak leaves have begun their chromatic transformation. My chain breaks and we stop along a ridge top beneath Great Blue Limestone ledges on Timpanogos.

When I'm done with the chain tool, I still have a stiff link and try several methods to get the chain to move freely. Scott says, "That's a fine example of the scientific method at work. Formulate a hypothesis, try an experiment, and test the results."

"Nah," I reply. "I confabulated all the experimental possibilities. I said a little prayer as I fixed the chain. We'll never know if the working chain resulted from experimentation or divine intervention."

21 October, Great Western Trail, Mt. Timpanogos

"Look at the new patches of red on the mountainside," I tell Sam as we ride along. "Too red, almost maroon, to be maples. Almost a sumac red."

"I'm not sure what it is," Sam admits.

We round a corner and the answer glows red in front of us. Good-sized dense bushes with small, newly red leaves.

"*Rhus trilobata*—Skunkbush, Lemonade Sumac!" Sam exclaims. "It's a member of the Sumac family, as are mangoes, pistachios and cashews." Sam abandons a description of malodorous leaves to try out his new back tire on the loose rocks leading up over the quartzite. The rubber knobs dig in beautifully and up he climbs, around one curve, past the root, onto the quartzite. Without apparent cause, his front tire jerks to the left and he falls in slow motion, downhill, shoulders and back taking the first blow, his bike swinging over him and then under as he somersaults down the rocks, banging his hip and elbows and knees.

"Did you hurt the bike?" I shout down to him.

Not badly, it turns out. Three broken spokes, which Sam, bleeding only from one elbow, wraps around adjoining spokes so we can continue the ride.

In the late-afternoon light, the cliffs of blue limestone just inside the canyon catch light and shadow like grey-blue drapery. Timp's flank stretches east to west like colorful kilim tapestry. High above Utah Lake, we stop to admire the crystal-clear valley.

"Just bought my son Ben Goethe's novel *Wilhelm Meister's Apprenticeship*," I tell Sam. "He read the first chapter aloud to me as we drove home, the great scene where Marianne comes home from the theater to declare that, for the two weeks until her rich suitor returns, she will not play the role required by society but will be herself, the person she chooses to be, the lover of the unfledged Wilhelm Meister. There at the turn of the eighteenth century, I told Ben, a new sense of self is emerging, a self that can unfold botanically, rather than molded to fit religious and social norms."

"You've got great kids," Sam says. "And that story is pretty interesting to me. Nanc and I have been talking about Rembrandt's 'The Anatomy Lesson' this past week. In a way, it's a similar story. Leaving medieval thinking behind, Rembrandt may be painting about the possibility and power of the individual. Look at this body! the painting seems to say. Don't suppose the body is some way because a philosopher or churchman said so. Each of us can come to truth and understanding without authority interpreting for us."

"I like that," I say. "And by the look of your bloody elbow, we had better get you down off this mountain so you don't end up on the table of some anatomy lab."

Sam dives off the hill and I holler after him: "Easy on the spokes."

THIRTY-EIGHT

Life's Essential Injustice

19 October, Cedar City, Southern Utah State University

Last night we rode south in David Keller's Audi Quattro for the Utah State Board of Regents meeting this morning. It's a honey of a car, except the German engineer must have been five feet tall. After the three-hour drive, I stepped out of the car's back seat and my stiff knee buckled. This morning, it's swollen. Now, after an hour's meeting in which the Regents voted to okay our four-year Philosophy degree and the division of Sam's Physical Science Department into three departments, Chemistry, Earth Science, and Physics, we drive back north. Good news for the College. Bad news for the knee.

19 October, Utah Valley State College *(by email)*

Scott—got home after the Regent's meeting in time to make the scholarship ball at the college. Nanc has shopped for a gown for the past coupla weeks and found a form-fitting, black, backless, halter-top dress that takes my breath.

I bought a new sport coat for the dance, but when I see Nanc's gown I head to the tux shop and rent a full-blown, brand-new European tux complete with patent-leather shoes, and a lace-front shirt. I haven't been this dressed since Nanc and I went to the high school junior prom 35 years ago. Nanc can really dance, as can our friends Frank (architect) and Lucille (Vice President for Academic Affairs). I stumble through, but it's worth it. Jeez, what a woman to be with and what company to share. In the hall, low-light and midnight, Frank and Lucille tango. By god, they sizzle.

20 October, Provo

"No Sam, I can't ride today. The knee's still swollen from Keller's Audi and hurts like hell."

"Shit. One little twitch and you're off your bike. Delicate sonofabitch."

21 October, Orem

Been workin' out in the gym every morning at six a.m. Half an hour on the weights and thirty to forty-five minutes on an elliptical trainer or stationary bike. Two reasons for not telling Scott. First, I'll nonchalantly kick his ass when we get back on the bikes. Second, workin' out in the gym is shit—not nearly as interesting as bantering about anything and everything with Scott. He's smart and a helluva friend, but I'll be damned if I'll breathe a word of that to him.

5 November, UVSC Campus

"Okay Sam," I say through a bite of enchilada, "I've pampered the knee for two weeks, iced it, wrapped it, let it rest. It's no better, and in fact, on Saturday, when I stepped down a step after walking for ten minutes, the sudden pain from the outside of the knee left me gasping."

"So you've made an appointment with your doctor?" Sam asks.

"No," I answer. "I can't go to Rosenberg and tell him I injured my knee riding in an Audi. I've decided to get back on the bike. Can you ride this afternoon?"

"Nope. I'm not riding with you again until you've seen your doctor. You've screwed up your knee good. I'm not being solicitous here, just don't want you to come back whining in two weeks that I made you ride and permanently ruined your knee."

"Okay, what can I say. But I hope the damn thing's hurt bad. If he doesn't order another operation I'll forever be a whiner."

"Don't worry about that," Sam reassures me. "The word's out already."

13 November, Park City, Utah

Rosenberg assesses my knee with practiced fingers. "Still a bit of swelling," he says. "About the same as your last visit." He probes the sides of the knee, asks about pain, listens to my account of riding in the Audi. "Muscle pain, most likely," he surmises. "Back off your rehab just a little, come back in three months."

"That's not going to satisfy my partner in crime," I plead. "Wouldn't I be better off with another operation?"

"Triple your glucosamine/chondroitin intake," he says. "That's the best I can do for you."

That afternoon, Sam and I scale the slope of Timpanogos (is this the thousandth time?). I tell him my story.

"Good enough," he says, as we stand at the top overlooking the thick, smoggy air filling Utah Valley. "Aren't you glad you saw Rosenberg!"

"The main thing I'm glad about today," I answer, "is that my son Joe just adopted a six-pound baby boy. He and Tracy will call the little tyke Jacob."

14 November, Great Western Trail, Mt. Timpanogos

Four p.m., sun dropping quickly toward the black line of the Oquirrh Mountains. We wheel up the mountain, happy to break a sweat. A small herd of deer bounds across the trail and disappears in thick oak brush. The valley below us is brown with dense smog.

"A cold winter will be bad news for this valley," Sam observes. "Inversions aplenty."

Higher on the trail, Timpanogos rising sharply into the sky above us, we spot a perched kestrel, bobbing its tail, looking out through its multicolored mask. "I read recently that in England they call kestrels wind-hovers. Prettier than chicken hawk, don't you think?"

"Remember when we used to see two kestrels here?" Sam asks. "I wonder if something happened to the other one? Do they mate for life? We ought to look that up. And, by god yes, wind-hover is beautiful."

The Birder's Handbook says that among the American Kestrels (*Falco sparverius*) "promiscuous matings occasionally occur before monogamous bonds form." On the opposite page, there's an essay on size and sex in raptors. Males are larger in most birds than females, but in many raptors, like kestrels, there is "reversed sexual size dimorphism." Why are the females larger than the males in these species? the author asks. In raptors that pursue sluggish prey, the difference is less pronounced, but in those that hunt birds, females may be half again as heavy as males. But why?

The first possibility is that the greater size allows females to protect themselves from aggressive males equipped with sharp talons and beaks and a killer instinct.

"If that's true," Sam says, "human females sure as hell ought to be larger than males."

Another hypothesis is that the different sizes may allow the males and females to hunt different prey and thus reduce competition for food. But if this is true, the author asks, why aren't males sometimes the larger of the two? Perhaps, he answers, it's because the female needs larger reserves to produce eggs.

"I love watching scientists at work," I say. "Careful observation and then creative thinking to explain what they observe. You guys are in a good profession."

"I used to be a scientist," Sam says wistfully. "I even practiced this sort of hypothesis creation and testing. Now I'm a dean and fight for money."

15 November, Great Western Trail, Mt. Timpanogos

We head up the trail, tense as worried cats, setting a pace neither of us can keep up long.

"Sam," I pant, "you're killing me."

"You're the one in the lead," he says. (Why doesn't he ever pant?)

While we wobble up the unrelenting trail, I tell him that our friend Alex Caldiero was one of the fifteen hundred employees "downsized" by Novell earlier in the day in a move to maximize profits.

"Remember that poem Alex wrote a couple of years ago after the brutal layoff that netted the Ashtons millions when they sold Word Perfect?"

"Sure do," Sam answers. "'This is not the time to think about / growing a beard. You just / got laid off and you're in / Utah and you're a minority...and / you're 45 years old and you don't know God personally.' Bad luck breeds good poetry. But it doesn't pay the mortgage."

"Alex has a more recent poem," I say as we look down at the Geneva Steel-fouled valley, the plant still pumping particulates into the air despite the layoffs its management just announced. "Listen to this bit of wisdom: 'in such a moment / acknowledge / life's essential / injustice / so you can get some sleep.'"

"I can't do that," Sam says. "Never in my life have I been able to do that. And so I never sleep through the night. I have learned to enjoy it, for the most part. I examine the weather, study the phases of the moon, think about my grown children, wonder what I can do to make a mark, walk outside to feel the Earth's breath on my skin. All good."

"Every time I think of Alex," I say, "I'm charged with creative energy. And I felt that way the other night while seeing my son Ben con the people of River City out of their money with his golden voice and incessant patter and then, unexpectedly, getting conned himself by Marian the Librarian. Or the week before, watching my son Sam dancing and singing as the lead in the *Technicolor Dreamcoat.*"

"You've got talented kids," Sam notes as he heads down the hill. "Their mother's genes must have been dominant."

20 November, Mad Dog Cycles, Orem

At four, I walk over to Sam's office, hoping for a ride. Inside are two vice presidents, a couple of deans, and various other shady characters.

"I take it you're not planning on a ride?" I ask Sam.

He winces, and I head to Randy's bike shop without him. I walk out with arms full of gear (always a better option than actually riding):

New cleats for my Speedplay frog pedals—$25.49.

New Shimano shoes—$46.74.

Two red sidewall Panaracer FireXCpro 26X2.1 All-around XC Tires, Aramid Bead with dual compound side knobs to ensure high cornering grip and an Anti Snake Bite Chafer to protect against pinch punctures—$67.98.

One Rema Tip Top Tour patch kit—$2.12.

Wait till Sam gets a load of these tires.

Thirty-Nine

Standing in the Snow Thinking About Plums

Sunday December 9, Great Western Trail, Mt. Timpanogos

The snow has had us off our bikes too long. We are tight, both physically and emotionally. We grumble our way up the trail, not cheered by the four inches of snow on the asphalt before we hit the climbs.

But Nanc has shown me a Mary Oliver poem, and I am determined to stand among the plum trees we have loved for all these years—trees planted by early homesteaders from Provo. We ride our bikes a short way up the trail, leave them when the snow reaches our pedals, and walk through the snow to the hundred-year-old trees.

"I gotta read you a poem about these trees and our lives," I tell Scott. "You ready for this?"

"You got a poem in your pocket?" Scott asks.

I take out a small piece of paper on which I have scribbled Oliver's words. I turn to face the sun and read in my most solemn voice, befitting these trees:

THE PLUM TREES

The only way
to tempt happiness into your mind is by taking it

Into the body first, like small
wild plums.

"I'll be damned," Scott says as I finish. "Wish I could tempt some happiness into my mind. For months I've been locked up in my head, the victim of anxious thoughts about being a mostly absent father. I love the poem. And I love the fact that a couple of grizzled old guys are standing in the snow thinking about plums and happiness. So many things are so good and I don't want to miss them. But it's all so goddamned risky."

Our feet are getting cold and we frost the air with each breath. But neither of us is in a hurry. The plums and plum mead these trees have given make us feel blessed by them. It's a forward gift from homesteaders three generations gone. The plums have blossomed and leafed in the spring, fruited through the summer, ripened during the fall, and prepared for winter. It's the life cycle we have come to know in our own bones. We hope we may have similar small gifts of sensuousness and wonder to give. Like these trees, we are becoming wild and unkempt and old. It won't be long until our time passes.

December 14, Pole Heaven, Hobble Creek Canyon

A foot of new snow on top of a splendid base! We tighten up the laces and buckles on our Scarpa T3 boots, zip our gaiters, skin up, fasten the cable bindings on our Rossignol Black Widows ("SHE MATES, SHE KILLS" it reads through the clear base of the skis). We shoulder packs with food and water, push mittens through pole straps, and we're off, stealing a morning from work, up before the snow machines.

Climbing the gentle road that will reach Camel Pass, then dogleg north to run behind Rock Canyon before dipping into Provo Canyon, we fall into a rhythm lain dormant since last March, a physical poetry that would scan with unaccented two-beat feet in day-long lines. The snow is dry like a good white wine, crisp and feathery, weightless and clean.

Our skis whisper through the untracked snow. Clouds chase over the ridge top to the south, spitting new snow, splitting now and then to reveal a patch of lightening sky. A pair of golden eagles hunts just over the north hill, great wings beating irregularly. The eagles sweep over our silent moving forms, double back, slide sideways like a skate's heel on a bowbend (thanks, G.M. Hopkins!), and beat their way on up the draw, the tips of their wings bent upward like a dancer's fingers.

Sam exhales. I can see his shoulders loosen, his head clear.

We climb on, step after step, skins fingering the snow to hold our weight as the road climbs. Sweat gathers between shoulder blades. Snowburdened trees hang heavy over the narrow road that switches back and forth until it ushers us into a big meadow.

We eat apples and cheese and quaff pints of cold water. The sun breaks through a tear in the clouds. Unmittened fingers pry the skins off our skis, fold them in on their gummed sides, and pack them up.

Gravity and the physics of slick skis on light snow do the work now. A knee bend here, a pole plant, shifting weight, the other ski forward (bless St. Telemark!) and we sweep off the hill. I whoop as I curve through aspen. Sam's dark figure flits serenely past a stand of conifers. The road flattens and we kick and pole toward the bottom.

Sam points to the hill hunted by the eagles an hour ago. Four dark forms bob across the snow, skirting oak brush. Wild turkeys. The lead turkey takes flight, long neck leading its heavy body, gliding a hundred yards before setting down. The other three make their way across the snow as awkward pedestrians.

Tired muscles relax in the warm car. The pungent scent of wet wool saturates the heated air. In another hour, we'll be sitting at a desk writing a new policy, trying to decide if a candidate for tenure should appeal a negative decision before or after the Board of Trustees' decision. Our heads will be clear, and we'll pay careful attention to the rights of the member of the faculty.

December 14, Orem

A quick note: Scott is a much better back-country skier than I am, though I work very hard to match him. On many days I can out-climb him and the climbs are what I live for. But his telemark turns are beautiful, and he always shows me what a beautiful descent should look like. I make "three-point" descents, my two skis to the side, and my ass dragging between. I am generally glad to get off the mountain.

December 21, Orem

Small Solstice gathering at our home—good friends, good food and drink, and fine conversation. Over the last few months, Scott and I have vinted a Chardonnay out of Okanagan Valley grapes and we share it with our friends. We also taste a wonderful Pinot Grigio made by Jim and Melinda.

Well into the evening, Scott announces that he's going to deliver an oration on the meaning of the word "solstice." Over the ensuing groans, he commences. "As you know, I'm working on a book called *On Standing: Human Erections Through the Ages*. It's about standing stones and phallic power structures and poetic stanzas and the *nunc stans* and the philosophical notion of substance and the legs of Louis XIV and Brigit Bardot and Rilke's standing acrobats and Dostoevsky's description of Holbein's horizontal 'Dead Christ' and all the words related to standing like stasis, constitution, ecstasy, statue, statute, prostitute, standpoint, substance, understand, standard, existence, and so on. As a species, we call ourselves wise (*Homo sapiens*) and argue that our language differentiates us from other animals. Even more basically, however, we define ourselves by our ancestors' revolutionary achievement of a standing posture (*Homo erectus*). The primacy of standing over language, the dependence of speaking on standing, has been repeatedly argued (in the eighteenth century by Herder and Humboldt and more recently by physical anthropologists). We are human because we stand…"

"Give it a rest, Abbott," I grumble. "What about all of the other human characteristics? And more to the point, what about the Winter Solstice?"

"I was getting to that," Scott says. "The word 'solstice' means 'sun standing.' It's that moment when the sun quits wandering to the south, stands still for a day, and begins to wander north again."

"Thank you, Professor," I break in before Scott gets off on another tangent. "One slice of Nancy's fruitcake is worth ten of your lectures."

As the evening winds down, Lyn produces a gift package from her sister, Michele. Last summer, Michele sent me a package of low-bush Alaskan cranberries bartered from their neighbors. The berries came by FedEx and showed up on our porch one afternoon. They were leaking and I had no idea what was in the box. My first thought was, *This looks like a donated heart or maybe a horse head.* I unpacked the box to find several pounds of the most tart cranberries I have ever tasted.

I went to work on a couple of brews to use this fine and thoughtful gift. During my long brewing cycle, Lyn and Scott headed to Alaska and I sent a couple of bottles of my plum mead (made from the canyon plums) to Michele and David.

Now Michele sends a cranberry liqueur, a true surprise, made with the same dark, sour berries. The berries have been alchemically transformed into a tart and sweet liqueur. The bottle comes with a beautiful and thoughtful card expressing solidarity and kinship between Alaskan and Utah brewers and mead-makers. Late in the evening, we open the small bottle and pour each a thimble-full.

"Here's to good friends," Scott toasts.

"Here's to the warm and welcome return of the sun and here's to the good gifts of the Earth," I chime in.

"Here's to a wonderful and beautiful shared new year," Nanc adds.

"And here's to generous Alaskans," Lyn concludes.

Fine friends touch glasses and meet eyes. A warm evening. A celebration of Solstice. A fine set of notions for a new year. As Mary Oliver suggests, we tempt happiness into our minds through the body, and, I would add, face the unknown future confidently with dear friends.

FORTY

I'll Bury Her Among Piñons

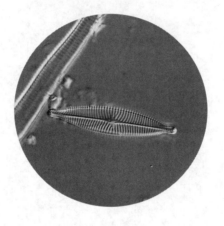

28 December, Fish Creek Cove, Teasdale

Nanc and I pack up and head to Teasdale for a few days with all our grown kids, now our equals—a rare event in these past years. The night is snowy and we take pictures on the porch, freezing thousands of snowflakes in place as they fall, stopping time for a moment, looking like we are suspended together in the Milky Way.

It is a strange thing. My grown and brilliant kids have surpassed me. I love the conversations to which they bring new information, new experiences, new ways of viewing and talking about the world. At first, this was difficult for me, but now I revel in the new pattern. It makes me believe the future will be okay in the hands of people like my grown offspring.

Midmorning it begins to warm, a few snowflakes fall languidly on the sage and we head up the county road toward the back of Fish Creek Cove. Sarah, Paul, and Marie are along for the walk. Good conversation, the sense that the holidays are winding down, a fine Christmas-gift breakfast of homemade buttermilk pancakes.

We decide after a couple of miles to climb a Navajo Sandstone ridge and have a look at the Henry Mountains sixty miles away. Paul has brought his young Australian Shepard, Java, and we have our old golden, Kiva. We start up the sandstone cliffs, both dogs eager to reach the top. Java makes it with ease, waiting for us to catch her. But it's a different story for Kiva, although this is her country. She was with Jed and me while we worked to build our cabin, keeping guard on the porch, fending off deadly coyotes. She has run off other dogs, kept the property cow-free, has been the keeper of the lower kingdoms at Teasdale. Today she can't make the climb. When she was a pup, before we got her, she jumped out of a still-moving truck and broke her hips. The vet said she would have to be killed. My daughter Marie said, "Look buddy, if you broke your hip would you want some jackass to give you an overdose of phenobarb? Fix the damn dog's hips—I'll make a monthly payment until hell freezes."

So Kiva, the dog with screws and pins and partially artificial joints, now past twelve, is stuck—she seems to realize her age and condition and still wants to get to the top of the ridge. I scale back down the rocks, grab the seventy-five-pound mutt, and hoist her tentatively, ledge by ledge, to the top. She sits quietly, looking hard east and west. This is the last time she will be here and she seems to want to imprint the memory. She comes to each of us, rubs against us affectionately, tongue lolling out, and again sits, looking across seventy-mile vistas. It's as though it has been enough, and being here right now with us is a bonus.

I'll bury the ashes of that old girl here in a year. It's her place. I'll put her among the piñons, deep in the forest, and in the rocks. It will take me all day, and I'll be sore in the shoulders when I finish, and dirty. I'll have blisters on my too-soft hands. Then I'll sit on the porch and drink good beer and talk with fine friends and my lover, and life will be good. I'll be lonesome, and full of memory and desire. I'll think about how many things I wanted to do, how much better I wanted to be.

29 December, Wickenburg, Arizona *(by email)*

Sam—I'm on my way back to Provo after a couple of days in Phoenix, where Lyn and I visited a friend of hers from grad school. Instead of driving home through Flagstaff, we headed northwest on the dogleg that will eventually take us through Lost Wages and other neon-Nevada hellholes. But first we had to drive through the little town of Wickenburg.

Wickenburg is unremarkable except for its mining and ranching history and its beautiful desert location, but in my mind it's interwoven with early attempts to establish myself as a person separate from my parents and family. In the late summer of 1972, the drilling crew I was working with moved our rig from Agua Caliente to a site near Wickenburg. We were there for several weeks and had all sorts of experiences, but I only made one entry in my journal:

> While we drill an exploratory well a few miles north of town, I've taken a room in an old motel crammed into the elbow of a highway-railroad intersection. My next-door neighbor is a wizened ex-contortionist who looked deeply into my eyes the first time I said hello and told me she would read my palm if I would come into her room. I begged off, claiming I had a vague palm. Her name is Maria, and in the relative cool of the evenings she maneuvers a hose to sprinkle a tiny plot of grass and flowers in front of our rooms. She wears a sleeveless blouse, a pair of loose shorts, and sneakers with no socks. She has tied white rags around her deeply tanned left calf and her equally brown left bicep, white semaphores that accentuate the contrast between the almost theoretical lines of her emaciated limbs and their pronounced joints. Galls. Burls. One evening she saw me staring at her bulbous elbows and went into a practiced explanation of how her mother used to tie her in knots when she was a baby so she would be limber. She made it clear that she had never regretted that turn of events, for it had led to her eventual greatness and the chance to mingle with the truly great people of this century. She is resigned to living out her days in Wickenburg, where the desert heat eases her arthritic joints.

It wasn't hard to find the railroad and the underpass in Wickenburg. Even today there are only 6000 inhabitants of the town, many of the shop owners betting that kitsch will be their economic redemption ("Renderings," "Rustiques," "El Chorrito Mexican Stuff," "Tumbleweed Gifts and Gallery"). I showed Lyn the bridge where I often leaned over the dry sands of the Hassayampa "River," churning with feelings of youthful strength and loneliness and adventure and melancholy and self-sufficiency. But thirty years of lost memory, coupled with changes in the town, left me walking the streets unable to find the four-room motel I stayed in. Lyn asked someone at the nearby Desert Caballeros Western Museum about the place, but for some (probably male) reason, I didn't want to hear the answer. I wasn't really searching for an actual building, but for memories, and I didn't want some Wickenburgian messing with my precious memories.

Year IV

Yet some of us have the nerve, the insolence, the brass, the gall to whine about the limitations of our earthbound fate and yearn for some more perfect world beyond the sky. We are none of us good enough for the world we have and yet we dream of Heaven.

Edward Abbey, *Appalachian Wilderness*

FORTY-ONE

Driving Off the Spleen

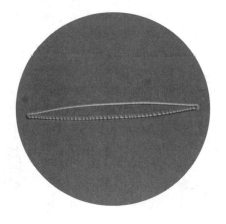

5 January, Great Western Trail, Mt. Timpanogos

Saturday morning, and still well below freezing. We're up early because frozen mud is better for a biker than regular mud. Nancy has bought Sam neoprene booties for Christmas, which he wears as added insulation over his biking shoes.

"You're a lucky man," I tell Sam before we leave his garage.

"Just because of the booties?" Nancy asks, sticking her head out the door.

When I answer "primarily," she throws a pair of socks at me.

Passing the Orem Public Cemetery, we turn up the steep road leading to the water tanks. Two runners wave hello as they descend from the hill. The bearded one turns in surprise and asks, "Sam Rushforth?" He identifies himself as David, a friend of Sam's and Nancy's daughter Sarah. "Are you biking and botanizing?" he asks.

"You read our column?" Sam replies.

"Whenever my wife leaves a copy of *Catalyst* in the bathroom," he admits. He looks at me. "Are you Scott?"

When I say I am, he asks how my knee is doing.

I'm flabbergasted. He does read us.

"I had the same operation three years ago," he says. "And last year I ran the Wasatch Ultra-Marathon. Now I'm helping train my friend here for the triathlon."

We say good-bye, and Dave hollers after us, "What are you guys talking about today as you ride?"

"Our main topic," Sam hollers back, "will be how smart we are to ride with each other and not with real athletes."

Above the water towers, the dirt road is indeed still frozen. We gain altitude and eventually we're riding through several inches of snow. At the top, overlooking the mouth of Provo Canyon, we're happy to climb off the bikes. The snow is like sand, and riding through sand uphill is not good for men of our age and girth.

Sam motions me over to the edge of the hill. Six deer lie splayed against the snow below us. We clamber down to look them over. There are no bullet holes. Four of the deer have multiple broken legs.

Back home, we call my son Joe, a Conservation Officer for the State of Utah. Ten minutes later, he calls back—it was his buddies who carried the road-kill carcasses up onto the mountain so they could reenter the food chain. Food for coyotes, eagles, and jays. Mystery solved.

6 January, Great Western Trail, Mt. Timpanogos

Another early morning ride over the frozen mud. It feels good once our blood begins to circulate. While we climb, Scott tells me that his son Ben got a wild hair last night and hiked up past the water tanks, up a section of the Great Western Trail, and laid out his tarp and sleeping bag on a flat place overlooking the valley. He woke up about four a.m. to the sound of what he thought were sirens, inexplicably close to him, insistent and loud. He finally distinguished yips and yelps between the sounds and realized he was hearing a pack of coyotes.

"Fresh tenderized deer meat," Scott told him, "not far below where you were sleeping."

I ride into a frozen rut as deep as my pedals and fall hard on my left butt-cheek.

"You won't sit comfortably for a few days," Scott points out. "I been trying all these years to teach you—it's really better you don't fall down."

I don't bother with a reply to such inanity. I'm a serious old man. I get back on my bike, start out, end up in the same rut after twenty feet, and fall hard on the other side of my ass. "I did that on purpose," I say. "I hate a sore ass only in one cheek. I seek balance in all aspects of my life."

1 February, Provo

"Scott," I say at lunch, "why do you suppose anyone is interested in what we've been writing?"

Scott answers, "I've been worrying that question from the other side: Why do we ride and write in the first place? Yesterday I picked up Melville's *Moby-Dick* and found at least a partial answer:

Call me Ishmael. Some years ago—never mind how long precisely—having little or no money in my purse, and nothing particular to interest me on shore, I thought I would sail about a little and see the watery part of the world. It is a way I have of driving off the spleen, and regulating the circulation. Whenever I find myself involuntarily pausing before coffin warehouses, and bringing up the rear of every funeral I meet; and especially whenever my hypos get such an upper hand of me, that it requires a strong moral principle to prevent me from deliberately stepping into the street, and methodically knocking people's hats off—then, I account it high time to get to sea as soon as I can. This is my substitute for pistol and ball.

"We can't write like Melville," I say, "but we know about depression, about that urge to get into a fight. And we keep asking and trying to answer those knotty questions: What has meaning, what doesn't? Why is intimacy so difficult? Why do men hide behind a palpable mist of testosterone? Why do we compete with each other and form hierarchies? How do we stave off sadness and a bleak existence? How do we escape the perils of mundanity? Better to ask them in print than to reach for a gun."

20 February, Orem *(by email)*

Sam and Scott, I was checking some plant records this morning at the NY Botanical Garden web site and came across this entry. Take a look at the collector's name in the 5th line. This is a 1916 collection. Looks like the second coming's come and gone... damn, I missed it!

Name: Brassicaceae (Mustard Family)
Arabis drummondii A. Grey
Image: Not Available
Location: United States of America. Idaho. Clark Co. Spencer.
Collector: J. H. Christ, 2817
01 Aug 1916
Description: Fruit.
Habitat: Sagebrush.

All the best,
Jim Harris

20 February, Orem *(by return email)*

Sweet Jesus, Jim, Sam and I missed it too! But it reminds me of a valuable piece of information. Do either of you so-called botanists know where the "H" comes from in the name Jesus H. Christ? If you'd think for a minute about virgin births and then about creatures with only half the normal number of chromosomes, you'd realize it stands for "haploid."

7 March, Great Western Trail, Mt. Timpanogos

"This will be a short ride," I remark hopefully as we head up the road from Sam's house. "Too warm for the mud to be frozen."

As we wobble up the hill, I tell Sam about Lyn's and my weekend trip to Ely, Nevada. "We drove out into the Steptoe Valley to see the charcoal ovens, big thirty-foot-high, beehive-shaped domes constructed in 1873 by Swiss-Italian charcoal burners (*carbonari*) to make charcoal for the silver smelters. What a strange sight that was, a stately row of empty rock domes nestled up against the eastern slope of the mountains. They looked like they might have been dropped there by randy feminist aliens from Trent Harris's film *Plan 10 From Outer Space*."

"I've seen them," Sam replies. "That austere series of basins and ranges across the center of Nevada is some of my favorite country anywhere on earth. Highway 6 is my drive."

"On the way home we stopped outside of Delta at the Topaz Mountain Detention Center. What in the world did the Japanese-Americans from the California coast think when they arrived on that arid piece of ground with desert mountains standing sentinel in the distance? The camp held about eight thousand of our fellow citizens for several years during the hysteria accompanying World War II. Lyn and I stood in front of a little memorial, its brass plaque blasted by some idiot's shotgun, and thought about the so-called Patriot Act passed almost unanimously by our representatives in Washington after the terrorist attacks on the World Trade Center. We're so damned predictable, so cravenly racist, so smugly patriotic, so easily ruled by fear."

We've reached the top of the climb, the last of it over a couple inches of snow and ice, and we stop, sweaty and cold, to look over Utah Valley.

Sam wipes sweat off his forehead with his do-rag. "When they dismantled the Topaz camp at the end of the war," he says, "sending the inmates back to the ruins of their former lives, they took a bunch of the barracks to BYU to use for student housing and temporary academic buildings, quarters for the young men and women returning from the war."

"Weeks after I was born in Greeley, Colorado," I interject, "my parents took me to Utah to live in one of those barracks while my father used the G.I. Bill to finance college. I didn't know they had come from Topaz. Gives me the shivers."

16 March, Utah Valley Regional Hospital *(by email)*

Sam—My son Joe and his wife, Tracy, had twins today, two little six-pound girls, Ciara and Regan. Long dark hair and angelic faces. The proud papa was glowing, not to mention the grandpa. While Tracy and Joe passed the new girls around, Tracy's mom held little Jacob, born and adopted last November. Twins and a half! Please remember my burgeoning progeny next time I fall behind on a trail. I'm a swiftly aging man. And I expect Joe will age a little himself over this next year.

23 March, Great Western Trail, Mt. Timpanogos

Woke this morning to the sound of two dozen Canadian geese flying north over our house in a beautiful, fluid wedge. I spent an important piece of my youth in the marshes west of Kaysville listening to and watching those geese. I call Scott early and tell him to hustle over to my place and we head up the mountain. Halfway up, deep in conversation about work, we are startled by a meadowlark. It makes us both stand off our bikes and listen. Those burbling notes are a balm in a crowded and busy world.

"You been followin' the gov's Legacy Highway stuff?" I ask Scott a little later. "Those guys have little legal right to begin construction, start anyway at the peril of some of the most important wetlands on Earth, and then have the balls to blame delays on the green community, who all along stated they would challenge the freeway in court. What are a few hundred thousand birds and the continuation of a millions-of-years-old flyway in comparison to a slower commute into Salt Lake?"

"No contest," Scott says. "I read that at a hearing on the environmental impact, they brought in a farmer who was going to make a killing by selling his land to the state. 'People keep calling these wetlands,' he said. 'It's nothin' but a damned swamp.'"

"Thinking about my decades of work against exploitation

of the environment reminds me of the lecture you gave last week at the college," I say. "You quoted lines from Rilke's *Duino Elegy*: 'And we: spectators, always everywhere, / Turned to the universe and never escaping! / It fills us. We order it. It falls apart. / We order it again and fall apart ourselves.' Aren't we all trying to erect something that won't fall apart, to create edifices of religion, science, art, architecture, environmental activism— in word, in paint, in stone, in analyzed data, even in our off- spring—that will endow us with a sense of meaning, of lasting purpose, of immortality? And isn't it all doomed in the end? Remember that dream I had during one of our so-called hu- manitarian trips to Mexico? I was trying to cross El Camino Real with several hundred children. The traffic was dense and moving at breakneck speeds. Most of the children were walk- ing, but some had skateboards. I surveyed the tools I had to help the group across the highway: a paper plate, a knock-off yellow Swiss-army knife, and three cents. During an unexpected break in the traffic, several of us raced across the highway. I looked back for the others. They had disappeared, filtered back into fields and orchards and houses."

"And then," Scott notes, "we fall apart ourselves."

24 March, Provo *(by email)*
Sam—Thinking about your dream and that trip to Mexico, I dug up some notes. The exchange still floors me, and Nancy's response may be the funniest thing I ever heard.

29 May, 1998, Provo
In our preparatory class for a trip to Tarahumara settle- ments in the Sierra Madre Mountains of north-central Mexico, we're having the BYU students read Susan Griffin's book *A Chorus of Stones*. One of the students objects to a passage that thinks about violence against homosexuals in

the context of Nazi hatred of Jews.

"Why does the book disturb you?" Sam asks the student.

"Because the book is pornographic," she answers, "and pornography leads to masturbation which leads to homosexuality which leads to necrophilia."

"Whoa," Sam responds. "Do you even know what necrophilia is?"

"Having sex with corpses."

"Okay. But how do you know that pornography leads so directly to necrophilia?"

"It's common knowledge."

She never comes back to class. Within a week, we're notified that she has filed an official complaint with the Academic Vice President. Our course, she claims, is not "God centered," as required by the university's mission statement.

"At least it's not godawful," Nancy points out.

FORTY-TWO

Draw Me No White Dresses on Corpses

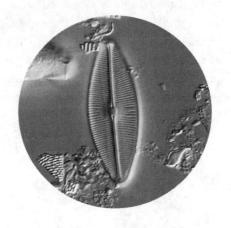

28 March, Springville Art Museum

Surrounded by colorful landscapes painted by Utah artists, Jed (Sam and Nancy's youngest) and his soon-to-be-wife celebrate their wedding. Two talented and goodhearted young persons looking to share a future together. Nancy is beautiful in crushed velvet and Sam resplendent in a tux. Sam reads a Mary Oliver poem asking, "What will you do with your one wild and wonderful life" and relates his father's last piece of advice to him: "I've learned over my life that there are no utopias. Don't waste your life looking for them."

I try to remember the last advice my father gave me and come up with three candidates: "When you go off to college have an open mind, but not so open that your mind falls out"; "Don't rev the engine so high before shifting up, this isn't a VW"; and "Do more than you're being paid to do and you'll do well."

What will my children remember me by?

5 April, Logan, USU *(by email)*

Sam—Wish you could have seen Ben and me tonight! As you know, Ben will be a student at USU next year, studying in the College of Natural Resources with a marvelous scholarship provided by the Quinney Foundation. Tonight was the College's awards banquet. I picked Ben up at three for the drive to Logan. There was my handsome boy, dressed in suit and tie. His head was shaved, excepting a ragged strip running front to back and an even more ragged strip slanting down behind one ear.

"What the hell?" I asked gently.

"Like it?" he asked in reply.

"You're going to accept a major scholarship in the College of Natural Resources looking like the victim of an alien hazing?" I asked.

"I asked Nora to the prom by writing on the back of my head," Ben explained.

Ben drew a lot of attention at the reception, but his moment of true glory came when the four Quinney Scholars for the year were introduced. Elegant Ms. Quinney read Ben's biography while he stood resplendent next to her: "The first Quinney Scholar is Benjamin Abbott from Orem High School. He's a drama student," she said, "which may explain his hair." When she finished, the cowboy-booted representative of the alumni association stood and, before announcing his scholarship, said dryly, "The last scholarship was for best hair-do, ours will be for..."

7 April, Great Western Trail, Mt. Timpanogos

Easter morning. The familiar winter landscape is altered only by the first green grass and by the low clusters (or umbels) of yellow flowers that are always the spring's first wildflowers: *Cymopterus longipes* (spring parsley). "We're aging," I tell Sam at the top, "and our rides are growing less and less wild, but there will always be wildflowers."

"Sure," Sam replies, "unless we destroy the planet. Let's ride down where they've been working to bury the green pipe and see what damage they've done."

The trail leads along a rocky cliff, a precarious ride for old men balanced tenuously on two-wheeled contraptions. Sam rides confidently, but I tighten up and slow down and make the ride even more precarious than it has to be, remembering the incident years ago when Sam, swatting at a wasp on his arm, lost balance right here and tumbled over and over down the slope between two cliffs. By the time I get off the cliff, Sam is sitting on the long, dry, matted grass of a sloping meadow. We bask in the sun, passing the time, happy to be alive. Then we're off to see the construction site.

8 April, SLC, NRC Hearing on Nuclear Waste *(by email)*

Sam—Lyn and I are just back from the demonstration against bringing high-level nuclear waste to the Goshute Reservation. Besides Mayor Rocky Anderson's speech against the plan and Chip Ward's eloquent and damning statement to the effect that the NRC had already decided and the hearing was a sham, my favorite moment was near the end of the demonstration when a woman handed our friend Larry Harper a sign. "I have to go," she said. Larry looked at the sign—MOMS AGAINST NUCLEAR WASTE—and said, "I'm not a mom." "Neither am I," she said. So there he was, handsome and hirsute, carrying his MOMS sign from the Gallivan Center to the Salt Palace.

21 April, Washington, D.C., Phillips Collection *(by email)*

Scott—I'm in town to do some lobbying for UVSC and got to spend a couple of hours in the Phillips Collection on DuPont Circle. They had a fine show entitled "Corot to Picasso." I was especially taken by Courbet's "Preparation of the Dead Girl." The painting originally depicted a group of somber women preparing a dead girl for burial. The main character was naked, her head flopped to the side and her arm dangling. In the early 1900s, the painting was coming up for auction and someone thought the public could not deal with the subject of death. So they painted a white dress on the corpse, straightened her head, lifted her arm and placed a mirror in her hand. The title of the painting was changed to "Preparation of the Bride."

The attempt to deflect our thinking from finality and death is wrong-headed. As I see it, our lives are like the wildflowers we enjoy so much. They can be beautiful and wonderful, but they are, naturally, short-lived. To deny the ephemeral nature of our lives is wrong—it robs us of the beauty of the moment. This Earth and our time here are not trivial or everlasting. It's what we have. We can't pretend this life is not important, hoping the next life is more important. We can't diminish the beauty of a relationship, the glance of a dear friend, the unexplained event that creates love and beauty, however temporary. Draw me no white dresses on corpses to pretend they're brides.

21 April, Provo *(by email)*
Sam—I wish I could have seen that painting with you. When my brother John died, the mortician tried to keep me from seeing John's body until they had, in effect, painted a white dress on him. Here's a description of the moment that changed the course of my life:

> We leave the café and drive to a mortuary. The mortician offers condolences. I say I would like to see him. He explains that most family members, especially after an autopsy, find it better to wait until the body has been worked on. I explain that I need to see for myself and follow him downstairs. The smell of pizza and the sound of laughter from a side door. Three bodies laid out on tables. The mortician points to a clear plastic bag on the center table. I pull open the folded plastic. Don't touch him, he warns.
>
> His face is drawn. An open eye leers upward. A scraggly growth of beard and moustache. The sagging jaw reveals uneven teeth.
>
> My teeth.
>
> From shoulder to shoulder, down the chest to the hips, a surgical Y. The top of the skull has been sawn off, then replaced. Severed locks of hair litter the forehead.
>
> I stand before the body. It is unspeakably present. His feet are livid.

FORTY-THREE

Who Has Once Met Irony . . .

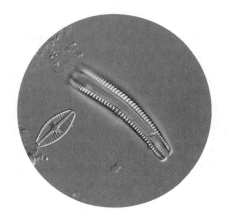

1 May, Great Western Trail, Mt. Timpanogos

For the first time this year, we come across evening primrose, the big fourmerous white flowers elegant against the fresh green grass. "The light of the night." "The hope of the Netherlands."

"Sam," I pant as we ride too fast up the hill, "look at the paintbrush." I jump off my bike and head across the hill to where the muted, orange-red flowers nestle among silver-green sage. Farther up, we stop to look at a bright yellow composite. At the top, overlooking Utah Valley, I tell Sam about a few lines from a poem I read in the *New York Review of Books*, a translation of a poem by Polish poet Adam Zagajewski: '. . . Who has once met / irony will burst into laughter / during the prophet's lecture.'"

"That's remarkable," Sam responds. "Somehow it reminds me of the thirty-year-old 'boy' who came to you at BYU and said he was not paying tuition to have you spout your academic-freedom arguments but to assure him that what he already knew was true. Glad we don't get that at UVSC."

"Like hell, we don't," I retort. "As chair of the philosophy department, I got a call just the other day from a man asking for a waiver for the required Ethics and Values course. 'I'm LDS,' he said, 'and I have my ethics and values already set for life.' 'That's good,' I told him, 'now that your values are set you can take the class to work on your critical reasoning skills.'"

5 May, Great Western Trail, Mt. Timpanogos

We ride past a deer skull, stripped white except for a hairy toupé, on the ridge above Johnson's Hole. It is nestled next to the bright purple flowers of an *Astragalus*, one of the locoweeds. Death camas are blossoming, their lily stalks rising up from long, thin leaves.

"Look at the oak brush up the hill," I tell Sam. "The strip at the top has brand new leaves, still rusty brown. Below, the oak leaves have turned green. Why is that?"

"When the leaves first unfold," Sam answers, "they lack fully-formed chlorophyll. This allows pigments such as anthocyanins and others to give that brown-red-purple cast to the young leaves. It takes a while for the chlorophyll to fully form."

"It takes a relationship a while to fully form too," I say tangentially. "But Lyn and I have reached an important milestone. Last week when she suggested, romantically, that we 'consolidate our things,' I couldn't have been more pleased."

11 May, Dolores, Colorado *(by email)*

Sam—Lyn and I just rode our bikes for a couple of hours with my sister Carol outside of Dolores. You remember Carol's near-fatal car accident last August and my trip to Grand Junction to be with her? She has healed wonderfully, although her broken ankles and feet and hip and elbow still hurt most of the time and she's got some damned fine scars.

She drove us up onto the mesa to where a single-track bike trail begins under big Ponderosa pines, a park-like landscape with most of the underbrush burned out by a quick fire several years ago. Carol wasn't very good with the gears of her Specialized Rock Hopper, but the gently winding trail was made for practice and she's always been a good athlete, so no problem. No problem, that is, until the trail turned down quickly over jutting rocks and there she was flying over her handlebar to land spread-eagled on her front. I had visions of re-broken hips and elbows and ankles. She was fine, other than a big knot on one knee. Lyn explained about keeping your ass back while descending and on we rode.

So good to see my sister healthy and alive!

12 May, Leadville, Colorado *(by email)*

Sam—Yesterday we drove north from Ouray to Paonia, Colorado. You probably know the place as the home of the *High*

Country News, one of our favorite environmental publications, but I was there in search of memories. When I was three years old, my dad took his first teaching job at the high school in Paonia. His subject was Vocational Agriculture, a field he knew in part because of work on his parents' dry-land wheat farm near Windsor, Colorado. The agriculture in and around Paonia is primarily related to fruit growing, not exactly my dad's strong suit, and for that and other reasons we only stayed there for a couple of years until we moved to Montpelier, Idaho and then to Farmington, New Mexico a few years later.

My memories from the Paonia years have been limited to an imprecise image of the front of our little log house, the thrill of a sled ride down an adjoining hill, and a dark warehouse where migrant workers were housed. I remember putting down my Golden Book to watch boxcars loaded with wooden fruit boxes rattle past our log house, and being led by my mother across the street to the warehouse. She knocked at a side door. It slid open. She reached warm bread and a pot of steaming pinto beans through the opening to a dark-eyed woman with a tiny, brown-skinned baby at her breast.

Now, with Lyn, I nosed the car through the little town, feeling my way toward a child's memories, easing toward a little hill on the south side of town. There it was, a small log house on a stretch of grass on the corner of 2nd and Orchard. Orchard led to a steep little hill. Across the street stood fruit warehouses. A railroad track angled behind the house.

Driving out of town, up through coal-mining country into the high mountains, I had a new sense for my past, for the landscape that shaped me. I'm a creature of the Intermountain West. I can't live without the crisp scent of sage, distant vistas, and plentiful public lands.

13 May, Leadville, Colorado *(by email)*

Sam—Just back from a great bike ride nearly 13 miles on the Mineral Belt Trail. Given their history of mining, given the realities of a landscape torn and ripped and blasted and left a wasteland of tailings and poisoned pools and twisted iron and broken timbers, the citizens of this town perched between some of Colorado's highest peaks have decided to make the most of the history of the region, a decision that included building a splendid trail right through claims like the Swamp Angel, the Dead Broke, the Modest Girl, the Last Rose of Summer, the Star of the West, and Blind Tom. Oxygen was not as plentiful as we're used to, and Lyn called my parentage into question while we climbed to 11,000 feet with her brake dragging, but what a great ride!

We visited the National Mining Museum this afternoon. EVERYTHING BEGINS WITH MINING, EVERYTHING!!!!!—so claimed four successive signs. Lots of interesting stuff about mining engineering and tough men. Not a word about environmental degradation and human casualties. It reminded me of the exhibition in the Mormon Church's Museum of Art and History that glorifies the pioneers without a single reference to polygamy.

Dinner in Rosie's Brew Pub. The brewmaster has named her beers after women, including a fine Hildegard von Bingen porter.

13 May, Orem *(by email)*

Scott—Nancy and I stayed in Leadville a year or two ago. Mary Foote lived there, the only married woman in town. Nancy has done research on Mary Foote for many years, looking especially at the lively letters she wrote from that mining town. Nanc has come to feel a wonderful sisterly bond with her and is at work on a play about Foote and her western life. You may also know that Wallace Stegner used, unattributed, many of Foote's letters for his novel *Angle of Repose*.

FORTY-FOUR

A World of Yellow Scent

3 June, Great Western Trail, Mt. Timpanogos

"My brother John's birthday," I tell Sam as we leave his house on our bikes. "He would have been fifty-one this year. Sure do miss him."

At the Canyon Glen trailhead (major construction on the green pipe by the wrecklamation people has blocked our normal route), Sam turns up the sudden trail and I follow him. We're sucking air and ignoring burning legs when a brilliant blue pocket of flax flowers, *Linum perenne*, cuts its way into my consciousness. After the sharp switchback that Sam rides but I don't even attempt, another flash of blue interrupts the pain. A male lazuli bunting, bright blue and orange and white and black. From its boxelder perch, it trills us up onto the first level. Gathering breath for the next climb, I have a sense of *deja vu*— two blue flashes in a row, lazuli bunting and flax on the same ride—this has happened before. There is, I think, an intimate pleasure in repeated experience.

Up another level, riding the ridge that curves around Johnson's Hole, I jump off my bike to look at a carpet of dusty-orange globe mallow, *Sphaeralcea coccinea*. Among the globe mallows are white blooms I figure are sego lilies but that turn out not to be lilies at all. The long stamens and cross-shaped style remind me of evening primroses, and some of the flowers are turning from white to pink like primroses. But they're along stringy stems and not rising out of a rosette of leaves. I turn to Sam.

"They're probably pale evening primrose, *Oenothera pallida*. And what a pretty sight, the white flowers among the orange in the openings between the stands of scrub oak."

At the top of today's climb, we reach the fire road and follow it toward the mouth of the canyon. Lazuli buntings sing conspicuously (conspicuous is the point of the plumage) from the dead branches of oak brush that burned in the fire a few years ago. In places, the oak that sprouted from roots that next spring is already as high as Sam's shoulders. Coming out of the canyon, we drop precipitously down a jeep road through yellow Dalmatian toadflax and purple sweet vetch and into a wave of scent, billows of sweetness that would be cloying if the plants giving off the generous odors weren't on this spare, clean desert hillside. Surrounded by the yellow flowers of cliff rose, *Purshia stansburiana*, a member of the rose family, we step out of time and motion (if there's a difference) and into a world of yellow scent.

"The Swiss pastor and physiognomist named Lavater," I tell Sam, "speculated at the end of the eighteenth century that our spoken language, conventional and abstract, can't possibly be the language of heaven. Instead, he suggested the direct language of scent."

"Can't say I would argue with him right now," Sam replies. "Although I see heaven as an abstraction and smell this cliff rose as earthy. I have come to where I hate all references to heaven."

"Tell me more about the cliff rose."

"It has superabundant yellow pollen centers," Sam begins, "which explains why it's one of the sweetest scented of all Southwest plants. The genus is named after Frederick Pursh, the guy who got first crack at the Lewis and Clark botanical collections. 'Stansburiana' comes from Howard Stansbury, early 19th-century explorer and naturalist whose name you know from Stansbury Island on the Great Salt Lake. Shut me up if I telling you more than you want to know. Cliff rose is among my favorite plants."

"Mine too," I say. "And as for the lecture, it's not your personality that keeps me riding with you, but what you know about plants. Go on."

"You asked for it," Sam says. "Smell the tiny leaves. They're acrid, a little like quinine. Later, they'll have seed-bearing plumes. Cliff rose sometimes hybridizes with its close cousin *Purshia tridentata*, which has always given me fits. I actually don't know which of the two these are. And shall we throw in the names *Cowania mexicana, Purshia mexicana, Cowania stansburiana*? I have spent twenty years trying to exactly separate these shrubs. Got some way to go yet."

"Okay," I say as we climb back on the bikes, "the careful descriptive language of science and the divinely earthy language of scent. We've got our bases covered."

"Not likely. Every time I think I know something in biology, I am chagrinned. The living world, to date, is much more complex than we can discern."

7 June, Great Western Trail, Mt. Timpanogos

We're greasing our chains before today's ride. "Sam," I say, "take a look at this list I found on an internet site. It was longer, eighty-three plants in all, but I just copied the names of plants we see often and may or may not have taken a liking to."

Absinth wormwood (Artemisia absinthium)
Bull thistle (Cirsium vulgare)
Canada thistle (Cirsium arvense)
Chicory (Cichorium intybus)
Chinese clematis (Clematis orientalis)
Coast tarweed (Madia sativa)
Common burdock (Arctium minus)
Common mullein (Verbascum thapsus)
Common teasel (Dipsacus fullonum)
Dalmatian toadflax, broad-leaved (Linaria dalmatica)
Dalmation toadflax, narrow-leaved (L. genistifolia)
Field bindweed (Convolvulus arvensis)
Houndstongue (Cynoglossum officinale)
Leafy spurge (Euphorbia esula)
Poison hemlock (Conium maculatum)
Puncturevine (Tribulus terrestris)

Rush skeletonweed (Chondrilla juncea)
Russian-olive (Elaeagnus angustifolia)
Russian thistle (Salsola collina and S. iberica)
Saltcedar (Tamarix parviflora and T. ramosissima)
Scotch thistle (Onopordum acanthium and O. tauricum)
Spotted knapweed (Centaurea maculosa)
Wild mustard (Brassica kaber)

"So what's the point of the list?" Sam asks.

"It's the State of Colorado Noxious Weed List," I answer.

"Okay," Sam says, "I hate tamarisk and I know how spotted knapweed can take over a field of wildflowers, but what would our section of the Great Western Trail be like without the yellow flowers of Dalmatian toadflax and mullein and the purple flattops of thistles? The flora and fauna of the world have a right to change. And change they will. But while they do, we've got to do everything we can to prevent extinction of the native flora."

Thinking of thistles, we stop when the first bunch of them appears beside the trail. "Are these bull thistles (*Cirsium vulgare*) or Canada thistles (*Cirsium arvense*)?" I ask Sam, a question we have considered before.

"They may be Scotch thistles (*Onopordum acanthium*)," he answers. "As your list indicates, ranchers see them all as a weed problem. I was reading recently that Scotch thistle was first found in Utah in 1963. In twenty-five years it had spread to cover tens of thousands of acres in twenty-two counties. A single thistle plant can produce forty thousand seeds."

"As we have noted before, they also seem to be amazingly attractive to insects," I say. We look carefully at a thistle flower that has dozens and dozens of little black bugs, just larger than gnats, burrowed down between the purple flowers. A single black bee, back legs heavy with pods of pollen, works the flower as well. A neighboring flower has dozens more of the little black bugs along with a copulating pair of dark-colored wasps, the female mining the flower, the smaller male atop her. A third flower sports a pair of copulating black bugs with red corners on their wings. "Red-winged black bugs," I joke.

"Those are true bugs," Sam says.

"As opposed to plastic bugs?" I ask.

"No," he says. "There are several dozen families of insects, one of which is true bugs, or *Hemiptera*. These little fellows aren't beetles or wasps, but bugs."

"Okay," I respond. "Whatever they are, they are clearly excited by whatever this thistle is producing. And we know that once the seeds appear, goldfinches will gather for a feast of their own. Wish we could get our minds around the whole cycle of relationships between these non-native thistles, the native plants they displace, the bugs that feed on them and pollinate them, and the birds that eat and spread the seeds. I don't care about how thistles inhibit sheep and cows from grazing—they're grazing on non-native grasses anyway, and destroying native habitat—but I'm interested in the whole complex natural-unnatural web that includes mountain bikers."

"Me too," Sam says. "We make 'management' decisions based on incomplete pictures that come around to bite us in the ass. We need much more research by private and governmental scientists and much less power by ranchers—and much more concern on the part of ordinary citizens."

22 June, Brighton *(by email)*

Scott—Marie and John are marrying today. As you know, I am the minister, thanks to the $25 internet ministerial certificate I procured. I've never done anything like this and it is pretty interesting. Marie is my oldest daughter and is perfectly beautiful in her white beaded gown. John is dressed in black formal pants with an ivory shirt. They are as handsome a couple as I have ever seen.

The ceremony is on the cabin deck, attended only by immediate family members. It's a wonderful sight, the men and women all in black and John and Marie in white. The sun chases in and out of clouds, throwing long strips of light on the mountains across the valley and making the deck a panoply of color and shadow. Nanc recounts a beautiful history of marriage as part of the ceremony. She looks more like Marie's sister than her mother.

But the interesting thing to me is performing the marriage of my own daughter, an adult who is wiser in most instances than I am and who has thought through and rethought her life, made decisions, and come to this place of her own volition. And, by damn, it's a pretty fine place.

22 June, Provo *(by email)*

Sam—Give Marie my best. She's got the best traits from you and Nancy in a single package.

A little family story from my place last night. Ben and Sam and Tim were over for the night. It was a happy evening, the kind that eases my lingering anxiety over how my choices will play out in their lives. We cooked a good dinner together and sat down to share the meal. Tim, who by some quirk of biology has overtaken Sam in height, despite the two-year difference, was telling Lyn a story when the phone rang. I should have let it go, but I always wonder if it is going to be another call like the one announcing that my father had been killed, and so I slipped into the next room and answered it. A man's voice said, "Mr. Abbott?" "Who's calling?" I asked. When he turned out to be a telemarketer I lit into him. "Why the hell would you call me now, in the middle of dinner with my family, disrupting our evening to sell us something we don't want? Why would you call us now?" "Because you're a dickhead," he said, and listened for a few seconds while I spluttered. We both hung up and I went back to dinner with a great story to tell.

23 June, Great Western Trail, Mt. Timpanogos

The pungent yellow flowers of the cliff rose are shot through their centers by fuzzy tendrils, four, five, six, or seven of them curling up out of the flower's cup like insect antennae feeling an inch-and-a-half into the universe. If you tug at one, it comes away from the flower with a little green foot of a seed. "Sam," I say, "imagine a hundred thousand of these corkscrewing down into Utah Valley on a stiff breeze, tough hybrid little bastards looking to colonize a domesticated landscape."

"Imagine," he answers, "the intoxicating scent of a valley bursting with yellow cliff rose. Whole new religions would arise out of the rumors coming back from the place about explorers who entered paradise and, having found it, refused to leave."

FORTY-FIVE

Happy Hour/Under God

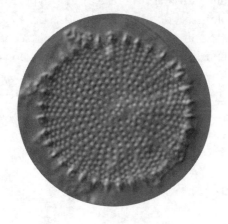

7 July, Great Western Trail, Mt. Timpanogos

"How long can the plants on this mountainside survive without rain?" I ask Sam as we race the early morning sun to the ridge above Johnson's Hole.

"They're all suffering," he answers, "but just like they are adapted as species for fire, they're also adapted for drought. The real question is how long the human species can mess with natural water systems in the desert southwest and still survive."

We're battling a stiff canyon wind that angles in at ninety degrees and threatens to shoulder us off the ridge, but I'm anxious to continue the conversation. "I've been thinking about water in the desert since David Cassuto's lecture on campus last week. He said that more water goes to grow alfalfa in California than is used by humans in the state, most of it provided by outrageously expensive and destructive 'reclamation' projects in deserts. And the profits from the so-called 'public works' go straight into the pockets of the wealthiest."

"We also created a multi-billion dollar project in Arizona," Sam says, "to take water from the northern mountains to the south-lands to grow goddamned cotton. So all of the diverted water of northern Arizona goes south to grow alfalfa and cotton for the good of a very few. You have any suggestions? Most of the Arizona and national politicians are complicit or directly benefit from this situation. Cotton and alfalfa are killing our western ecosystems."

"Charles Bowden," I add, "writes that giving new water to any city in the west is like sending an alcoholic a case of whiskey. It solves the problem only in the short run."

We reach the trailhead for Frank and stop to consider the shape we're in.

"What do you think?" Sam asks.

"I dunno," I answer.

"Guess we better give Frank his due," Sam says. "There will

come a time soon when we'll just have to wave when we ride past." He kicks off, snaps his loose foot onto the pedal, and up he goes.

I'm sluggish this morning, lacking calories or will or muscle or something, and I follow reluctantly, slowly, blocking out every thought of keeping up with Sam, focused only on finding the easiest line and keeping upright and moving forward. I make it to the C-turn and swing up and around ready to capitulate, but there I am, by some quirk of momentum, still on my bike and still moving. Riding at a snail's pace (and snails don't have to balance on two thin wheels), I reach the S-turn, make its twisting climb, and face the rocky double chute that is Frank's *piece de resistance*. Since I'm still on the bike, I give it a half-hearted try, sliding and bouncing up the first chute, finding enough energy to speed up my cadence slightly, summoning up some scrap of will and there I am! safe on the somewhat flatter piece of trail between the chutes. The second chute isn't as difficult or long as the first, and I attack it with new-found vigor, riding it well till I'm one crank from the top. I lean back with satisfaction and up comes my front wheel, courtesy of the bike-hubris gods, and I'm lying on my back in the oak brush. It's not a bad place to lie, your bike still between your legs, gazing up at a brilliant blue sky, the dusty scent of oak brush sharp in your nose, grateful for the chance to fill empty lungs. But Sam's waiting somewhere up the trail, so I unclip my cleats from the pedals, pull myself out of the brush, and ride on, slow in the morning's gathering heat, up the ridge Frank follows, past dry grass, milkweed pods growing fat, sunflowers celebrating their namesake, through a little grove of overhanging maples, up the last technical climb before the meadow (how is it possible that my tired legs and heart are still pumping?), and into the meadow.

What a sight! A sea of blue lupine flowers punctuated by thousands of yellow toadflax. A riot of reproduction even in this drought. But where the hell is Sam? This is the top! I ride on up the meadow, climbing out of it onto Nude Knob, where I find Sam sitting on a rock overlooking both Provo Canyon and Utah Valley.

"You sorry son of a mangy bitch," I pant. "You couldn't stop in the meadow, could you?"

"Glad you could make it," Sam answers. "I saw vultures circling and figured maybe I would inherit your bike."

15 July, Dublin, Ireland *(by email)*

Scott—Nanc and Anita drop me off in O'Neil's Pub while they go to the Irish Tourist Board nearby.

After an hour, a man my age sits at the bar and orders a whiskey. He shakes hands and introduces himself as Alex. He has a beard much like mine, but he wears a workingman's coat and has strong, working hands. We talk for an hour. I ask him what he does for his keep and he says he's a welder. But what he really does is fish. He bends closer and lowers his voice: "and I work to keep the fookin' Brits outta me homeland. Two years more and I'll leave the job," he says, "and I can fish the day through. And one more thing. I'll listen to Bob Dylan all day too by God."

I tell him I am going to see Dylan perform at the end of August and he lights up.

"A whiskey for me friend here," he speaks to the keep. "Powers." He bends closer and sings Dylan's "Forever Young," low and lyrical and very Irish: "May your heart always be joyful, / May your song always be sung, / May you stay forever young, / Forever young, forever young, / May you stay forever young.

"You 'tink of Alex now when ye see Dylan. You taste the Powers, started in 1791 it was. And maybe we'll see one another again someday."

I go for a pee and Alex is gone, smoke rising in a slow curl out of the ashtray he was using.

19 July, Great Western Trail, Mt. Timpanogos

An early ride this morning with my son Ben, he of the rubber band legs and iron lungs and, lucky for me, patience beyond his years. It's possible I'm still a better technical rider than he is, but he has power and stamina I can only remember. Just inside the mouth of the canyon, Ben stops suddenly and points to a big hawk, maybe a redtail, landing on the limestone cliff above us. While we admire the dark head and powerful breast through binoculars, two vultures and then two more circle into sight above the perched hawk. Behind us, from the thick growth along the river, we hear the varied calls of a yellow-breasted chat.

At Canyon Glen, we turn up the Great Western Trail, Ben ahead of me with his quick cadence. He has inserted colorful bird feathers into the holes of his helmet. I follow him up to Johnson's Hole, up the ridge, and back toward the canyon's mouth on the fire road.

Ben points out a spotted towhee, then another. We're looking for a lazuli bunting, which I've told him about but he's never seen. Perhaps we're too early this morning, or maybe it's just too damned hot and the breeding season is over. Whatever the reason, we wend our way toward the mouth of the canyon without a single sighting. A quick ride up an arm of the Great Western brings us to an overlook where we stand and talk philosophy— whether metaphysical certainty or grounding is necessary or even helpful for human society. We agree that it's not necessary and perhaps counterproductive as religions and nationalisms run amok. Ben cites the recent flap over the words "under God" in the pledge and I describe for him the *New Yorker* cartoon that puts the patriotic pietism in perspective: A picture of Eddie's Bar and Grill with a sign in the window announcing "HAPPY HOUR / UNDER GOD / 4-7."

A bird lands in a dead tree in front of us, the blue bird of heaven we've been looking for, a male lazuli bunting in all its glory, fat and blue and orange and black and white, its head brilliant blue in a sliver of morning sun. A couple of red-headed finches join the bunting in the tree, then a female bunting and another male stop by. Just down the hill, a colloquy of magpies engages in its own raucous black-and-white debate. Ben and I roll off the hill burning with a distinctly non-metaphysical sense for this mountain on this day.

20, 21, 22 July, Great Western Trail, Mt. Timpanogos
A string of early morning rides, inspired by daily reports from the Tour de France. As I ride up familiar climbs, I imagine I am Lance Armstrong attacking the mountain with steely resolve and unlimited strength. If Sam were here, our conversations would keep me from such silly fantasies. Doesn't a man ever grow up? Will I go to my grave still thinking I am as talented as the author whose book I'm reading, as handsome as the actor in the film, as immortal as a child?

FORTY-SIX

Canvas for Paint, Paper for Ink

7 August, Great Western Trail, Mt. Timpanogos

Scott's full of news about his and Lyn's trip to the East Humboldt Range in north-central Nevada, a place I've often visited to collect water samples.

"We camped near Angel Lake at about nine thousand feet," Scott tells me as we rise rapidly along a ridge. "We hiked around the north end of the mountain for seven hours and didn't see another human being."

"The last time we saw another rider on this trail was three rides ago," I note. "The West is big and open and still not as claustrophobic as it will someday be."

"We hiked up to a waterfall in the cirque above the lake," Scott continues as we stand overlooking Utah Valley, hazy with smoke blown in from Oregon fires. "After the good snow year, there were wildflowers everywhere: monkey flowers, elephantheads, red and yellow columbines, purple and yellow asters, a rainbow of yarrows, green gentian, horsemint, goat's beard, coneflowers, sunflowers, curlycup gumweed, goldenrod, lupine, sweet vetch, larkspur, toadflax, bind 'flower' (delicate plants like these surely can't be called weeds, Lyn argued), wild geraniums, mustards, penstemons, paintbrush, masses of fireweed, bluebells, monkshood, shrubby cinquefoil, and on and on. And here's the kicker: a couple of monarchs floated by, then a dozen, and hundreds more wobbling past us from east to west, a long thin cloud of monarchs stretching out in time for twenty, thirty minutes, thousands of them, tens of thousands following an age-old urge that would find the survivors hanging in an Oyamel fir tree in Mexico or, more likely in this case, on a eucalyptus tree in California."

"You lucky bastard," I say. "Nevada is still wild, the opposite end of the world from urban Dublin where I was a month ago. And damned different from what the Wasatch Front is and is going to become. If we cared to, we could still engage in planning that would make the future a better place. But that never seems to happen—we're going to see the Wasatch Front become Los Angeles."

11 August, Great Western Trail, Mt. Timpanogos

Sam and I greet the Sunday morning on our bikes, riding east up Provo Canyon into the sun just risen in the canyon mouth. Quickly we leave the river and swing up the Great Western, up the trail that so routinely strains our hearts and lungs and wills, the trail that acts almost like canvas for paint, like paper for ink, affording us a robust medium for conversation. Standing at the brink of Johnson's Hole after the first two scrambles, we reflect on a decade of riding together.

"We've never regretted a ride," Sam says. "Not the Moab slick-rock concussion ride, not the boulder field shoulder separation ride, not the bloody oak brush slash-across-the-brow ride—although that one took a long time to heal."

"How many more times will we be able to ride Frank?" I wonder.

"We'll be riding Frank when we're seventy I hope," Sam figures. "There's really no other alternative for guys afflicted with as much testosterone as we are."

"We haven't heard a single bird today," I note.

"The annual August silence," Sam says. "Breeding season's over and the songbirds fall silent. Remember reading Lisel Mueller, who taught us to notice this?"

"Sure I do," I say as we start down the hill. "Some writers teach us new things, others say better what we already know. If we get down alive, I want you to read a passage from a book I've just finished, Charles Bowden's *Blues for Cannibals*." We speed down the flank of Timpanogos without serious incident and I pull out the book. "Bowden is mourning the death of a young artist he knew," I tell Sam. "In that context, he disparages religion and pop-psychology and writes that he doesn't trust the answers or the people who give the answers.

I believe in dirt and bone and flowers and fresh pasta and salsa cruda and red wine...These things I know. The answers I don't know, nor am I interested...

There will be more blooms this spring, the cactus grew at least ten feet last year. They will open around nine in the evening and then close at dawn. I'll sit out there with a glass of red wine and the lights out.

When I tell people about the blooms, about how they open around nine and close before sunrise and do this just for one night, they always ask, 'Is that all?'

Yes. That's all."

"That's it," Sam says, "that's it."

18 August, Great Western Trail, Mt. Timpanogos

Our gears let us gather momentum and then relinquish just enough power to avoid spinning in the thick, late-summer powder gathered on the trail. Our fat tires grip the quartzite slide. Our brakes guide us forward over sudden turns and pedals act as counterweights on ridges. Contoured seats are steering devices and handlebars carry our weight.

"Amazing inventions, our mountain bikes," Sam comments. "Think where they get us!"

Where they have gotten us today is high on the mountain, poised to ride Frank again, although it's clearly too hot for such foolishness. Up Sam goes, and I follow. As always, Frank's a tough, relentless foe, but by hook and crook and a little luck Sam and I both ride the C turn and the S approach and the two successive chutes and the steep meadow and the rocky stretch under the maples and the sudden rise into the burn and then we're at the top. We admire the remarkable vista while our hearts gradually slow their hammering.

"Just read a report about the effects of the drought on sage and black brush and other shrubs," Sam says. "There's a helluva lot of die-off goin' on."

"Isn't that a natural cycle?" I ask. "A constant change as the climate ebbs and flows."

"Sure," Sam answers, "although there's been a lot of human intervention, most of it through sheep and cattle. I don't know of a stream, large or small, in the west that hasn't been stripped of vegetation by grazers and left to dig deep into the earth. That speeds up runoff, changes the water supply to the surrounding vegetation, dries springs, all of which make the effects of any drought more severe. Look how even the oak brush is shriveling at the edges."

I look around and find every clump fringed with desiccated leaves.

At home, curious about the hardy scrub oak that has greeted so many of our falls with welcoming arms, I do a little research. The scientific name is *Quercus gambelii* (Gambel's Oak), named after William Gambel, a nineteenth-century collector of western plants and the Assistant Curator of the National Academy of Sciences. The male pollen-bearing catkins produce lots of yellow pollen to pollinate the female, acorn-producing parts on the same tree (oaks are "monoecious"). Wild turkey, deer, bear, and squirrels all eat and spread the acorns, as do various birds. The extensive root system can spread stands of oak brush by as much as a foot per year, which accounts for quick recovery after a fire. As Sam has pointed out, the new spring leaves are rust colored because chlorophyll has not yet masked the original colors. In the fall, the chlorophyll fades and the browns and reds reappear.

In northern Utah, scrub oak hosts quail, pheasants, scrub

jays, magpies, chickadees, and rufous-sided towhees as perma-
nent residents. As we have witnessed, mule deer and elk browse
scrub oak occasionally. Oak brush does so well in dry conditions because deep roots, xeromorphic leaves, and efficient
water transport all keep the plants alive in conditions like this
year's. The plants are very high in tannic acid.

Later, talking with Sam about my findings, I wonder about
the tannin. "You know how the scratches fester that we get
from oak brush? Remember that slice across your forehead and
around to your ear? I wonder if it healed so slowly because of
the acid."

"Could be," Sam answers. "The scrub oak obviously produces various sorts of chemicals to protect itself from insects
and browsers and mountain bikers."

FORTY-SEVEN

Too Old a Dog

23 August, Provo *(by email)*

Sam—A most remarkable trip to Logan. On the way home, I stopped in a Salt Lake coffee shop to sketch out the events.

Ben loads his mountain bike into the back of my van, throws in a backpack bulging with a tent, sleeping bag, and cooking equipment. He adds a cloth bag full of books and a little duffle bag holding a few clothes. He tosses in a bike helmet, and we're off, headed from Orem to Utah State University in Logan.

Although I've been biting my tongue through Salt Lake and past Bountiful, I finally can't keep myself. "You have plenty of money. Tell me again why you are so intent on camping in the canyon for the semester?"

"I wouldn't stay up the canyon out of necessity," Ben answers decisively. "It's something I *want* to do."

"I'm worried you'll spend so much time surviving that you'll neglect your chemistry and calculus and American lit."

"The time I'll save from social activities in the dorms will more than make up for the lost time."

Driving through Ogden, I continue to press my objections. "Now I'm worried about your state of solitude. There's a good chance you'll become a new Unibomber."

"No, Dad," Ben starts, but I break in. "It doesn't matter what you argue, I'll just have another worry based on your latest conclusion. Let's change the subject."

Ben describes last spring's bike trip from Logan down to the Bear River Bird Refuge and back. He's a fine raconteur, and by the time he's finished, we're entering Logan. So are lots of other parents and students. I look at their cars jealously, certain they have a house or a room with an address to go to. Ben guides me up the hill, past the dorms, through a quiet, well-cared-for neighborhood, up a road leading to a little cut in the hills northeast of town, and onto a gravel road. A couple of restrooms stand at a trailhead. We drive on up the canyon, and Ben announces that this is the place. He takes out his bike, his bags, and gives me a big hug.

"Take care," I say, and hand him five twenties. "Security funds. Security for my wandering mind."

"Thanks, Dad. Take care yourself."

"I will," I promise.

3 September, Great Western Trail, Mt. Timpanogos

Slow, mostly flat ride today. I mention to Scott that we drove out to see Robert Smithson's *Spiral Jetty* at the tip of Promontory Point yesterday. "Smithson made the Jetty in 1970 at a time when the lake was very low. He built it of black basalt rocks found in the area. The lake is low again and the jetty is emerging, white now with salt crystals, quite different from its original form. The white jetty is all the more dramatic because it's emerging from water colored red by a microscopic alga, *Dunaliella salina*, a green alga loaded with red pigments. I've done research on that part of the lake for many years. Never saw more than a couple of cars there. Yesterday we must have passed three hundred cars. It's a helluva phenomenon."

"Can't wait to see it," Scott replies. "Smithson knew the sculpture would change dramatically with time. And, of course, there's the irony that he was killed just the next year or so."

We're not climbing much today, so Scott has breath to continue. "Sam, while you were braving the crowds at the edge of one receding lake, Lyn and I were at Ruby Marsh on a remote Nevada flyway looking at birds in the remains of another ancient lake: great blue herons, great-, snowy- and cattle- egrets, cormorants, pelicans, snipes, white-faced ibis, sandhill cranes, northern harriers, red-tailed hawks, and ducks aplenty. Nature is an inventive and imaginative creatrix."

"I love the Rubys and the associated marshes," I respond. "I fished there a time or two as a kid. In later years, Jack Brotherson, a BYU ecologist (and dear friend) and I traveled the west studying the marshes and springs in the deserts and mountains from the San Juans in Colorado to the Sierra Nevadas in California. In 1981, Jack and I traveled more than twenty thousand miles in his old yellow Chevy pickup, collecting algae and studying the terrestrial vegetation of many dozen hot springs. It was an amazing adventure. I collected hundreds of samples, and provided organisms for at least two of my graduate students' theses.

"The springs were all different—some large with variable temperatures and beautifully inhabited by naked spring-lovers. Others were scalding and dangerous. Once Jack and I walked out onto a crusted mud flat at Mono Lake (largely dewatered now due to human demands) toward a prominent spring I wanted to collect. Jack went through the crust, waist deep in very hot mud. I hauled him out, all the while thinking I would soon join him and some damned coyotes would have barbequed stupid. Fortunately, I did not break through, and Jack was more angry than scalded. We had just come from a spring earlier that day that was above 200F. Jack claimed this mud was plenty hot too: 'my love-life may be over, cooked like well-done scallops.'

'Take down your pants and blow on your balls,' was the best advice I could think of."

13 September, Great Western Trail, Mt. Timpanogos

It's a beautiful morning after weeks of rain. The trail is hard-packed, which is good, but rutted, which is bad, so the storms have brought no net gain to bikers. The vistas, however, feel different. "Everything feels softer," I tell Sam, "even the dry grass."

"Is it softer," Sam asks, "or clearer? Seems to me the rain has washed months of dust off the scrub oak, off the grasses and the blue limestone and out of the air. The colors are brighter for sure."

"Perception is a tricky business," I add. "It takes a lot of thought to figure out what it is we're seeing. I've been reading a new book by Robert Richards called *The Romantic Conception of Life: Science and Philosophy in the Age of Goethe*. I told you before that Goethe was an advocate of direct observation of the kind we do with our butts in the air. But then Goethe's friend Schiller got him to read Kant and Goethe wrote this as the forward to his *Theory of Colors*:

> The most amazing demand is sometimes made…that one should undertake experiential observations without any theoretical assumptions…But we cannot make any progress through mere observation of something. Every observation becomes a consideration, every consideration becomes a reflection, every reflection becomes an inference—so one can say that we theorize every time we attend to something in the world. But we should be conscious of this, we should be self-aware of it, and undertake it freely—and, to use a bold expression—with irony."

"Well I'll be damned," Sam replies, "Goethe had some sense after all."

"Speaking of perception," I continue. "You remember Laraine Wilkins, one of my grad students in German? She wrote a great thesis on the grotesque woman's body in German cinema, then headed to Harvard for a Ph.D."

"Sure I remember her," Sam says. "And her daughter, Lena."

"I had lunch with Laraine last week," I report, "and she asked me if I had changed since leaving BYU. She said she had heard someone claim that I had undergone a radical shift in personality, a change evident in our *Catalyst* column. I pressed her for details, but she left it at that. What do you think? Have I changed radically in the last four years?"

"Not radically enough for my taste," Sam answers quickly,

"but it's interesting the question would come up in that form. You have certainly fought with depression, especially after your divorce. You don't church or tithe any more. Maybe that's what they mean. When I look at you I see the same person, the same moral commitments, the same basic goodness, the continuing fight for justice, for economic fairness, not to speak of the recurrent bad taste, stupid sense of humor, and loud mouth. Naw, Laraine's friend is full of shit. You're too old a dog."

21 September, Great Western Trail, Mt. Timpanogos

"Sam," I wheeze, "the trail is riding me rather than the other way around."

"Quit bitchin," Sam replies sympathetically. "Greta pays you good money to move your butt off the couch onto your bike seat. Still, I've been thinking that maybe we've used up all our best notions. We've written about biking and aging and the natural world for *The Salt Lake Observer* and the *Catalyst* forty-six times now. That's more columns than either of us has words, more words than we have sense. You think it is time to hang up the bike shorts?"

"I guess I hope the riding never stops," I answer. "But it's probably time to quit repeating our old stories. Are you going to tell Greta, or shall I?"

"You do it," Sam replies. "Let's write for November and December and then slip into the sunset."

FORTY-EIGHT

God Stories

13 October, Great Western Trail, Mt. Timpanogos

We slowly work our way through the newly destroyed homestead orchard, hundred-year-old trees (our plum trees!) bulldozed helter-skelter and cute little plastic and faux wood park pavilions peppered throughout, asphalt "trails" between. "Scott, I've been having a helluva time figuring something out. Nanc and I were married many years ago. We both wanted to work hard to create a religious home. It was something we had in our generational blood and seemed the right thing to do."

"I come from the same background," Scott replies, "and making a religious haven was on my young mind as well."

"I have been thinking why it didn't work in my case. I read all the sacred texts of my childhood many times. I went to church, said my prayers, and did everything I could think of. I remember leaving an experiment I was doing to sit near a radio listening to semi-annual Mormon conference speakers pontificate in that standard sing-song pseudo-reverential voice, trying like hell to get into their frame of mind, trying to see the world from their point of view, maybe even catch their vision. I wanted to fit in, to believe in a sweet hereafter. But nothing ever worked. And the harder I tried, the less happy I was. In fact, I became convinced that trying so hard was actually harmful, robbing the present of its beauty and substance. It's lousy to spend your time between fear and bullshit. And, by god, this Earth is no rental car, a trial to get through so you get the better model."

Scott responds, "There was a moment for me when belief simply fell away. It was in Princeton, walking home after a long day in the library, an utterly paradoxical and unexpected epiphany, as close to revelation as I have ever come. I was brought up short—in midstep and midthought—by the realization that I was no longer a believer. And then the miracle: the sudden knowledge didn't destroy me. I could still stake my life on the patterns that had proven so productive, or—I could choose

(Why, after all these years riding together, is he still so much more powerful than I am?)

"He's a hell of a smart guy," I answer, "so I'm not sure exactly what he said. I think I partly misunderstood his original point, and I think he said that like you and me, he sees human existence as absolutely contingent. But that god stuff confused the issue for me."

By this time, we're at the top of the climb, on a flat trail leading toward the mouth of the canyon.

"Those god stories," Sam says, "those stories I tried so hard to believe, have turned out to be more destructive—for me and I believe for the world—than they have been enabling. And for my money, they're the stories that have evolved, spun by people through the ages, added to, detracted from, by people who don't even have the humility to know the stories are human constructs."

At the mouth of the canyon, Sam dives off the hill at breakneck speed. I follow at the same speed, thrilled by the motion, the air, the light. We sweep past sage and oak brush and blue limestone, the cold air whistling past our ears. Inexplicably, Sam turns off the already steep trail onto a suicide cutoff. "I get your bike," I shout, just before he loses his line and hits a stump with his front wheel. Over the handlebar he flies, smacks his ass on a flat rock, then rolls awkwardly down a grass-covered decline, coming to rest fifty yards below his bike. Not until I see him get up and take his first tentative steps do I shout down, "I think Hauerwas underestimated the commitment potential of stories that end with death!"

23 October, Great Western Trail, Mt. Timpanogos

Riding in front of a fast-moving cold front. The sky in the northwest is black and threatening with occasional lightning. We shoot up the steepest and fastest of our routes to try to beat the storm.

Scott tells me he's just got a letter from his son Nate, who is a Mormon missionary in Hong Kong. "I sent him Ed Abbey's response to a missionary," Scott says. "'So you're going to Christianize the savages. Aren't they savage enough already?'"

"How did Nate answer?"

"'Dad,' he wrote, 'I love you.'"

"You're a lucky man, Abbott."

"Don't I know it. There's news from Tom as well. He met a singer who is in the New School University's jazz program and she convinced him to audition. The subway busker has been accepted into a new and challenging world."

Still some hold-out blossoms. A single Dalmation toadflax blossom on a desiccated stem, three sage plants with waning flowers, a handful of purple "daisies" on flattened stems. A single blazing star on an aged stalk. I have an affinity for this melancholy beauty: black ominous sky, hopeful old blossoms, sun strikes across the golden, dried grass. Makes me realize how close the final curtain is and how wonderful the trip has been.

FORTY-NINE

A Trillion, Trillion, Trillion Years

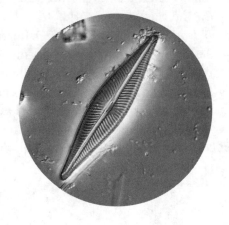

29 October, Provo *(by email)*
Sam—Ben just sent this from Logan. He's having a hell of an experience exploring the freedoms and possibilities of college.

Pops,

I've gone mobile and given my farewells as Green Canyon turns yellow and red. All my "necessaries" fit inside my backpack. It gives me such flexibility and freedom. I'll study at the library until closing time, then stagger into the moonlight, unroll my bag, and sleep. I feel so sleek. I'm condensed. I do miss the peace of the canyon. Wherever I sleep on campus, there's a lingering fear of discovery and a definite lack of privacy.

There's that old Puritan idea of Satan residing in the woods. Nature's an uncivilized place of carnal and pagan character. Coming out of the woods, I've gotten quite the opposite impression. The canyon was wholesome. Oak trees have no hidden motives. Grass is for the sake of grass.

The way I live now is closer to a true homelessness, just what I wanted. Strangely, I feel the change from canyon tent-dwelling to itinerant nook-sleeping was a bigger change than the house-to-canyon transition. I have fewer luxuries, but the current organization of my possessions is more convenient than ever. Because each of my possessions carries with it a cost (I've got to carry it), I'm much more discriminating. Most single-purpose items have been eliminated, leaving me with an adaptive set of tools. I can cut open cracker packages, fix bikes, listen to the radio, brush my teeth, have a flashlight, and tell which way is north (actually I ditched my compass—too big), all with things I carry around with me. I think it is more efficient for me to carry around my room than it was to live in it.

Just one more thought between my American Literature class and a dull economics class. "Wow, heavy load," my teacher said as I lumbered out of class with my thirty-seven-pound pack. "Not nearly as heavy as all the things you tie yourself to," I answered.

31 October, Great Western Trail, Mt. Timpanogos

Late afternoon ride on Halloween, a Celtic holiday celebrating the ending of the "season of the sun" and beginning the "season of darkness and cold." Jesus, it's a metaphor for my life. I have always tried to be cheerful, or at least functional—my colleagues and acquaintances, I believe, never guess how dark I feel—just a few intimates notice and a few I tell. Even so, every fall I wonder if the sun will come back or if the gloom is irrevocable, deepening into final darkness and cold. Or is it me that may not come back? My heart is dark and my belly is anxious. So it has been for fifty-five years. So, I suppose, it will be for a few more years.

In Latin America, the holiday is Los Dias de los Muertos, the Day of the Dead, the day the monarch butterflies return to the sheltering fir trees of the Mexican mountains for the winter, bearing the spirits of the departed. "The spirits of the departed"—what does that mean? When I am departed, how will a kindred monarch find me? How will I be recognized? And what happens when the fir trees that shelter our sister monarchs are chopsticks and toilet paper? Where will the butterflies go then? Where will the spirits go? What will happen to the order of the world?

Scott and I are riding with Jed and my son-in-law Paul, pedaling fast up the front of the mountain, racing the departing sunlight, cresting our climb as the sun disappears west of the lake. It's suddenly cold without the sun. The valley slips deeper into twilight as we head down the steep trail. All the way, as so often, I wonder about the meaning of my life. Have I made any difference? What is a single, simple life worth? Who decides? Who remembers? Does anyone care? Write a book, carve a bust, give seminal talks across the country. Who cares. Get a good night's sleep and love, those are the keys. And, of course, have a lucky genetic composition.

Scott and I have ridden together for more than a dozen years in these mountains. We have ridden through my sister's death and Scott's split with his wife. We have ridden in brilliant sun and horizontal snow. We have survived frightening falls and testosterone-fueled races. We have worked through the timid mean-spiritedness of BYU, the stupidity of the Gulf War, and the Balkans debacle. We ride now with an incompetent U.S. president threatening world stability—our bodies are electric with rage. We have ridden melancholy and quiet and filled with the ebullience of novelty and unexpected grace. But we have ridden—day after day in the same part of Earth and we have seen and listened and smelled and remembered. And we have found pattern and order. We have seen the resurrection green of spring and the waning of the green season to the umber and barrenness of autumn. We saw the entire mountain burn and rode the next day through smoke, ash, and destruction and finally, months later, through growth and regeneration. And it has mattered, or at least has seemed to matter, or at least has seemed to matter to us.

10 November, Provo

Sitting by my fire, I watch the snow spit outside, think about a bike ride with Sam to loosen tight muscles and an anxious mind. The morning stretches into afternoon, the snow turns to rain. We won't ride today, I finally tell myself. Mud on the Great Western Trail makes short work of our derailleurs. The afternoon lengthens. The weight of undone work is heavy on my mind, discontent gathers. I stare fixedly into the still crackling fire. Its meager comfort dissipates. The grey light fades into evening. I lean my aching head against the chairback, close my eyes…Sam and I turn up the trail into Provo Canyon.

"Colder than a welldigger's ass," Sam exclaims. I stretch stiff legs, try to warm my arthritic shoulder. Near what used to be the old homestead, we stop and pick the last of the Potawatomi plums, shriveled by the cold, still sweet and tart. My CamelBak bladder swells with memory, grows heavy on my back. Sam's potent plum mead flows through the mouthpiece, filling my mouth with the heady taste of fermented honey flavored by these very plums, the remnants of the natural cycle we have witnessed for years.

We climb steadily, turn along the green pipe, follow it up canyon to where it dives into the earth and the Great Western snakes up over the quartzite. I've been nipping at the mead and am starting to sweat a little, so I stop to unzip my coat. "Is it just me," I ask Sam, "or is the weather changing? We've lost the snow, the mud is drying as we climb."

"Probably the mead," Sam replies, and powers his way up the switchback, up over the quartzite slide onto the bench. I follow him into Johnson's Hole, where I stop again and shed my coat entirely. A flash of yellow and black flits from the top of a thistle.

"Wrong time of year for a goldfinch," I note. "But then it's entirely wrong for sego lily and death camas too, and look at them, flowering all the way up the ridge."

We're higher now, a spring sun is shining, and from a branch above the soft new leaves of oak brush comes the trill of a lazuli bunting, then a flash of bright blue. Our old friend Frank welcomes us up his serpentine reaches and steep chutes. In a high meadow, we stop to admire a field of lupine, to watch a small herd of elk melt into the maples, to talk.

We ride on up into the unfolding summer, past spring beauties and perfect little steersheads. Yellow violets mark the way to the saddle of Little Baldy. Monkey flowers and elephant heads nod close to a snow-fed stream. Utah Lake sparkles far below. We wind through flowering sage, past tall green gentian, around the point of the mountain into American Fork Canyon, up to the ridge trail at the top of the Alpine Loop. Without stopping for breath we turn north on this stretch of the Great Western— Mineral Basin to the west, Heber Valley to the east—riding now into deep summer. Sam's mead sustains us, lends fire to thighs and calves, makes route-finding child's play. Before we know it, we're flying up the last sheer climb to the sharp ridge that looks down into both Little and Big Cottonwood Canyons.

A cold autumn wind whips past our ears and I slip my coat back on. The plum mead warms from within as we spin past Brighton and climb toward Guardsman's and then Scott's Pass. On the Wasatch Crest Trail, we're forced to dismount several times to cross snowbanks, duck under trees to escape a severe winter thunderstorm. A pair of noisy Clark's nutcrackers squawks at us from a limber pine. "*Pinus flexilis,*" Sam reminds me with a grin. "Remember all our conversations about the horny goat weed ads I get and your prostate saver saddle? About penis size and testosterone poisoning?"

"Yeah," I answer, "and we've talked a lot about love and loss as well. These bikes have carried us far and high. Shadowed by blue limestone and above cottonwood lined rivers, we've talked about anything and everything. I've learned a lot from you about a lifelong love, that rare marriage of passionate equals you and Nancy are involved in. And maybe you've learned a few things from me as well."

"Sure have," Sam answers, a bit slow for my taste. "But best of all, our readers have read generously. One of my favorite responses was the rumor we heard among the gay community that we were lovers."

"I wasn't quite as flattered by that as you were," I say. "I could surely find a better looking guy." I turn off the ridge, heading west into a darkening Millcreek Canyon, the cold sun setting ahead of us. "Friendship between men, banked and buffered by gruffness and insult, isn't as common as it ought to be. We've been lucky, my friend."

The fire is cold when I wake up, and my neck is stiff.

12 November, Orem *(by email)*

Scott. It's deep night and I'm awake, obsessing again about the End Game. As a biologist and melancholist, I swim in the past, dwell on the future. We are the only animals on Earth who do this. I have put on my dad's ruby ring after 30 years, trying to conjure his memory.

In great detail I examine the early photographs of my mother—trying to see the character deeply ingrained in her face that would come out later at difficult times in her life. She is beautiful in her youth—trusting eyes, auburn hair, head tilted slightly sideward as if trying to figure something out, something just beyond brilliance.

Mom and Dad—both of them wondering about their relationship, puzzled about who they were, why they couldn't make their lives work, why they felt battered and betrayed, trying to relate with their children, wondering what their own lives meant. Two people unprepared to live together, perhaps even deep lovers who were beyond the hard tasks of a life together, unable to allow their initial attraction to ripen into long-term mutual respect. Trying to figure out how to deal with a brilliant clutch of children that appeared along the way. Most people appear to be in this swirl. It seems to me to be one of the central issues of life.

This afternoon, a phone call telling Nanc about her mother's death, Vera's leap into the abyss. Leaving us as the elder generation—older but not wiser.

I find myself examining all the potential endings of the future. I live in this instable state constantly. How can I understand that our god—the sun—will run out of hydrogen in 4.5 billion years and swell to the size of the orbit of Mars? What does it mean that Earth will evaporate when this happens? No wonder the ancients worshipped the sun. And in the middle of all this, I am so happy to have a moment now, in the middle of Earth's life, with people I adore.

It's more and more clear that the end of the Universe will occur in a cold, meaningless darkness, structureless, void of insight and meaning. Most physical data point to this unexpected emptiness, this dark abyss, endless expansion into nothingness. A trillion, trillion, trillion years from now, the universe will likely be gigantic beyond comprehension, featureless, cold, atoms the size of solar systems. Not a spark of warmth, not a shred of sentience, not a speck of light.

So what does this leave us? It leaves us more than we can comprehend: *the now of our lives*. It leaves us friends, autumn, the haunting eyes of a stranger passing in an airport, a few more changes in season, the wan smile of a lover. We have dawns, storms, the sound of wind at night, rain in the desert, dark-roast coffee, good food. We have revealing, late night talks with our lovers. We have consciousness and memory, gifts of Nature, the surprise of a thunderstorm, a full moon breaking through the clouds, an unexpected second crop of corn, the love of a grandchild, the ending of a war, the healing of souls, the worship of a day.

And hell, it's been interesting and fine to write these words with you these past years. To share our thoughts and feelings with each other, with friends, strangers. What a fine thing to SEE, to really pay attention, to write, to think. And the past month has been wonderful, dozens of *Catalyst* readers asking us to keep writing, suggesting our column has somehow made a difference for them. Makes a guy smile, reach for a beer, think about what else there may be to say.

"Reach for a beer"? Now that I'm being reflective, let me add this. Alcohol has been a mixed "blessing" for me for several years. When I was a 15-year-old, I drank heavily and regularly paid my bar bill to the Twin Pines (which were actually spruces) once a month. Brews were two-bits a toss and it was easy to buy your partner a drink. The evenings glided away with what seemed to be "smart time, friend time" but which was certainly something else, some sort of counterfeit existence. My life was coming apart, I was failing school, I was playing cards in a rough part of Ogden, I was lying to my mom and dad about who I was. They couldn't do much, because their lives were coming apart too.

I got a construction job, made a bucket-load of money, and lost it all to alcohol and blackjack (greased by "free" drinks in a casino in Elko, near where I worked). You know, for two years, I felt sort of normal. I could fake it in school, I could do hard physical labor, I was tough, and I felt like a blue-collar rogue. I continued this through my senior year in high school and first year of college (Weber State University). Damn, I was the hot stuff. I remember being beaten up one night by a coupla guys who lifted my wallet. But even then I thought I was "tough."

Then I began seeing the love of my life again, Nanc. My drinking and carousing slowed and the cost / benefit ratio shifted. We married and I went to Weber State full time and managed an automobile station for a buck an hour. Nanc worked at the First National Bank of Layton for the same salary. Hell, we were rich! Weber State University for me, Weber State University for Nanc, and a very different and happier life pattern. I stopped drinking.

I graduated and took a graduate studies position at BYU (what?!?!). Good money, good studies, cheap apartment, camaraderie with Nanc like nothing before. We were pregnant, and a child portended things changing for the better. It was blissful.

Nanc was bed-ridden mid-pregnancy when we had planned

to go to Davis County for Thanksgiving with both of our parents. So, at 5:30 in the morning I grabbed my .410 single-shot, a half-a-dozen shells, and headed to the marshes. I killed two pheasant cocks before 10:00 in the morning, came home, cleaned, de-feathered, and stuffed them with apple slices and nuts. I roasted them, baked potatoes, made a salad and we had a helluva Thanksgiving feast for us and our families. And so things continued for many years.

But years later, when periods of blinding darkness descended again and again, I was left to negotiate one of the most difficult parts of my life. Self-absorbed, sad, frightened, seeking some sort of relief, I found that alcohol was a powerful, short-term answer to long-term problems. Of course, it often created even more problems.

I am indeed my father's son.

Year V

He called and called. Standing in that inexplicable darkness. Where there was no sound anywhere save only the wind. After a while he sat in the road. He took off his hat and placed it on the tarmac before him and he bowed his head and held his face in his hand and wept. He sat there for a long time and after a while the east did gray and after a while the right and godmade sun did rise, once again, for all and without distinction.

Cormac McCarthy, *The Crossing*

FIFTY

Not the End, Yet

Great Western Trail, Mt. Timpanogos, Scott's Version

Sam and I head up Provo Canyon just before noon on a clear, cool Saturday morning. We're feeling good as we turn up the dirt road that takes us to the green irrigation pipe, bracketed by heavy equipment. By next summer, it will have disappeared into the ground. Things change.

"How's the eye?" I ask, wondering about the outcome of Sam's surgery on Thursday to have a plastic lens inserted.

"Feelin' pretty good," he says, "although everything I'm seeing has a blue tint. Jesus, one operation after another, a colonoscopy here and a skin cancer treatment there has left me feeling more mortal than usual."

"We're aging fast," I agree. "Just getting up in the morning is more of an adventure than it used to be. I wake up with a stiff shoulder and a tight bladder and can scarcely totter over to the toilet."

"Big deal," Sam says. "We've complained like this for years."

My sphincter tightens as we approach the Great Western Trail, and it has nothing to do with age. As so often before, we make the familiar but still tricky sharp turn off the dirt road onto the trail that climbs steeply up toward Johnson's Hole. It's loose and rocky as always after a dry summer. I've got good momentum heading through the first turn, get lucky when my wheel bounces between two babyheads instead of over one of them, have enough power left in my legs to force the bike up over the protruding root, teeter over the quartzite slide, and make a last scramble up to where the trail levels off for a few yards.

"Good ride," Sam shouts from where the root has dislodged him from his saddle. "Damn good ride."

We up the ridge, through oak brush still rust-colored with late leaves, and fight up the series of sudden hills that have for years tried our strength and balance and endurance. At the top of the last one, I look back and don't see Sam. When he joins me a minute later he's got dust on his back.

"Taught that hill a lesson," he grumbles. "I whacked it good."

From here, it's an easy, winding ride back toward the mouth of Provo Canyon. Our conversation is easy and winding as well. I drop off the hill in high spirits, hardly touching my brakes, feeling young and strong, seeing the trail well, sensing the sharp turns through the precise mechanisms of my bike. I slow a bit and Sam passes.

"What a ride!" he shouts. "What a morning! What a life."

I follow him down the steep switchbacks and watch him shoot faster than usual over the lip of the steep chute above the new houses that have replaced the orchard. We stood at the top of this shortcut twenty times before finally daring to launch ourselves down the short but nearly vertical drop. Since then, we've taken the route a hundred times, each time with a little more bravado. Just before gravity throws me down the slope, I slam on my brakes. Sam lies twisted at the bottom. Dust settles around him.

"Sam," I call. "Sam!"

I've seen him like this before. He always stretches gingerly once he's got his breath back. When he lost the trail and dislocated his shoulder half a mile east of here, he was stunned at first, but eventually got up and rode home.

Now, he's lying on his side, curled up like a baby. His left leg is twisted awkwardly, still attached by the cleat to the bike pedal. The bike's front wheel has collapsed. Sam is breathing—I can tell because of the bubbles in the blood his face is lying in. He's not conscious. He doesn't respond to my shouts. I should move him. Has he broken his neck? His back? He's sucking blood into his nose. I don't think I should move him. So much blood. He's a pile of meat.

I'm gingerly turning Sam's face out of the pooled blood when he groans. He turns his head more, raises it. He pulls the leg still attached to the bike. I lift his heel, twist it hard to disengage the cleat from the pedal.

"What happened?" Sam asks, trying to get up.

"Don't move," I say. "You crashed your bike."

"What happened?" he asks again.

"Your front wheel tacoed," I answer. "Lay back on my Camel-Bak."

"Where am I?" he asks, raising himself.

"Don't move! Sam! You've hurt yourself. Lay back."

"What happened?" Sam asks, grasping, fighting for clarity. I've never seen him like this before. People lean on Sam for clarity, for insight, for information, for support, for strength.

"We're at the bottom of the hill. You went over the front of your bike. You're hurt. I've got to get help."

"I don't need help," Sam says.

"You need help," I insist, "but I can't go get it until you tell me you'll lie here. Do you know what happened?"

"I crashed my bike," he says. "Let me up."

"You've got to stay here, you sonofabitch. Lay down. Lie still. I'm going to get help. Will you lie still? Lie still!"

He lies back on the CamelBak, blood oozing through his beard, through his hair. I run toward a house under construction a hundred yards away. A young man hands me his cell phone. I call Nancy and leave a message. I call 911 and direct an ambulance. I run back to Sam.

"I called an ambulance," I tell him.

"I don't need an ambulance," he says. "Get me home."

"I'll get you home," I say. "But we've got to get that cut fixed. And check your head and neck."

"Where's my tooth?" Sam asks.

"Looks like you've still got your teeth," I say. "But you're bleeding." I take off my sweaty do-rag and press it against his forehead, just above his left eye, where blood pulses from a deep cut. "Hold this," I tell him, and he does.

The ambulance arrives, accompanied by a fire truck. Sam answers questions about where he is. He tells them he'd rather go home and have a beer. They strap him onto a board. Nancy arrives, white-faced. She leaves with Sam in the ambulance. I put our bikes in the back of her car and meet them in the emergency room.

Over the course of a long Saturday afternoon, Sam lies on the hard board. He's wheeled into X-Ray, into MRI, into who knows where. He drips blood into the evening, leaking slowly while an IV drips into him at about the same rate. Nancy and I learn, as the hours pass, that his neck isn't broken, that his brain doesn't seem to be injured. All the bones in his face have been smashed: the orbitals around his eyes, his nose, his cheeks, his upper mandible, his left eye socket. Sam's left eye has fallen deep into his cheek. The thick smell of blood permeates the room.

I hear a doctor tell someone on a phone that the patient had done a "faceplant." I want to grab his shirt and tell him to speak respectfully.

Sam is drugged with some serious painkillers, but he is mostly conscious. "Go home," he keeps telling me, "no reason for you to waste your Saturday."

"I'm not worried about you, you sack of shit," I answer. "I'm here for Nancy." The day stretches into night. They take Sam off the board. He looks like he was in a bad fight. This will make a hell of a good last column.

Sam's Version

"Some sonofabitch is gonna ask me if I was wearing a helmet," I remember thinking on my way to the ground. Then, as I hit— "Good god, this is harder than I thought a person could hit."

I was wearing Sarah Jane's Cal Arts ball cap. I worried it

will be lost, ruined or stolen. But I have no power to make this known. Scott will not take me home—I do have a slight memory of my request. The ambulance shows up with a bunch of tough EMTs.

"What day is it?" they ask. "Where are you?" Where are we going?"

"Look," I respond, "I'm in an ambulance because of that damned Abbott. You are takin' me to some hospital. Suppose we stop off for a beer? I'm buyin.'"

Nanc is reassured. I am acting as bad as ever. In fairness, I have only the slightest remembrance of any of these events. For the next several hours, I can only remember the occasional view of the emergency room full of blood and mud. I wonder what poor bastard has been there before me.

"Well, his neck is not broken," I remember them telling Nancy. After seven hours, they take off the neck stabilizer. Later, "He doesn't seem to have any brain damage."

"How would you decide?" I ask.

Friends come by. I have no idea how I look except by the mirror of their faces and I conclude I have probably hurt myself. The docs tell Nanc, "This is not life threatening. We can rebuild him as long as he has an intact spine and no brain damage." They add, "His nose is all over his face. Both cheekbones are broken. His upper mandible is broken badly. His eye sockets are both broken, the left in several places. His zygomatic arches are both broken. He has several crushed sinuses."

I am irritated as hell. There is no need to make this a big deal for Nancy—it is not a big deal. I can get by with repairing all of this shit and there is no need for her to worry. After several hours, we are moved upstairs to an intermediate care room. Friends continue to come. I am embarrassed by the attention, especially the obvious worry I have caused Nanc. Eventually, she sleeps in a bundle of lumpy white blankets on the floor. I spend most of the night awake, worrying about her, my friends, my kids, the meaning of life, how I dodged death and why.

Jeff Tayler, a physician and a dear friend of mine, hears about the accident and, as a physician-cum-CEO of a major medical corporation, flies into action. I have access to the best care in Salt Lake City. I have an appointment with David Thomas, one of the best plastic surgeons in the west. He doesn't have time to do the surgery and so calls two of his colleagues. They don't have time either. In the end, I suggest to Thomas, "Surely a face like mine is more interesting than a steady diet of tits and noses." He agrees and schedules surgery while I'm on the phone with him. I hear him giving directions. "I'll need a bone saw, a bone drill, a set of wires, a full set of face plates, and a partridge in a pear tree. This guy is busted up."

After the surgery, he hands me a mirror. "Shit, doc. I just gave you several thousand dollars and this is the best you can come up with?" Actually, I am pretty pleased—he has brought up the left eye at least three-quarters of an inch, my deep cuts are all stitched shut, and I look more or less human.

Ok, so what have I learned? Friends matter. When given the chance, it's better to be alive than dead. Family matters. Colleagues who care matter. A beautiful day matters. So many people care—people you didn't even know about. An aspen tree in the wind is exceptional. A kind word is inestimable in its worth. Life is so short, but so rich.

And Jesus, a good friend will save your life and retrieve your best Cal Arts ball cap (even though it is muddy and bloody) and put it in your garage on your twisted bicycle so you can find it and quit worrying.

Epilogue

He went back the way he had come, again taking his time, seeing everything now from its opposite side. It was as though he made the place dimensional and substantial by his walking both ways over it, granting it the same interest in going as he had in coming. To his mind it was old beyond knowing and yet new, timeless and yet momentary, so that watching it as once more it opened before him, old as he was, he was renewed.

Wendell Berry, "At Home"

26 May

Sam, when I read what we wrote nearly a decade ago, I feel renewed, to use the words from Wendell Berry's fine story. We returned to that stretch of the Great Western Trail so many times and we wrote about that stretch so often that we gave it subjective substance of sorts.

We marveled that Paul Richards, an "old man" of sixty, could be up on our trail. Now, you're two-thirds of the Mark of the Beast and I'm sixty-three. How did that happen?

1999 was my fiftieth year. I'm reminded of Goethe's story "The Man of Fifty Years." Goethe's character feels his splendid powers waning and tries to forestall the loss with a traveling cabinet full of makeup and restoratives. It's a melancholy story of resistance to inevitable change. Our obsessive riding at that approximate age was a better restorative for me than makeup, for sure, but it was also an agent of difficult and risky change. In the long run, those have been important choices for me. And they have taken their toll. Fortunately, riding and writing are powerful medicines.

Our account notes that the population of the earth reached six billion in 1999. Today, there are seven billion of us. One billion added in thirteen years. Headed for eight billion. My beloved grandchildren are adding to that number. There are too many human beings on this beautiful and fragile planet. It's partly my fault. I wouldn't have it any other way. It's deeply paradoxical.

Sam, we have both been working at UVSC (which then became UVU) since the turn of the millennium. What if we had kept working at BYU? We would never have been able to write openly about the profound discussion we had under the influence of six big cans of Budweiser after our seven-hour, dehydrating ride along the Great Western Trail from Sundance to Brighton. But then, we have never been able to write coherently about those insights anyway. All we know is that it was one of the most profound conversations ever held. I'm still proud to have been one of the interlocutors.

BYU is still on the AAUP "Censured Administrations List" for egregious violations of academic freedom. That was a good piece of work we did.

Lyn and I have remained "consolidated." We designed and built a house together. And now we're writing a book about how barbed wire has been construed in advertising and literature *(It was a nun they say invented barbed wire.* James Joyce, *Ulysses).*

Despite my inadequacies as a father, my seven children seem to be making good lives for themselves. I think that would make a good epitaph.

We almost had to write an epitaph for you, Sam, after that brutal fall. Glad you're still around. I miss those daily rides, those daily conversations.

30 May

Scott..........I guess I don't know where to start. At the "front" of my "fall" those years ago, I thought I was fine. What the hell. After all, I had taken a hundred falls before, some of them less than comfortable, some of them more severe than I thought this one was. You are a more "selective" rider than I am (no insult intended) and often more likely to avoid danger. As in my life, I am a curmudgeon of a rider and a "just-go-for-it" person. Stupid, to say the least, as many people have pointed out to me throughout my life.

My Executive Assistant and dear friend, Kerri Howlett, was furious. I had had Lasik surgery two days before my crash and she wanted to know what in god's name I was doing on the trail riding like the maniac I can be. She suggested to me she does not want to work for anyone else and does not want me dead.

Five surgeries later, my jaw is wired together, my left eye is blind—though lifted back to match the other after harvesting five slabs of bone from the iliac crest of my pelvis to rebuild an eye platform. Trouble is, I don't like being one-eyed and limping like a sailor with a wooden leg. While this makes me melancholy, I can live with it. Good god, I don't have Lou Gehrig's disease or terminal cancer! I simply have terminal, unrelenting, skepticism with a large dose of stupid. But I still have Nanc and my kids. And in the middle of all of this, I have three grandchildren I never expected to meet and would have missed if I had been just a bit more injured. Who gets this? Who is as lucky as me?

I am afraid this is the way I have lived my entire life. Seems like every day I find or cause some sort of trouble or dilemma. I remember very few days of full joy and unhindered happiness. As I write these words, I am sad, afraid, and wondering what the future will bring to my loved ones. Nanc and I talk about this sort of thing relentlessly, and though she is the compass of my life, she also has her own doubts and fears. It is not easy to age. Getting toward the end of life is an especially unsettling place where it takes courage and strength to avoid a withering of the spirit.

So, my epitaph will have to wait for a while. But let it say something like, "I wanted to be better than I was. Though I never became what I wanted, I loved you all fiercely and was your advocate in life and, if possible, will be in death . . ."

About Torrey House Press

The economy is a wholly owned subsidiary of the environment,
not the other way around.
—Senator Gaylord Nelson, founder of Earth Day

Love of the land inspires Torrey House Press and the books we publish. From literature and the environment and Western Lit to topical nonfiction about land related issues and ideas, we strive to increase appreciation for the importance of natural landscape through the power of pen and story. Through our *2% to the West* program, Torrey House Press donates two percent of sales to not-for-profit environmental organizations and funds a scholarship for up-and-coming writers at colleges throughout the West.

Torrey House Press
www.torreyhouse.com

Visit our website for reading group discussion guides, author interviews, and more.